T0302444

Lafayette at Brandywine

Books by Bruce E. Mowday

TRUE CRIME

Stealing Wyeth*

Jailing The Johnston Gang: Bringing Serial Murderers to Justice*

HISTORY

Pickett's Charge: The Untold Story*

J. Howard Wert's Gettysburg

September 11, 1777: Washington's Defeat at Brandywine Dooms Philadelphia

Unlikely Allies: Fort Delaware's Prison Community in the Civil War

SPORTS

Richie Ashburn: Why The Hall Not. The Amazing Journey to Cooperstown*

BUSINESS

Selling Your Book*

Life With Flavor: A Personal History of Herr's*

Selling of an Author

FICTION

First Date Homicides

LOCAL HISTORY

Spanning the Centuries: The History of Caln Township

Chester County Mushroom Farming

Six Walking Tours of West Chester

West Chester in Modern Day

Along The Brandywine River

West Chester

Coatesville

Downingtown

Parkesburg

*Published by Barricade Books

Lafayette at Brandywine

THE MAKING OF AN AMERICAN HERO

Bruce E. Mowday

Barricade Books

Published by Barricade Books Inc.
www.barricadebooks.com

Library of Congress Cataloging-in-Publication Data

Names: Mowday, Bruce E., author.
Title: Lafayette at Brandywine : the making of an American hero / Bruce E. Mowday.
Other titles: Making of an American hero
Description: Fort Lee, NJ : Barricade Books Inc., [2021] | Includes bibliographical references and index.
Identifiers: LCCN 2021019212 (print) | LCCN 2021019213 (ebook) ISBN 9781569808283 (hardcover) | ISBN 9781569808290 (ebook) ISBN 9781569808306 (paperback)
Subjects: LCSH: Lafayette, Marie Joseph Paul Yves Roch Gilbert Du Motier, marquis de, 1757-1834. | United States--History--Revolution, 1775-1783--Participation, French. | Brandywine, Battle of, Pa., 1777. | Generals--France--Biography. | Generals--United States--Biography. | Statesmen--France--Biography. | France. Armée--Biography.
Classification: LCC E207.L2 M74 2021 (print) | LCC E207.L2 (ebook) | DDC 973.3/47092 [B]--dc23
LC record available at https://lccn.loc.gov/2021019212
LC ebook record available at https://lccn.loc.gov/2021019213

10 9 8 7 6 5 4 3 2 1

Manufactured in the United States of America

Dedication

Lafayette at Brandywine: The Making of an American Hero is dedicated to everyone who endorses Lafayette's belief in freedom, independence and individual rights.

As an article in the *Illinois Intelligencer* on June 10, 1825, stated, and we should heed today, "When Lafayette is forgotten our enthusiasm in the cause of liberty will have departed and the hour of our slavery will have arrived."

Graphite drawing by Adrian Martinez 2020

Contents

Foreword

It is probably true that every author has at least one ideal reader in mind as he or she writes. For Bruce Mowday, that reader was me. As I have been a "Lafayette-ist" for more than a dozen years now, this book spoke to me in a way no other book has. It is not simply a biography or a description of events, but a detailed explanation of the genesis of Lafayette's ascent to hero status.

It was enthusiasm that brought Bruce Mowday and me together. At first it was Lafayette's enthusiasm that brought us separately to him. Then it was our joint enthusiasm for Lafayette that brought us together. After our first conversation, Bruce Mowday quickly became a member of the American Friends of Lafayette. It was like two kids realizing they both adored the same superhero.

This book certainly goes a long way in fulfilling our common goal: making sure that Americans understand that Lafayette and the Franco-American alliance were indispensable components of ensuring the United States' independence from England. Sharing Lafayette's legacy with the general public is a top priority of The American Friends of Lafayette. This extraordinary book clearly proves that Bruce has the same goal.

Lafayette at Brandywine: The Making of an American Hero does a perfect job of helping us understand what motivated a "Boy General" to put himself in harm's way at his very first battle. He did not stay on the sidelines like most aristocrats of the day, but went where musket balls and artillery fire whizzed by him. Not because he was told to be in the "thick of it," but because he chose to be.

"Lafayette-ists' like me take great pride in the Battle of Brandywine. This is where our hero was born. This is where he legitimized himself at a mere twenty years of age. This baptism by fire is the start of fifty-seven years of involvement. Lafayette was never idle. Until his death, Lafayette was always involved in some way . . . for some cause.

However, *Lafayette at Brandywine* goes beyond the events of September 11, 1777. Bruce Mowday sets the stage perfectly. He helps us understand what led Lafayette to that fateful day. He also summarizes the events afterward deftly and succinctly. Like Lafayette, Bruce Mowday does this fearlessly. A complete biography of Lafayette would take many volumes (as most historians have figured out).

I am asked about Lafayette films quite often. My answer is that it would be impossible to cover his long, complicated and fascinating life in a two-hour movie format. Maybe a ten-part mini-series could capture it all. *Lafayette at Brandywine* provides its readers with both detailed descriptions and broad overviews. The images at Brandywine that Bruce Mowday conjures up in the reader's mind play out like a movie. Firsthand accounts place us in the middle of the action. The chapters leading up to the battle and the subsequent post-battle chapters round out his life like a mini-series might.

As I read the chapter *A Hero is Born*, I came upon a phrase that gave me goosebumps: "As Lafayette's blood mingled with American soil" Could this be the exact moment? Not in Silas Deane's office, not on *La Victoire*, but here? Did Lafayette realize at that moment, as his boot was filling with blood, that he had found his purpose? As his blood seeped into the Pennsylvania battlefield, his fate was sealed and a hero was born.

Sure, Lafayette was seeking glory, and possibly revenge, but certainly not riches. This book reinforces the notion that Lafayette's enthusiasm was selfless. Major General Nathanael Greene characterized Lafayette as having "noble enthusiasm." I wholeheartedly agree with the great Revolutionary War General, who was not insinuating an aristocratic attitude, but rather an honorable one.

I would add that Lafayette's enthusiasm was simply pure, just as Bruce Mowday highlighted perfectly in this book. Lafayette brought the purest enthusiasm with him in 1777 and, thankfully for the United States, just in the nick of time.

Chuck Schwam
The American Friends of Lafayette
March 17, 2021

Acknowledgements

While drafting a book's manuscript is a solitary endeavor, a large team of compatriots are needed to complete a book. So many people deserve to be acknowledged for their expert help and encouragement on this project, *Lafayette at Brandywine: The Making of an American Hero*.

At the top of the list is Simsun Greco. Simsun was a tremendous help as she immediately delved into the life of Lafayette and advised on sections in this book. Simsun provided constant support during my work on all aspects of this book.

Early in the project I contacted The American Friends of Lafayette, a wonderful organization dedicated to keeping the memory of Lafayette, the American hero, alive. Kim Burdick, Resident Manager at the Hale-Byrnes House in Delaware, suggested I contact Chuck Swam, treasurer of The American Friends of Lafayette organization. Chuck used his many contacts to assist me in gathering pertinent information. Chuck graciously consented to write a wonderful foreword for this book. Kim provided information on Lafayette spending his 20th birthday at the Hale-Byrnes House.

Alan R. Hoffman, President of The American Friends of Lafayette, provided access to valuable information on Lafayette and his life, especially Lafayette's celebratory trip to the United States in 1824 and 1825. Alan translated the work of Auguste

Levasseur, Lafayette's private secretary during the tour. Alan is also a fine editor and made many excellent suggestions and corrections to the manuscript. Friends' member Mackenzie Fowler used her social media skills to seek out answers to my research questions. Mackenzie also shared information on an ancestor who fought with Lafayette at the Battle of Brandywine. When a question arose concerning details on the death of Lafayette's father, American Friends of Lafayette President Emeritus Robert Rhodes Crout, a Lafayette scholar, supplied answers.

Though introductions from The American Friends of Lafayette, I had the opportunity to talk with Glenn E. Campbell, senior historian of the James Brice House of Historic Annapolis, Inc. He provided valuable input on Lafayette's early days in America. Also, Diane Windham Shaw, Director Emerita of Special Collections and College Archives of Lafayette College gave me permission to use information she gathered for a talk on the "abolitionist Lafayette." Diane is a longtime member and curator of the Friends organization.

Through The American Friends of Lafayette, I've had communications with Julien Icher of the Lafayette Trail, Inc. Julien is an enthusiastic supporter of all things Lafayette.

A great artist and good friend, Adrian Martinez graciously offered the use of one of his outstanding paintings, Lafayette being wounded at Brandywine, for the cover of this book. The painting is an American masterpiece. Adrian captures so many aspects of Lafayette in his painting, along with the patriotic fervor of Brandywine. Adrian and I spent several hours one hot July morning walking the field where Lafayette was wounded. A model for Adrian's painting was Ben Goldman, a well-known Lafayette interpreter and re-enactor. Ben spent time talking with me about Lafayette and my book project during an anniversary re-enactment at the Sandy Hallow portion of the Battle of Brandywine. Linda Kaat, a great proponent of the preservation of history and especially Brandywine, introduced me to Ben. Linda directed the

Sandy Hallow event. She is also working to have a monument placed at the location where Lafayette was wounded.

Carmela Cohen of Barricade Books, Inc., did a wonderful job utilizing Adrian's painting in the cover design. Barricade Publisher Jonathan Bernstein has been an enthusiastic supporter of this Lafayette project.

Another outstanding artist, and good friend, Heather Davis contributed her paintings of buildings that still exist on the Brandywine battlefield. Heather, who lived in Chester County near Chadds Ford, now resides in Everett, Pennsylvania.

Craig Caba, curator of the J. Howard Wert Gettysburg Collection,™ provided some of the illustrations for this book. The items were photographed by Hunter Winters.

During the early stages of my research, I had an opportunity to talk with Harlow Giles Unger during a joint book signing at the Union League in New York City. He wrote *Lafayette*, a biography. He spent time talking with me about my idea of Brandywine being the place where Lafayette took a substantial step in becoming an American hero.

An early step in the research process began with a Christmas gift selected by my young grandson, Kaleb Reutter, for me and purchased by my daughter, Melissa. Kaleb pointed out *The Marquis: Lafayette Reconsidered* on a table at a Barnes & Noble store and said it would be a fine gift. Kaleb was correct. The book provided excellent details of Lafayette.

A breakfast meeting at Hank's Diner, on the Brandywine battlefield, with Karen Marshall, Heritage Preservation Coordinator for the County of Chester, and Andrew Outten, director of education and museum services for the Brandywine Battlefield Park Associates, resulted in encouragement for the Lafayette book project. Karen also offered assistance in reviewing the latest research done by the Brandywine Battlefield Task Force.

Cliff C. Parker, Archivist for the Chester County Archives, kindly set up a time for me to review the task force records. That review took place during the COVID pandemic. Cliff made sure all safety precautions were in place.

Staff members at two research centers near the Brandywine battlefield, the Christian C. Sanderson Museum in Chadds Ford and the Chester County History Center in West Chester, provided help in researching records. Chuck Uhlmann, curator at Sanderson, pulled records for my review one Saturday afternoon. Conor Hepp, President, Ellen Endslow, Director of Collections and Curator, Kathryn Martin, Librarian, and Margaret Baillie, Assistant Librarian, all aided me in my research at the History Center.

Another organization assisting in my research was the Brandywine Conservancy & Museum of Art. The Brandywine Conservancy has a rich history of preserving the land associated with the Battle of Brandywine. I remember a trip to Washington, D.C., a number of years ago with Associate Director David Shields to seek federal funds for preservation efforts. I was President of the Friends of the Brandywine Battlefield group at the time. David, along with Director Ellen Ferretti and Shelia Fleming, Manager for Municipal Assistance, are involved in the Conservancy's Birmingham Hill Preserve project. I served as a member of a task force on the project.

The Brandywine Conservancy & Museum of Art's Birmingham Hill Preserve was the site of the first and second defensive lines of the Continental Army during the afternoon's Battle of Brandywine on September 11, 1777. It is hallowed ground where Americans fought and died to establish our liberties and a new nation. The preserved land, 113 acres, also was the site where Lafayette was wounded. The Preserve was acquired in two parts over a period of eleven years. This land is the location where Linda Kaat is coordinating the placement of a marker designating the area where Lafayette was wounded.

As I was doing research, I discovered that a relative of Jim, Duie and Peter Latta, three prominent businessmen running the family's A. Duie Pyle Company, was a participant at a reception for Lafayette in West Chester, Pennsylvania. Jim, the family historian, provided family history. Friend Susan Coman, who is related to Lafayette, offered her family history of a French relation who fought for the British and was captured at Saratoga.

Kevin Farris, a friend, writer and editor, gave me an introduction to author Tim McGrath who recently authored a book on President James Monroe. Tim graciously consented to an interview. Another author and friend, Gene Pisasale, who has researched and written about Lafayette and Brandywine provided assistance. Randall Spackman of the Chadds Ford Historical Society, and owner of the Thornbury Farm Trust, which is part of the Brandywine battlefield, provided assistance on this project. Artist friend Karl J. Kuerner, who lives on a section of the Brandywine battlefield, shared his knowledge.

Margaret Chew Barringer provided information on the Benjamin Chew House and Cliveden in Germantown, where Lafayette stopped during his grand tour.

During my years of doing research, I've encountered a number of people interested in our country's rich history and are always willing to discuss the fine points of our past. For this book, Ken Woodward, Clair Leaman, Dr. Lark Eshleman, Mary Walsh, Patty DeFroscia, and Kenneth Lawson all offered encouragement.

When I sought published books, Larry Weindorf was my key contact. Larry owns *For The Historian*, a great bookshop in Gettysburg, Pennsylvania.

I also acknowledge Colin Hanna for his encouragement and offer to give a talk on Lafayette and Brandywine at an anniversary event at Radley Run Country Club. The club sits on land where the British formed to charge Washington's army during the afternoon of September 11, 1777.

INTRODUCTION

Two personal epiphanies, intertwined, developed during my years of research for my new book, *Lafayette at Brandywine: The Making of an American Hero*. Those two discoveries formed my idea for this book.

I'll begin with my second discovery. The baseline for my research was my rudimentary understanding of Lafayette. He was a great proponent of American freedom, a singular fact taught in American history. Quickly, I became aware that Lafayette was an extraordinarily courageous person. He certainly was a unique individual, maybe one of a kind. America was extremely fortunate to have attracted Lafayette's fancy. This young Frenchman risked his life, spent his fortune and put in jeopardy his relations with his family and home country to help secure the independence Americans enjoy today.

A sad realization was that Lafayette's selfless deeds and uncompromising integrity are fading from today's American consciousness. America's rich heritage is being forgotten, ignored and rewritten. By doing so, America places itself in dire peril, a danger that was forewarned. An article in the *Illinois Intelligencer* on June 10, 1825, stated the consequence of depreciating our past. The article read, "When Lafayette is forgotten, our enthusiasm in the cause of liberty will have departed and the hour of our slavery will have arrived."

The time has come for America to reacquaint itself with Lafayette, his deeds and his ideals. While excellent books and periodicals abound on Lafayette's many-faceted life, America needs to be reminded of his dedication to America's freedom.

The genesis of Lafayette's journey to becoming an American hero began with a meeting, with of all people, the brother of the King of England, the Duke of Gloucester. The Duke's brother, King George III, was waging war on his American colonies at the time of the meeting between the Duke and Lafayette. During the evening, the Duke of Gloucester made it clear he didn't totally support his brother's bellicose engagements with the colonies.

Lafayette's escape, yes, an escape, from France to assist America was full of dangers. France was silently cheering on America against England, France's despised foe of the time. The time wasn't quite right, France's rulers believed, to officially support the American rebels against England. When news leaked that Lafayette planned to offer his services to the colonies, Lafayette's family and the King attempted to block Lafayette's voyage to America. They wanted the rambunctious young Frenchman to remain in France.

A determined Lafayette eluded the King and his minions, financed his trip to America and safely landed in South Carolina. His stay in America was almost short-lived as Congress at first decided to turn Lafayette away at the doors of Independence Hall. Too many previous French and European officers were given commissions, only to be deemed costly failures. In the weeks preceding Lafayette's appearance, General George Washington informed Congress he wouldn't accept any more such foreign military men.

Upon setting foot on American soil, Lafayette had many obstacles to overcome to become an American hero. Besides convincing Congress to give him a commission, the young foreigner had to master a new language and earn the respect of his comrades in arms, including Washington. Even though he was an officer in the French army, Lafayette had no battlefield experience.

As General Washington embraced the teenaged Frenchman, some say as a son, Lafayette matured as a military officer, as a statesman and as a leader. His character was tested on many occasions while he was in the service of the United States. While courted by foes of Washington, in both America and France, Lafayette stayed true to his commander and father figure, Washington. Indeed, Lafayette was one the few people Washington could depend upon for an honest evaluation of events during the American Revolution.

On the issue of slavery, Lafayette urged Washington and other Founding Fathers to do away with the destructive and immoral practice. Lafayette even established a community for former slaves. Alas, Lafayette's sage advice was not heeded.

While a rich man before coming to America, he spent his fortune in the cause of American liberty. Lafayette and his family were destitute later in life. Decades after the American Revolution, Congress finally restored some of the wealth of the American hero.

There is little doubt that America became victorious over England because of France. France supplied needed soldiers and a mighty navy to neutralize England's superiority over the Americans. France's aid, to some extent, came to America because of the efforts of Lafayette. Lafayette was a tireless supporter and cheerleader for his adopted home.

America might have won independence from England without Lafayette's individual efforts, but surely America would have failed without the assistance of France.

In the years following the winning of freedom from England, America recognized the importance of Lafayette's contribution. His grand tour of the United States, orchestrated by President James Monroe, was a clear demonstration of the love and admiration America held for Lafayette. No other person has ever received a 13-month celebration in the United States.

My initial inspiration for this book came while thinking about a book I wrote on the Battle of Brandywine. The book, *September*

11, 1777: Washington's Defeat at Brandywine Dooms Philadelphia, was the first detailed look at the battle. The book, which took more than five years to research and write, came about after a realization that no such work had been done on Brandywine, the pivotal battle of the Philadelphia campaign.

Why was no book written on the engagement?

Brandywine involved a number of notable persons of the American Revolution. George Washington, Alexander Hamilton, Lafayette, Nathanael Greene, John Sullivan and others were there fighting for the Americans. William Howe, Charles Cornwallis, Wilhelm von Knyphausen, Banastre Tarleton and others took to the fields surrounding Chadds Ford, Pennsylvania, for the British.

The main defense of Philadelphia, home to the Continental Congress, was made along the shores of the Brandywine at Chadds Ford. The battle comprised the largest land area of any conflict in the war.

Surely, Brandywine was worthy of recognition.

Documentaries and histories of the American Revolution either totally ignore Brandywine or briefly mention the battle. Again, why was Brandywine not noted in such treatises? The answer lies with the winner and loser of Brandywine.

The winner, the British, lost the war. During my research in London, I was told at the Public Records Office, the British version of the National Archives in Washington, that they "had heard" of the American Revolution. When queried about the Battle of Brandywine, the clerks indicated they weren't familiar with that engagement.

A major victory in a British lost cause was forgotten.

Brandywine was an embarrassment for George Washington. As the Italian proverb states: "He that deceives me once, it's his fault; but if twice, it's my fault." The British used the same successful flanking movement utilized at Long Island the year before to defeat Washington at Brandywine.

The defeat was total. American causalities were twice the number suffered by the British. Some British officers claimed that if two more hours of daylight had been available to fight, Washington's army would have ceased to exist that day. Afterwards, Washington appeared to have put the nightmare of Brandywine out of his consciousness. At least, Washington didn't discuss Brandywine or write about the conflict much after the battle.

So, both the winner and loser had reason not to dwell on Brandywine. Little wonder, the battle faded from the nation's consciousness.

Americans tend to look for silver linings, even during disasters. During my original research, many connected with Brandywine at the Pennsylvania state park pointed to one bright spot. They contended that elements of Washington's forces battled the vaunted British troops on even terms for several hours during the late afternoon. The soldiers then, according to the modern-day conviction, took that memory of standing up to the British to Valley Forge and used the experience to make them better soldiers, soldiers that eventually defeated the British.

True, the Americans stood and bravely fought the British at Birmingham Hill and Sandy Hallow near the Quaker Birmingham Meeting House during the late afternoon of September 11, 1777. However, the second part of the speculative theory is questionable. Did the Americans take the memory of those several hours with them to Valley Forge?

Since the survivors of Washington's army didn't even camp in Valley Forge until three months after Brandywine and weren't properly trained for another few months, did the troops really remember those few hours in a losing battle?

Some of Washington's soldiers were involved in battles, losing ones at Paoli and Germantown, between Brandywine and Valley Forge. Paoli was another total disaster. Some label Paoli a massacre by the British. The battle cry "Remember Paoli" was coined to rally American troops against the British.

Paoli appears to be more of an inspiration for the troops at Valley Forge than Brandywine. And why, in the first place, would troops be inspired by a losing battle? Wouldn't American troops be more emboldened by the American victory over the British at the battle of Saratoga in October 1777? True, a different segment of the American army secured the triumph at Saratoga but the battle was a clear victory for the rebel army.

So, if the memory of two hours of hard fighting in the loss at Brandywine wasn't a catalyst for better soldiering, did something special, important, that impacted America's freedom take place during the Battle of Brandywine?

Yes, emphatically.

The possibility of a monumental occurrence being overlooked at Brandywine bothered me for some time. Lafayette kept entering my consciousness, and the more I researched, evidence mounted that Brandywine marked the beginning of Lafayette's rise to the status of an American hero.

In the early morning hours of September 11, 1777, Lafayette was just another European officer offering his service for America. American soldiers had seen such officers before, and most came with fancy titles and ranks and departed by offering little of substance to secure America's freedom in exchange for their high pay. Just weeks before Lafayette's arrival, Washington told Congress to stop offering commissions to European officers.

Lafayette, because of his wealth and influence and personality, was accepted by Washington at the urging of Congress. But Lafayette was untested in battle and had not gained the acceptance of his fellow officers and the soldiers of Washington's army. He was a young man with no military experience and little knowledge of the English language. He was a long way from an American hero on that warm and foggy morning along the shores of the Brandywine River.

By the end of the long day of fighting and suffering, Lafayette was on his way to becoming an American hero. One historian reported Lafayette left the field at Brandywine a hero.

When Washington received word that the British had outflanked the Americans, Lafayette sought permission to join the embattled troops about to be routed by the British. Lafayette jumped into the middle of the action, rallying rebel soldiers under the command of General Thomas Conway, stationed just west of the Birmingham Meeting House.

A British musket ball entered and went through Lafayette's left leg. An aide saw the blood filling Lafayette's boot and helped the wounded Frenchman onto his horse and led him to the shelter of a nearby woods.

The Frenchman was no longer an unknown and untested foreign officer. Lafayette spilled his own blood in the cause of American freedom. His bravery won the faith of Washington and the rest of the American army.

No longer should Brandywine be lost in history. Brandywine should be remembered and celebrated for marking the beginning of Lafayette's journey to becoming an American hero.

Bruce E. Mowday
March 2021

Author's Note

Lafayette at Brandywine: The Making of an American Hero was written to reintroduce—sadly to introduce—Lafayette to the American public. This book is designed to make the text easy to follow for the 21st century reader. Some of the original passages with archaic spelling and grammar are updated without altering the original intent. Too many "sic" insertions and unfamiliar constructions break the flow of the text and make it difficult for readers to follow. Actually, those irritations cause readers to stop reading. In a portion of Lafayette's memoirs, Lafayette writes about himself in the third person. Those third person references were changed to first person.

Some of the 18th century letters and reports are flowery, long and laborious to read. I've purposely not used full texts in most instances. For those wanting to experience the exact words, footnotes indicate where the material can be found. Much of the information for this book came from Lafayette's memoirs, the files of the National Archives, and Auguste Levasseur's *Lafayette in America in 1824 and 1825: Journal of a Voyage to the United States.* Levasseur's book, translated by Alan R. Hoffman, contains wonderful details of Lafayette's grand tour of the United States, and interesting historical highlights.

Lafayette was an intricate man. He had many facets to his life. What this book is not is a biography of Lafayette. There are many fine books on Lafayette's life and relationships. This is not a history of the American Revolution. This is not a history of the two French Revolutions. This is not an academic tome full of obscure references. This is a book about Lafayette's contributions to American freedom and the events that impacted Lafayette. Also, this book stresses the importance of the Battle of Brandywine to Lafayette's shedding of blood at Brandywine.

Artist Adrian Martinez created the excellent painting used on the cover of this book. Upon close scrutiny, the painting reveals hints of what Lafayette might have thought about on September 11, 1777, at Brandywine. Was this a painting of a young Lafayette? Maybe an older Lafayette was reflecting on the day? Take time, if you can, to closely view the painting in an artistic light. This is not a representative caricature of Lafayette. Adrian creates sophisticated artistic historical paintings.

Lafayette Timeline

1757 to the Present

(Courtesy of The American Friends of Lafayette)

1757 **Sept 6**: Marie-Joseph-Paul-Yves-Roch-Gilbert du Motier, Marquis de Lafayette, is born at Chateau Chavaniac in the Auvergne region of southern France.

1759 **August 1**: Lafayette's father, Michel Louis Christophe Roch Gilbert Motier—a colonel in the Louis XV's army—is killed in action in Minden, Germany while fighting against the British during the Seven Years' War.

1759 **November 2**: Adrienne de Noailles, the future wife of the Marquis de Lafayette, is born in Paris.

1768 **September**: At age 11, Gilbert moves to Paris and attends the Collège du Plessis.

1770 **April 3**: Lafayette's mother, Marie Louise Jolie de La Rivière, dies at the age of 33.

1770 **April 11**: Gilbert decides to join the King's Musketeers, influenced by his grandfather's military experiences in the unit.

1770 **April 24**: Lafayette's maternal grandfather dies. He inherits great wealth from the La Rivière estate that includes a thousand acres of land, farms in Brittany, and business investments in the Indies. At 13, he becomes one of the wealthiest aristocrats in Europe.

1770 **September**: Lafayette makes application for appointment to the King's Musketeers in the corps d'élite.

1771 **April 9**: He receives official appointment to serve in the King's Musketeers and begins his martial education at the Military Academy at Versailles.

1773 **April**: Thanks to the influence of his future father-in-law, the Duc de Noailles, Lafayette becomes a Brevet Lieutenant in the prestigious Noailles Regiment.

1774 **April 11**: Gilbert, 16, and Adrienne, 14, marry in the Noailles family chapel.

1775 **August 8**: Lafayette meets the Duke of Gloucester, brother of King George III, while on maneuvers at Metz, France.

1776 **July 4**: The signing of the American Declaration of Independence. A sacred document even for Lafayette who adopts it as his clarion call to action.

1776 **November**: Johann de Kalb introduces Lafayette to Silas Deane, the American agent hired by Congress to recruit foreign officers to serve in the Continental Army for the American cause.

1776 **December 7**: Lafayette signs a contract with Silas Deane in Paris and accepts the commission as Major General in the American army.

1777 **March 16**: Lafayette and de Kalb secretly leave for Bordeaux where they make plans to sail to America.

1777 **April 20**: Lafayette recruits a dozen other men and uses a disguise to hide from the police who were ordered to arrest him for leaving without permission. Lafayette escapes across the Spanish border and boards ship off the coast of San Sebastian. He sails on this date.

1777 **June 13**: He arrives in South Carolina.

1777 **July 31**: Arrived in Philadelphia to receive his commission as major general in the Continental Army.

1777 **August 10**: He becomes an aide-de-camp for General Washington at Moland Headquarters in Bucks County, PA.

1777 **August**: With General Washington and General Nathanael

Greene, they reconnoiter the British from Grey's Hill near the village of Head of the Elk in the Chesapeake Bay.

1777 **September**: Sets up his HQ at Chadd's Ford with General Washington in preparation for the defense of the city of Philadelphia to stop the British invasion of the capital city.

1777 **September 11**: General Lafayette receives his baptism of fire in the Battle of Brandywine in Chadds Ford, Pennsylvania, and is wounded with a bullet through his left leg.

1777 **September**: Is carried by chair to a Moravian Hospital at Bethlehem, PA.

1777 **November**: Lafayette joins Washington at Peter Wentz' farm in Worcester Township, PA, near Philadelphia.

1777 **November 24**: Lafayette is given command of Continental troops to reconnoiter British General Cornwallis in New Jersey. Although outnumbered, his troops attack Hessians near Gloucester, New Jersey and send them reeling in defeat.

1777 **December 19**: Lafayette marches into Valley Forge with Washington and the Continental Army with 12,000 troops.

1778 **February 6**: The French Alliance is signed in Paris, the treaty of alliance and commerce between America and France.

1778 **February 17**: Congress sends Lafayette to invade Canada. Arrives at Albany. Mission aborted.

1778 **February 24**: Great Britain declares war on France.

1778 **March**: Lafayette accomplishes projects in New York State. He gets pledges from the Oneida Nation to support the American cause. He recruits forty-seven (47) Oneidas and sends them to Valley Forge to join him there.

1778 **April**: Lafayette returns to Valley Forge.

1778 **May 18**: 2,200 troops under Lafayette's command move from Valley Forge to Barren Hill to scout British in Philadelphia.

1778 **May 20**: Lafayette's spectacular escape from 16,000

troops commanded by British generals Howe, Grant, Clinton and Grey.

1778 June 19: Washington orders General Benedict Arnold to march back into Philadelphia and take over as military governor.

1778 June 28: Battle of Monmouth Court House (Freehold) New Jersey.

1778 August: Lafayette commands troops during the Battle of Rhode Island in the invasion of Aquidneck Island.

1779 January 11: Lafayette returns to France on board American ship *The Alliance* to get aid from the French government.

1779 February 12: Has important conference with Vergennes and Maurepas and argues for more aid to be sent to General Washington.

1779 December 24: Adrienne, the Marquise de Lafayette, gives birth to a baby boy. Lafayette names the infant George Washington Lafayette.

1780 February 29: Lafayette, dressed in his American major general's uniform, goes to the Court of Versailles to take formal leave of the King and Queen of France on his mission to resume his duties for General Washington. He is given a formal send-off.

1780 March 17: Embarks on *The Hermione* to America.

1780 April 28: Lafayette arrives at Boston Harbor and is enthusiastically greeted as a hero.

1780 May 10: Lafayette arrives at Morristown Headquarters and greets Washington with King Louis' message: the French Expeditionary Force will arrive in America with more than 6,000 elite troops, artillery pieces, munitions, ships, and money.

1780 May 15: Congress, by resolution, honors Lafayette as gallant and meritorious.

1780 September: Conference held at Hartford, Connecticut. Washington, Lafayette, Rochambeau, Chastellux and General Henry Knox are present.

1781 **January**: Continental unrest. Pennsylvania and New Jersey troops mutiny. Washington hopes such actions inspire no repeat performances in other battalions.

1781 **February**: Nathanael Greene commands Continentals in the Southern campaign. He asks General Washington to send Lafayette to help him counter Benedict Arnold's destruction of Virginia. Lafayette takes command of a corps of troops and saves Virginia from the British army's scorched earth policy.

1781 **August through September**: After maneuvering more than a thousand miles, Lafayette pursues, harasses, and finally corners Cornwallis at Yorktown. The French West Indian fleet under Admiral de Grasse arrives.

1781 **September 14**: Lafayette meets Washington and Rochambeau at Williamsburg to assure them that Cornwallis is trapped.

1781 **September 17**: The siege of Yorktown begins.

1781 **October**: French and American troops cannonade the British into surrender after nine days of blistering artillery fire.

1781 **October 19**: Cornwallis surrenders at Yorktown. The last major engagement of the American Revolution concludes.

1781 **December 23**: Lafayette gets permission from Congress to return to France. He leaves Boston Harbor on the ship *Alliance.*

1783: Adrienne gives birth to a daughter, Virginie, named after George Washington's state of Virginia.

1783 **September**: The Treaty of Paris, signed by Benjamin Franklin and French and British officials, officially ends the American Revolutionary War against Great Britain. America wins its complete independence.

1784 **June**: Lafayette leaves Paris to visit the United States and spends time at Mount Vernon as Washington's honored guest.

1784–1787: Virginia, Maryland, and Massachusetts make Lafayette an honorary American citizen.

1789: Lafayette is elected as representative of the nobility to the Estates General at Paris. He becomes a leader of the liberal aristocrats and an outspoken advocate of religious freedom and the abolition of the slave trade.

1789 July 11: Lafayette becomes the first Frenchman to introduce a version of the Declaration of the Rights of Man and of the Citizen at the National Assembly in Paris.

1789 July 14–15: The French Revolution begins.

1789 October 6: Lafayette's troops save King Louis XVI and Queen Marie-Antoinette from a furious crowd that invades Versailles.

1791 December: Lafayette is appointed commander of the army at Metz to check the Austrian invasion of France.

1792 August 14: Danton and Robespierre demand the arrest of Lafayette and all other aristocrats and plan to prosecute them for treason and execute them.

1792 August 19: Lafayette leaves France and flees to Belgium, where he is turned over to Austria and held prisoner.

1792 September 10: Adrienne de Lafayette is arrested by police at Chateau Chavaniac and is confined there indefinitely.

1793–1794: The duration of the Reign of Terror.

1794: Lafayette is made prisoner in Olmutz Prison in Austria (now in the Czech Republic).

1794 May: Adrienne is transferred to a prison in Paris. Adrienne's mother, sister, and grandmother are all guillotined.

1795 January: Adrienne is liberated thanks to pressure put on French officials by minister plenipotentiary, James Monroe, Elizabeth Monroe, and other Americans.

1795 April: Fifteen-year-old George Washington Lafayette is sent to America to stay with George Washington until the crisis ends.

1795 September: Adrienne de Lafayette asks permission from the Austrian monarchy to allow her and her daughters Anastasie and Virginie to visit Lafayette in prison at Olmutz.

1795 **October 15**: The Lafayette ladies arrive at Olmutz and join him in prison. Their living conditions in adjoining cells are abominable and unsanitary.

1797 **September 19**: Lafayette and his family are liberated thanks to Napoleon's military victories and American help given with the blessing of President George Washington.

1798 **February**: Georges Washington Lafayette returns to Europe from the United States and joins the rest of the Lafayette family in exile.

1799: Napoleon refuses to let Lafayette into the country because of his liberal democratic ideas. Lafayette defies him by ignoring intimidation and returns anyway to become a gentleman farmer at his wife's chateau La Grange.

1807: Adrienne, the Marquise de Lafayette, dies at age 47.

1815: Napoleon is defeated at Waterloo by British General Wellington. Napoleon is sent into exile. Lafayette is relieved that France has survived another political catastrophe.

1824 **August 15**: Lafayette arrives in America as an honored guest of the United States of America at President James Monroe's invitation. He is received with wild adulation. When asked by hosts how he wished to be introduced to his audiences, he replies: "As an American General."

1824 **September 28-October 6**: Lafayette makes a memorable visit to Philadelphia with his unforgettable speech at the State House, today's Independence Hall.

1824 **October**: The town fathers at Easton, Pennsylvania decide to name their institution of higher learning in honor of General Lafayette after listening to his State House speech in Philadelphia. Lafayette College becomes one of America's greatest memorials to General Lafayette.

1825 **September 9**: Gilbert departs for France after his spectacular visitation to each of the 24 states of the Union. He sails aboard *The Brandywine*, a frigate named in his honor.

1830 **July**: Lafayette commands the National Guard that helps overthrow King Charles X and installs Louis-Philippe on the throne of France.

1834 **May 20**: Lafayette dies in Paris four months shy of his 77th birthday.

1834 **May 23**: Lafayette is buried at Picpus Cemetery in Paris next to his wife. His son George Washington Lafayette scatters American soil around his casket. He rests as he wished—buried in American soil. Since the 1890's an American flag has flown at his grave site as a mark of respect for a man who risked his life and fortune for a country he loved as much as his own beloved France.

2002 **August 6**: The Marquis de Lafayette becomes the sixth honorary citizen of the United States of America by the virtue of legislation sponsored Senator John Warner of Virginia.

2007 **May 22:** The House of Representatives of the United States passes resolution honoring Lafayette on the 250th anniversary of his birth.

·1·

A Hero Emerges

A warm September day born in morning fog, concluded in darkness and embarrassment for General George Washington's fledgling American army. The last flickering rays of daylight actually saved Washington's troops as the British army halted their deadly and effective offensive against the battered American army. With an additional few hours of sunshine, several British officers contended, Washington's army would have ceased to exist that day in 1777.

History, for the most part, has relegated the Battle of Brandywine to the category of lesser events of the American Revolution. Modern day historical treatises and historians give Brandywine fleeting, if any, mention. The first in-depth book on the battle wasn't published until more than 225 years after the engagement. At that time, primary source material was sparse and scattered throughout the United States and England. When contacted by the author, a member of the British Public Records Office, the holder of Great Britain's important records, indicated he wasn't familiar with Brandywine. The representative said he never heard of the engagement, even though Brandywine was a major British victory in England's lost cause to retain control of its colonies.

Legitimate reasons existed for the lack of notoriety Brandywine received. Since losing the war, the British haven't paid much attention to the American Revolution, even to the British army's victories, such as Brandywine. The loss of the country's American colonies was just a minor blip in Britain's long history. General Washington certainly didn't pay much attention to Brandywine after the fact, as the battle was one of his major defeats.

Washington, a great leader and the one man most responsible for America's independence, had few military victories to his credit, especially early in the war against England. He was a master of leading and inspiring men. Washington miraculously kept his army together during the many dark days of the revolution. Brandywine is noted as just one of a series of engagements where the British professional army outclassed Washington's brave band of patriotic citizen soldiers.

At a quick glance, Brandywine was similar to the battle of Long Island. On August 27, 1776, the first major battle was fought after America declared independence. General William Howe's troops outflanked Washington's army and drove the American army from the environs of New York. The British held the strategic port of New York for the rest of the war.

Howe utilized the same flanking maneuver at Brandywine to foil Washington's attempt to protect the Continental Congress, then sitting in Philadelphia. After the battle, Howe was able to take the nation's capital at his leisure and did so 15 days later. By that time, the Continental Congress had fled first to Lancaster, Pennsylvania, on September 27, and then to York, Pennsylvania, for the winter.

The banks of the Brandywine River in Chester County, Pennsylvania, was the defensive position selected by Washington to stop the British army. Howe's path to the prize of Philadelphia led through the rich countryside of the Brandywine valley. Believing Howe would force a crossing near Chadds Ford, Washington braced his troops behind the water barrier. Though not a major river, the Brandywine came to a man's waist that late summer's day in 1777 and was wide enough to slow down attacking British and Hessian soldiers.

Washington received little friendly assistance from local citizens and his own scouts before and during the battle. He commanded an army utilizing misleading and incorrect information. A frustrated Washington, for all purposes, was militarily blind while fighting at Brandywine.

First, Washington was assured that the British army would take days to outflank his army to the north of his defensive position. The local information was proved wrong, as a friendly Tory knew a way to ford the Brandywine at two points and led Howe's forces on a march that took hours and not days.

Second, Washington's scouts failed to provide accurate and timely information. Washington was uneasy about relying on the information given to him. After all, Howe had outflanked him in previous battles. So, Washington's scouts were scattered throughout the area with a warning to be vigilant and an order to report any sightings of the British army. A little more than half of Howe's army, about 8,000 men under the command of General Charles Cornwallis, was able to evade detection for most of the morning and execute the flanking maneuver.

While Washington struggled to hold his flawed defensive position, Howe executed his intricate offensive plan almost perfectly.

As ordered, General Wilhelm Knyphausen took about half of the British army on a march from nearby Kennett Square to the banks of the Brandywine. Knyphausen's orders were to force American General William Maxwell's light infantry back from the front of Kennett Square, where the British army camped the night before the battle, to the shores of the Brandywine. Knyphausen tricked Washington into believing he commanded the whole of the British army. The ruse gave Howe and Cornwallis time to encircle Washington's army.

As Knyphausen attacked in the morning hours, the troops under Howe and Cornwallis executed their lengthy trek—approximately

17 miles that took about nine hours—around Washington's right flank, protected by American General John Sullivan's division. During mid-afternoon, Cornwallis lined his men along Osborne Hill and attacked Sullivan's forces. At the sound of the fighting, Knyphausen's men forced a crossing of the Brandywine and drove back the American defenders under the leadership of American General Anthony Wayne.

Despite some stubborn and spirited fighting by American troops, especially on Birmingham Hill and nearby Sandy Hallow, the Americans were in full retreat by nightfall and fled on the road leading to Chester, Pennsylvania.

September 11, 1777 was a disastrous day for General George Washington's army.

The date of September 11 has been cursed for Americans. On September 11, 2001, nineteen Islamic terrorists hijacked four airplanes and carried out suicide attacks. Two of the planes were flown into the twin towers of the World Trade Center in New York City, a third plane hit the Pentagon just outside Washington, D.C., and the fourth plane crashed in a field in Shanksville, Pennsylvania. Almost 3,000 people were killed.

Ironically, on September 11, 1941, groundbreaking took place for the Pentagon. On the same date in 2012, an attack on a United States diplomatic outpost in Benghazi, Libya, killed U.S. Ambassador Chris Stevens and three other Americans. And, on September 11, 1976, a bomb planted by a Croatian terrorist at New York's Grand Central Terminal killed one police officer who was trying to defuse it.

Was there any good news for Americans on September 11, 1777?

In the late 20th century and early 21st century at Brandywine, a prevalent theory centered on the fighting at Birmingham Hill and Sandy Hallow. For several hours the Americans held off the British advance and allowed Washington's surviving troops to retreat to Chester.

The Americans, according to the theory, believed they could

stand up to the British army because of their actions on Birmingham Hill. That memory, supposedly, aided Prussian General Baron Friedrich Wilhelm von Steuben when he trained the troops at Valley Forge the following year.

Von Steuben is credited for turning Washington's troops into a disciplined army. Von Steuben drafted a drill manual using the latest Prussian military techniques to instruct the American soldiers. By the time the 1778 campaign began, von Steuben's drills had prepared Washington's army for the coming battles with England's professional army.

Did the inspiration the Americans received from the few hours of fighting in a losing battle have any impact on their readiness in 1778? The Brandywine theory is certainly suspect for several reasons. The time between the afternoon engagement at Brandywine and the drilling at Valley Forge under von Steuben was more than five months. Washington's army was involved in other battles and skirmishes with the British—most notably Paoli and Germantown—between the time of Brandywine and the harsh winter at Valley Forge.

Paoli was another American disaster; some called the loss a massacre. The British, under the command of General Charles "No Flint" Gray, routed General Wayne's Americans at Paoli. Gray received his nickname because he ordered his solders to remove flints so no accidental shots could be fired to alert the Americans. Gray's troops attacked with just bayonets. Reports of the British bayonetting to death surrendering American soldiers led to Paoli being called a massacre. "Remember Paoli," became the fledging nation's first battle cry. Wouldn't the thought of revenging the slain Americans at Paoli be more of a motivation to become better soldiers than the brief fighting at Birmingham Hill?

And wouldn't a victory be more inspirational than a disastrous loss?

In the days after Brandywine, American troops fought the British at Saratoga, New York in several crucial engagements. British General John Burgoyne marched his force from Canada in the hopes of linking up with other British forces based in New York City and western New York. The British hoped to divide the New England colonies from those in the south. England could then subdue the radicals in New England and turn its full might on the southern states.

Neither of the supporting British armies arrived to assist Burgoyne at Saratoga. The British general attempted to force his way past the American forces under General Horatio Gates and failed on two occasions. The first battle took place on September 19, eight days after Brandywine. The second engagement commenced on October 7, 1777. Both failed to dislodge the British forces from Gates's clutches. Burgoyne surrendered his army to Gates on October 17.

Americans winning a decisive victory at Saratoga must have been more encouraging than two hours of spirited combat during a monumental loss at Brandywine. Actually, von Steuben had much more to do with the improvement of Washington's army than the memory of Brandywine, Paoli or Saratoga.

Was Brandywine a complete loss for Americans which earned its place in historical purgatory? Or did something positive take place at Brandywine, something that has been for the most part overlooked by those studying the American Revolution?

The answer to the last question is a definitive yes. Not only did a positive event take place during the disastrous defeat at Brandywine, but one that was crucial in the winning of American independence. The event took place on Birmingham Hill.

As British generals Howe and Cornwallis were smartly marching from Osborne's Hill, the portion of the American army under the command of General John Sullivan was poorly forming on Birmingham Hill. The British army drove the Americans from their defensive positions towards the field at Sandy Hallow.

An American hero—Marie-Joseph Paul Yves Roch Gilbert du Motier, Marquis de La Fayette—known in America as Lafayette —was minted during the furious battle. He shed his blood that day fighting for America's freedom. On the afternoon of September 11, 1777, at Brandywine, Lafayette took a substantive step in his journey to becoming an American hero.

While many dedicated and brave individuals contributed to the winning of independence for the United States, it is highly unlikely that the American Revolution would have been successful without Lafayette and the assistance he procured from his native France for the American cause.

Ironically, the young French general—he had celebrated his 20th birthday earlier in the month—almost didn't participate in the conflict at Brandywine. Lafayette came close to returning to France without taking up arms in defense of the colonies.

Arriving in America, Lafayette was imbued with an extreme desire to see the colonies become free and be rid of English rule. He had a promise of an officer's commission. Congress, at first, ignored the promise. Lafayette and other aspiring French and European officers who arrived with him were informed their service wouldn't be required. The rejection was due to Washington's strong urging that Congress stop handing out such commissions. Too many incompetent European officers preceding Lafayette were ineffective and drained the scarce funds available to the American military.

Lafayette did receive a commission as major general even though Washington believed the appointment was only honorary and didn't involve commanding American forces. Lafayette was initially resented by Washington's generals. Those officers had fought alongside Washington for more than a year. The young Frenchman, who didn't speak English well and had never taken part in a battle, suddenly outranked them.

On the morning of September 11, 1777, Lafayette was an unknown and untrusted volunteer member of Washington's staff, with no combat experience. By the end of the day, Lafayette was emerging as an American hero, embarking on a journey where he would play an integral part in America's freedom.

Brandywine deserves an honored place in American history because of Lafayette.

Musketeers of the Guard were equipped with Muskets.
It was also a name for the royal bodyguards of the King of France.

2

Young Lafayette

A young, decorated French colonel by the name of La Fayette commanded Grenadiers during action at the medieval town of Minden during the Seven Years War. France and its allies were in the midst of fighting its detested rival England and England's partners during the war that engulfed Europe and beyond, a forerunner of the World War I and World War II conflicts that occurred almost two centuries in the future.

Minden, situated along both sides of the River Weser in the northeastern North Rhine-Westphalia section of Germany, became a focal point of fighting during the summer of 1759. A major battle, a British victory, took place on August 1. The French-led force was the victor in a lesser engagement on July 9.

French commander Victor François, Duc de Broglie, victorious at a previous battle at Bergen on April 13, was determined to force his way past the army of King George II of Great Britain. King George II was a Hanoverian Elector, a prince that is, who was eligible to participate in the choosing of the Holy Roman Emperor. At that time, the royal families of Europe co-mingled and family connections were major factors in alliances. The strongest alliance had the most power.

Minden posed a difficult problem for Broglie. The medieval

city had a formidable defense made of walls and bastions constructed two centuries before the Seven Years War. Below the walls of the city, flowed the Weser River to the North Sea.

The French suffered about 7,000 casualties during the August 1 battle of Minden. One of the dead was Colonel Michel Louis Christophe Roch Gilbert Motier, marquis de La Fayette, a Knight of the Order of Saint Louis. He was killed by a British cannonball.[1] One of the British artillery officers that day was Captain William Phillips. Years later, Phillips, then a major general, and La Fayette's son would face each other as foes in the American Revolution during a campaign in Virginia.

Marie-Joseph Paul Yves Roch Gilbert du Motier, Marquis de La Fayette, to be known throughout America as Lafayette, was two years old when his father died on the fields of Minden. Lafayette wrote in his memoirs of his father's death, "The Prince de Chimay, an intimate friend of my father's, was killed at the head of the first battalion. My father was to succeed him. He took his place and was carried off by a cannonball, shot from an English battery."

Besides leaving the young Lafayette fatherless and greatly affecting Lafayette's upbringing, the death of Colonel La Fayette was a factor in Lafayette eventually controlling a large inheritance. Lafayette used his vast wealth to assist America in its upcoming struggle for freedom from England.

Lafayette was born on September 6, 1757, at his family's 18-room mansion, actually more of a fortress than a home, at

[1] References have listed La Fayette's death as both July 9 and August 1, 1759, even though most references cite August 1. Robert Crout, a Lafayette historian affiliated with the American Friends of Lafayette wrote, "I would suggest the most authoritative source would be Lafayette's personnel file at the French army archives that identifies his father's death at August 1, 1759 'a Minden.' It doesn't say battle of Minden or the overall 'operation.' Lafayette received a pension for the death of his father in combat until the end of 1785."

Chavaniac, in the province of Auvergne in south central France. The less than elegant abode was about three hundred miles south of Paris.

His parents were Colonel Motier, marquis de La Fayette, and Marie Louise Jolie de La Rivière. The Motiers were known by their noble title of La Fayette. Besides the title, the Motier family's wealth was rooted in its land. Marie Louise Jolie de La Rivière was an heiress to the Breton fortune. Her family also had close connections to King Louis XV and were descendants of Louis IX.[2]

Upon his father's death, Lafayette inherited the title of marquis. Colonel La Fayette's estate was controlled by Lafayette's mother. After the 1759 death of her husband, Lafayette's mother moved to Paris to be with her father and grandfather at the Luxembourg Palace. Lafayette remained at Chavaniac and was raised by his paternal grandmother Marie-Catherine de Suat de Chavaniac.

For the early part of Lafayette's life, he was surrounded by formidable women. Lafayette's grandmother was well-respected in the community. Living in the home were her two daughters and a granddaughter, a year older than Lafayette. Lafayette's mother did return to Chavaniac during summer months to be with her son.

Lafayette's character was formed by the women in his life, mother, grandmother and aunts. His respect for individuals and their rights was instilled in his early life. This attitude was far different from the nobles and especially the royal families of France. Lafayette's support of the tenets of the American Revolution would cause Lafayette to greatly suffer during the French Revolution.

Lafayette's early education was administered by a Jesuit priest. At the age of 11, Lafayette moved to Paris and attended the

---

[2] Jason Lane, *General and Madame de Lafayette*, Taylor Trade Publishing, London, 2003, p. 5.

Collège du Plessis of the University of Paris. As Lafayette's education progressed, his career path was limited but clear. Lafayette was destined to follow the family's military tradition and become an army officer. During his early years, Lafayette was regaled with stories of military honors won by family members. As a youngster, Lafayette saw paintings daily of his military ancestors and dreamed of leading an invasion of Britain to avenge his father's death. He also fancied winning glory for himself and adding to the honor of his family.[3]

The military tradition in Lafayette's family began with Pons Motier in the year 1000.[4] One of Lafayette's ancestors was Gilbert de Lafayette III, who served with Joan of Arc's army during the siege of Orleans in 1429. His ancestors also took part in the Sixth Crusade. Lafayette's great-grandfather was the Comete de La Rivière, and he served as commander of the Mousquetaires du Roi, the king's personal horse guard. Lafayette's uncle Jacques-Roch died while fighting the Austrians at Milan in the War of the Polish Succession in 1734.

Destiny propelled Lafayette forward to his place of honor as a hero of the American Revolution. Some go as far as to call Lafayette the hero of two worlds, America and France. His native France still doesn't embrace Lafayette as a national hero.

Lafayette's formal military career started when he enrolled in a program to train future Musketeers. The Musketeers of the Guard, also known as the King's Musketeers, was a military branch of the Maison du Roi, the Royal Household of the French monarchy. The Musketeers was an honored organization in France, operating from the 17th century until the 19th century. Training with Lafayette were three future kings of France. Lafayette was gaining powerful associates in his sphere. He would put his royal acquaintances to good use later during the American

---

[3] Lane, p. 5.

[4] Harlow Unger, *Lafayette*, John Wiley & Sons, Inc., Hoboken, N.J., 2002 p. 3

Revolution. Those same royal connections almost ended his life during the French Revolution and caused years of suffering in prisons.

Young Lafayette, four months shy of his 14th birthday, was commissioned an officer in the Musketeers in May 1771. His rank was lieutenant, and among Lafayette's ceremonial duties were participating in parades and presenting himself to King Louis XV. The King personally gave instructions daily to the assembled Musketeers.

The year before joining the Musketeers both his mother and grandfather died, just three weeks apart in April 1770. His mother was just 32 years old at the time of her death. The death of his grandfather meant Lafayette was lord of the La Rivière lands in Brittany. Lafayette's inheritance from his mother and her family made him a wealthy Musketeer.

Arranged marriages were a custom in noble and royal circles at the time, linking families for financial or influence considerations. On April 11, 1774, 16-year-old Lafayette married 14-year-old Adrienne de Noailles, a daughter of a wealthy, noble family and related to the French royalty. The marriage was arranged for Lafayette by his great-grandfather when he was 14 and when Adrienne was just 12. Adrienne's father, Jean-Louis-Paul-François de Noailles, Duc d'Ayen, arranged marriages for his five daughters.

Adrienne was not informed of the agreement for more than a year. The proposed marriage came with conditions as Adrienne's mother, Henriette d'Ayen, had severe reservations about Lafayette and the coupling of her daughter. Lafayette was to live in the family's elegant mansion in Versailles prior to the marriage, under the watchful eye of Adrienne's family. Lafayette could only accompany Adrienne while chaperoned. Then for a year after the marriage, the couple was to live at the family's mansion, the Hôtel de Noailles, in Paris.

While at Versailles, Lafayette was enrolled in a riding academy and met the King's grandsons, future kings of France. Adrienne and her mother both warmed to Lafayette and the marriage was eventually welcomed by daughter and mother. The wedding itself was a grand occasion held at the Hôtel de Noailles's chapel. Two future kings of France, Louis XVIII and Charles X, attended.

Love was not the primary inducement in arranged marriages. The custom of the time was for both husband and wife to have affairs. Lafayette's brother-in-law even encouraged Lafayette to seek female company. Lafayette quickly became loyal to Adrienne, and Adrienne, demonstrated by many of her actions during their marriage, was as committed to Lafayette.

Along with the marriage, came a placement in the Noailles regiment of dragoons. Lafayette's father-in-law arranged the transfer from the Musketeers with the rank of captain. His first posting was to the citadel at Metz. There he was introduced to Freemasonry. During the American Revolution, Lafayette would bond with a number of the Freemasons, including George Washington, Thomas Jefferson and Benjamin Franklin.

When not attending to his military duties, Lafayette was spending time participating in the royal court life in Versailles. "Not yet 18, a captain in the famous regiment, married into a family close to the throne, and favored by fate to emulate his ancestors in glorious deeds of leadership," Lafayette's fate was secure.[5]

D'Ayen arranged to have his son-in-law considered a member of the royal household, ensuring that Lafayette would have access to wealth and choice military assignments. Lafayette would then be more of a royal courtier than a military officer. The palace lifestyle was an uncomfortable fit for Lafayette, who was depicted as a shy and quiet youth and lacking in necessary royal graces. "He was now fully grown: nearly six-feet tall, large boned, fair skinned, with hazel eyes under a mop of reddish blond hair. He was considered awkward, possibly because he was taller by nearly

[5] Stanley Idzerda, *Our Marquis: A Biographical Essay on Lafayette*, Lafayette College, Easton, 2017, p. 5.

five inches than the average member of his set, and because he lacked the polish, grace and savoir-faire of the court nobility who moved easily between Versailles and the salons of Paris."[6]

Lafayette rejected a position in the court of King Louis XVI.

Despite attempts by Adrienne's family to keep the husband and wife apart during the early years of their marriage, Adrienne wrote to her husband in the spring of 1775 that they were to become parents. Daughter Henriette was born on December 15.

[6] Idzerda, pp. 5-6.

·3·

A Glorious Cause

Lafayette's posting at the French city of Metz launched and ignited his fervor for American freedom. The man responsible for initially guiding the young French officer towards his destiny was Charles-François Comte de Broglie, who had served with Lafayette's father at Minden, governor of Metz and a grand master Freemason.

Broglie invited Lafayette and two of Lafayette's close confidents, Lafayette's brother-in-law, Louis Vicomte de Noailles and Louis Philippe, Comte de Ségur, to join the Masonic brotherhood. Lafayette's passionate nature was roused. He became an ardent member of the Masonic fraternity. Lafayette's Masonic membership and his relationship with Broglie led to a dinner invitation on August 8, 1775, with a special guest, the younger brother of the King of England. The dinner was a defining moment in Lafayette's life.

Prince William, Duke of Gloucester and Edinburgh, a Mason, by no means supported the way King George III, his brother, was waging war on the American colonies.

The Duke of Gloucester was a member of the British army as he was appointed a colonel of the 13th Regiment of Foot in 1766. The next year he was promoted to major-general.

His military career was interrupted in 1771, as he was made Chancellor of Trinity College in Dublin. The outbreak of the conflict with the American colonies spurred the Duke of Gloucester to seek service on behalf of his country. He sought a command in the British army in America, but his brother, George III, declined the request.

The Duke was spurned by the King. The two brothers were once close but the Duke's secret marriage to Maria, Dowager Countess of Waldegrave, in September 1766, strained their relationship. After the marriage was finally revealed in 1772, King George III was offended that his blessing was not sought before the marriage.

The Metz dinner took place as the Duke of Gloucester and his wife traveled through France during the summer of 1775. The royal British couple was allowed to tour French fortifications and to inspect French troops, since England and France weren't fighting each other in a war, at least not at that moment.

Before the Metz dinner, the Duke of Gloucester received dispatches concerning the war in America. The Duke shared some of the information as part of the dinner conversation. The subject of American independence captivated Lafayette, and the young French officer had many questions for the Duke about the conflict. Lafayette wrote, "I became excited about a people fighting for liberty. The (conversation) had a strong influence on my imagination. Before I left the table, I had the idea of going to America to fight in the quest of liberty. The cause seemed just and noble."[7]

After the dinner, Lafayette made a reconnaissance trip to Paris to find out additional information on the War for American Independence. While visiting Adrienne, Lafayette told her of the courage of Americans out to foil France's old foe, England.

---

[7] George Morgan, *The True La Fayette,* J. B. Lippincott Co., Philadelphia, PA, 1919, p 52.

While Lafayette and the citizens of France were awakening to the reality of the American conflict, French leaders were already closely following the spirited and deadly-serious mutinous actions of the American rebels. Many French aristocrats were quietly cheering on the colonists. France had no love for Britain and was pulling for an American victory. Such a victory could lead to France reclaiming some of the land lost to Britain in the Seven Years War.

Julien Alexandre Achard de Bonvouloir, a representative of French King Louis XVI, was dispatched in 1775 to Philadelphia to conduct a secret meeting with American officials. French Foreign Minister Vergennes had specific instructions for Bonvouloir. He was not to identify himself as an official agent of France. If asked, he was to say he was a merchant from Antwerp. Bonvouloir was to make no promises but indicate France was open to trading with America. Benjamin Franklin was to be Bonvouloir's contact.

Bonvouloir utilized a Frenchman living in Philadelphia to make an introduction to Franklin. At first, Franklin wasn't sure if Bonvouloir was a British spy. Eventually, Franklin came to the conclusion Bonvouloir was acting in behalf of the French government. A night meeting was held at Carpenter's Hall, and two additional gatherings took place in December 1775.

The meetings, even though no promises were made, encouraged America. France's assistance was in the offing. Silas Deane was then sent on a secret mission to France. Bonvouloir reported to Vergennes that the Americans were serious about challenging England for their independence.

France was extremely cautious about publicly backing the colonists and infuriating England. A possibility existed that England would reconcile with the wayward colonists, and both countries could unloose their military on France.

The more Lafayette discovered about the American quest for independence, the more he embraced the cause of freedom.

Lafayette wrote, "Such a glorious cause had never before rallied the attention of mankind. Oppressors and oppressed would receive a powerful lesson; the great work would be accomplished or the rights of humanity would fall beneath to ruin. The destiny of France and that of her rival (England) would be decided at the same moment. . . . I gave my heart to the Americans and thought of nothing else but raising my banner and adding my colors to theirs."[8]

The lure of America gave Lafayette an opportunity to act upon a closely held belief. This was "his chance to give more than lip service to his credo: 'I am persuaded that the human race was created to be free and that I was born to serve that cause.' "[9]

As Lafayette's intense interest in the American Revolution grew, so did the interest of many citizens in Paris. George Washington, even though far away fighting the British, was celebrated in French society. Later, Franklin captivated the imagination of the French. Lafayette was not alone in France in cheering on the Americans.

Lafayette's ill-feelings towards England was another reason why Lafayette supported the Americans. His attitude could not have been otherwise after the death of his father at the hands of the English army at the battle of Minden. In his memoir, Lafayette wrote about his feelings and that of France.

> After having crowned herself with laurels and enriched herself with conquests, after having become mistress of all seas, and after having insulted all nations, England had turned her pride against her own colonies. North America had long been displeasing to her: she wished to add new vexations to former injuries, and to destroy

[8] Unger, p. 15.

[9] Robert Leckie, *George Washington's War: The Saga of the American Revolution*, Harper Collins, 1992, p. 340.

> the most sacred privileges. The Americans, attached to the mother-country, contented themselves at first with merely uttering complaints. They only accused the ministry, and the whole nation rose up against them. They were termed insolent and rebellious, and at length declared the enemies of their country: thus did the obstinacy of the King, the violence of the ministers, and the arrogance of the English nation oblige thirteen of their colonies to render themselves independent. Such a glorious cause had never before attracted the attention of mankind: it was the last struggle of Liberty; and had she then been vanquished, neither hope nor asylum would have remained for her. The oppressors and op-pressed were to receive a powerful lesson; the great work was to be accomplished, or the rights of humanity were to fall beneath its ruin. The destiny of France and that of her rival were to be decided at the same moment: England was to lose, with the new States, an important commerce, of which she derived the sole advantage, one-quarter of her subjects, who were constantly augmenting by a rapid increase of population and by emigration from all parts of Europe—in a word, more than half of the most beautiful portion of the British territory. But, if she retained possession of her thirteen colonies, all was ended for our West Indies, our possessions in Asia and Africa, our maritime commerce, and consequently our navy and our political existence.

When the American colonies declared independence, France didn't believe it possessed the resources to openly support the fledging country against England, even though the French military wished for an opportunity to intervene and win back some of its honor lost in the Seven Years War. "So pervasive was enthusiasm for the American fight that the economist and author André Morellet—an astute social observer who often accompanied Franklin on his rounds—quipped in 1777 that 'there is more support for American independence in Paris than in the entire province of New York.'"[10]

One Frenchman who closely followed the conflict in America was the Comte de Broglie, the governor of Metz and former ambassador to Poland who introduced Lafayette to the Masons and arranged the dinner invitation for Lafayette with the Duke of Gloucester. Broglie was aching for a chance to seek revenge on England and more importantly gain personal advancement. Broglie saw the young, rich, and idealistic Lafayette as a perfect associate to assist in advancing his plans to humiliate England.

"Lafayette, who knew nothing of these background intrigues, perceived only the best in Broglie. Broglie was not generally well-liked—contemporaries describe him as a small, headstrong man whose 'sparkling eyes' signaled a 'restless spirit' and whose overweening ambition kept him on constant alert for new prey."[11]

Broglie made a number of miscalculations from his faraway French vantage point, including deeming George Washington unfit to lead the American army. Washington was the only man in America capable of leading the young nation, as Lafayette and many others recognized. Also, Broglie underestimated Lafayette's determination, leadership and character.

A number of French and European military officers wished to serve in General Washington's army. Most were flocking to America for selfish reasons; glory and riches. Lafayette was not

---

[10] Laura Auricchio, *The Marquis: Lafayette Reconsidered,* Alfred A. Knopf, New York, N.Y., 2014, p. XXI

[11] Auricchio, p. 24.

interested in riches. While motivated by the thought of the noble American cause and the chance to follow in his ancestors' pursuit of family glory, Lafayette might have had another consideration. His fledgling career as a French army officer—Lafayette had yet to see battle action—was in jeopardy.

France's new minister of war, Comte de Saint-Germain, was in the midst of reorganizing France's fighting forces. From his experience as a French military officer, Saint-Germain was determined to make sure French army officers received promotions on merit rather than royal connections and wealth. Since France was at peace and in a precarious financial condition, the country had no need for a large force populated by young noble officers. Lafayette and others were placed on inactive service.[12]

Even though he was a new father with a young wife, the lure of America filled Lafayette's thoughts. Lafayette believed not only would his family oppose such a venture, but King Louis XVI was unlikely to give his approval.

Americans had not given up hope of French aid after the initial meeting with Bonvouloir failed to secure solid commitments. In fact, American leaders realized help from allies would be essential if freedom was to be obtained.

Deane, a lawyer from Connecticut, was doing his best to make unofficial contacts with French officials. Deane was under orders not to publicly disclose his mission. England was not to know of his true goals. If asked why he was spending time in France, Deane was to say he was a merchant businessman, akin to the cover Bonvouloir used. One of Deane's first goals was to have a private meeting with the French foreign minister, Charles Gravier, Comte de Vergennes.

Deane had a large request for Vergennes's consideration and

[12] Auricchio, p. 26.

little to offer France in return. America needed supplies and arms for 25,000 men and some military advisors. One hundred artillery pieces were also on Deane's shopping list. The military goods would have to be sold on credit as the new American government had almost no money. Lack of financial stability hindered America throughout the Revolution, as Lafayette would discover. Lafayette spent a substantial portion of his rather large fortune on America's independence.

Deane's secret interview with Vergennes on July 10, 1776, was almost immediately reported to the British. "Dr. Bancroft, Deane's secretary, recorded the conversation. Unfortunately, Bancroft was a British spy, and he reported the interview to London. According to Bancroft, Vergennes said France was not ready to recognize the United States and did not even think it proper to discuss a declaration of independence, until it had taken place."[13] France wouldn't receive word of the American Declaration of Independence until the next month.

The French wanted access to trade with America after the war, and a deal was struck. America would get its much-needed military supplies. Vergennes reported to King Louis XVI that by helping the Americans, British commerce would suffer and the enemy's power in the world would decrease. Contrastingly, France's power and commerce would increase, Vergennes reasoned. Vergennes held out hope that possessions lost to England in America and Canada might be recovered.

Vergennes was cautious, knowing that a good possibility existed that England would reconcile with the colonies. Vergennes also took steps in case a peace could not be reached. He instructed French representatives in Spain to see if a joint recognition of America by France and Spain could be arraigned if a war developed. By doing so, American ships would be allowed to dock at ports in both companies.

---

[13] Idzerda, *France and the American War of Independence*, Lafayette Papers, Cornell University, 1975, p19.

While an initial success, Deane's secret mission was no longer secret. He was known throughout Paris as an American agent. Once Deane was identified, he was inundated with visitors seeking introductions to Congress and a guarantee of military employment. "I have a levee of officers and others every morning . . . I have had occasionally dukes, generals and marquises and even bishops, and comtes and chevaliers without number,"[14] Deane wrote John Jay, an American diplomat who later served as President of the Second Continental Congress.

One of the visitors Deane received was Lafayette.

Deane received assistance by the end of 1776 as Benjamin Franklin and Arthur Lee arrived as the first American emissaries to France. Deane needed the help as the flood of applicants for military positions continued to descend on Deane. Deane doled out military commissions to many of those seeking his approval. A problem existed; Deane did so without Congressional authorization.

At first, Lafayette didn't seek Deane's support. He planned his trip to America and confided in his two military friends, Noailles and Segur. The young officers eagerly volunteered to join Lafayette in his adventure and join General George Washington's army. The three Musketeers made a pact to do so in October. Lafayette was aware of the repercussions he and his friends would endure from family and King, if his plans were made public. Lafayette asked Noailles and Segur not to mention his involvement.

According to Lafayette's memoir, he also consulted with Broglie. Broglie indicated Lafayette's plan could work but tried to dissuade Lafayette from an independent foray to America. Broglie did introduce Lafayette to an important military man helping France with its relationship with the rebels, Johann Kalb, known as Johann von Robais, Baron de Kalb.

A Prussian, de Kalb was born in Huttendorf, Germany,

[14] Auricchio, p 31.

in 1721. He learned English and French and was trained in the French military. He earned a military commission in the Loewendal German Regiment of the French army in 1743. During the war of Austrian Succession and the Seven Years' War, de Kalb honorably served the French and earned the Order of Military Merit in 1763. De Kalb resigned from the army in 1764 and married an heiress to a cloth manufacturing fortune, Anna Elizabeth Emilie van Robais. Even though he used the designation Baron, de Kalb had no legal right to the title.

De Kalb's association with America began during the Seven Years War. In 1768, France dispatched de Kalb to the colonies to secretly observe the colonists. The French wanted to know if the colonists were dissatisfied with England. The English arrested de Kalb as he was suspected of spying. Eventually, de Kalb was released as no evidence proved he was a French agent. When de Kalb returned to France, he reported that British rule wasn't widely embraced by the Americans. France would utilize de Kalb's knowledge of America during the American Revolution.

Broglie suggested to Deane that de Kalb would provide valuable assistance for the colonists and that de Kalb and other French officers should be sent to America. Deane agreed with Broglie and informed Congress that de Kalb and his staff would soon join the American leaders in Philadelphia.

Lafayette became friendly with de Kalb and the Prussian/French military officer later accompanied Lafayette to America. The two men spent the winter of 1777/78 together at Valley Forge and fought for American independence. De Kalb gave his life for America's freedom.

Noailles also met with de Kalb but was unwilling to proceed without official approval. Noailles wrote to an advisor of King Louis XVI. No reply was given. At the time, the King didn't mind French officers aiding the Americans; he just didn't want to do so officially and commit France to the American cause. Noailles then contacted Lafayette's father-in-law who informed Noailles to tell de Kalb to forget Lafayette's wild scheme.

Noailles withdrew from the venture, but Lafayette was impatient to go forward. He wanted to begin his service to America as soon as possible and met with Deane and de Kalb. Lafayette wrote in his memoirs that he presented his "boyish face" to Deane and spoke of his ardor for the cause of America's freedom. Unlike all of the other volunteers, Lafayette indicated he would serve America without pay. Lafayette did want a place in Washington's army with a high military rank. The rank would be needed, Lafayette reasoned, to ease the expected wrath of his family and country.

Negotiations between Deane and Broglie continued, and Broglie's French officers were enlisted in the American army. Plans were made to have two French frigates take 16 French officers to America. Lafayette was not on the list. The French contingent was at Le Havre, ready to sail, when the mission was cancelled. The disclosure by Noailles that three members of the King's Musketeers would take up arms for America meant probable war between France and England, a war France didn't desire at the moment. Vergennes forbade the frigates from sailing and ordered French ports closed to American ships. French military men were ordered not to take up arms to help America. The approval for secret aid to American was withdrawn, leaving Deane in fear of being booted out of France.

Lafayette was falling out of favor with the court of Louis XVI.

Deane had not given up on Lafayette. On December 7, 1776, Deane signed a document giving Lafayette the rank of major general. The document noted Lafayette's high birth, his alliances, his considerable estates, his personal merit, his reputation and above all his zeal for liberty of America.[15]

The agreement with Deane elevated Lafayette's participation in the American Revolution from just talking about his ardent

---

[15] Auricchio, p. 32.

fervor for individual freedom to being actively engaged in the American quest for freedom.

Lafayette was fully committed to the cause of America's independence.

Next, Lafayette had to execute an escape from France. To succeed, Lafayette knew his plans had to be kept from family, friends, the King, ministers, French spies and English spies. British Lord Stormont—David Murray, 2nd Earl of Mansfield—kept a watchful eye in Paris for any indication of French support for the rebels in America. De Kalb later wrote that the meetings Lafayette had with him and Deane weren't that secret. De Kalb indicated that he believed Lafayette's actions were sanctioned by Lafayette's family and the French government.

Lafayette's memoir differed from de Kalb's memory. Lafayette wrote that he needed a "miracle" to make his way to America and join the fight for freedom.

An impediment to obtaining France's aid for America arose as Lafayette made his preparations. News was received that General Washington suffered a major defeat at Long Island, a battle also known as the battle of Brooklyn or Brooklyn Heights. On August 27, 1776, the British Army routed Washington and substantially drove the Americans from New York City and isolated the rebellious New England states from the rest of the colonies.

Washington's army was forced to flee its defensive positions after the British army split its forces and outflanked Washington. The same tactic was successfully used a year later against Washington at Brandywine, where Lafayette shed blood for America and took a great stride in becoming an American hero. At Brandywine, the casualties for Washington's army were estimated to be between 1,500 and 2,000 soldiers, including Lafayette. Three hundred Americans reportedly died in the battle. The total British losses—dead, wounded and missing—were reported to be less than 500.

Washington's major defeat at Long Island made it impossible for France to give aid to the Americans. France couldn't afford to be involved in another losing war against England. Even the American representatives in France were reported to be despondent after the Long Island debacle. Vergennes believed Washington was not the right general to lead the Americans and urged Deane to replace Washington with a French officer. Vergennes proposed General de Broglie, Lafayette's commander at Metz, to replace Washington.[16]

Lafayette considered visiting Franklin, the highly popular American diplomat, making a positive impression on the Parisian community, but rejected the idea. Lafayette being seen with Franklin would betray his plans to aid America. Lafayette did contact Franklin through Deane's aide, William Carmichael.

Lafayette's father-in-law was furious at him for causing the family embarrassment at court and almost starting a war with England. Also, he was angry at Lafayette for even considering leaving his daughter Adrienne and his young family to go to America. D'Ayen suggested that Lafayette visit England for three weeks and see d'Ayen's brother, who was the French ambassador to England. Lafayette agreed to the trip to lessen his father-in-law's ire.

During the visit, his uncle arranged a meeting with King George III of England, whose troops he planned to fight as soon as possible. At English gatherings, Lafayette reported he "often defended Americans" and talked of Washington's victory at Trenton. Just before Trenton, Washington's army was in jeopardy of dissolving as the year 1776 was drawing to a close. The number of soldiers dwindled following the losses in New York because of disease and desertion. Of the remaining troops, enlistments of many of the men would expire with the dawning of 1777.

---

[16] Unger, p. 18.

A miracle victory was needed, and Washington orchestrated one beginning on Christmas night. During horrible weather, Washington was able to cross the Delaware River from Pennsylvania to New Jersey with most of his forces. The next morning at Trenton, Washington surprised and defeated Hessian forces fighting for the British.

The much-needed American victory saved Washington's army and gave hope to Lafayette and American supporters in France.

While in England, Lafayette was invited to inspect seaports outfitting British ships with supplies to support the British army in America. Lafayette wrote that he declined because he was afraid of committing "an abuse of confidence." By gathering such military intelligence while planning to be a British foe, Lafayette would be committing an act of espionage. Lafayette's honor would not allow him to do so.

During the England trip, Lafayette's memoirs reported, Lafayette danced at the houses of Lord Germain, minister for the English colonies, and Lord Rawdon and attended an opera. Lafayette blamed his brazen, reckless and dangerous conduct in London on his youth. He also noted he was extremely careful not to reveal his true intentions of taking up arms against the British army. The trip to London ended abruptly as Lafayette told his uncle he missed seeing his family.

Upon returning to Paris, Lafayette was ready to embark on his American adventure. Lafayette promised Deane he would purchase a ship and transport the officers Deane recruited for America to the colonies. Lafayette invested almost a year's income to purchase a slow merchant ship, *La Belle M*ère and renamed it *La Victoire—Victory*. Lafayette had the ship lightly armored for the expected voyage to America. Lafayette's memoir noted Broglie's aid in securing *La Victoire*.

In Lafayette's memoirs, he wrote that he owed much to "M. du Boismartin, secretary of the Count de Broglie, and to the Count de Broglie himself, whose affectionate heart, when all his efforts to turn me from this project had proved in vain, entered into my views with even paternal tenderness."

After his London trip, Lafayette was invited to visit court at Versailles but decided instead to spend three days with de Kalb and visit friends. He was avoiding the King and his father-in-law. Lafayette assured de Kalb that he had the blessing of his family for the American adventure, when, in truth, Lafayette had not informed them. At the conclusion of the visit with de Kalb, they set out for Bordeaux where he received some unwanted news. His latest plan to fight in the colonies was known at Versailles.

Lafayette's frenzied flight to America began in earnest.

In mid-March 1777, Lafayette sent letters to his pregnant wife and father-in-law informing them of his intention to travel to Bordeaux and then to America. Lafayette's letter to Adrienne acknowledged that he was leaving at a difficult time but he pledged his love to her. As for d'Ayen, he told his father-in-law that he was now a general officer in the American army, an appointment won by his zeal for the American cause.

D'Ayen was outraged by Lafayette's conduct and took measures to stop his son-in-law. D'Ayen contacted King Louis XVI who then issued orders forbidding Lafayette's departure. An arrest order was issued for the young Marquis. While King Louis XVI was outraged, Queen Marie Antoinette reportedly applauded Lafayette's daring actions. The King's arrest order reached Bordeaux after Lafayette departed.

Lafayette's ship stopped in northern Spain at Los Passajes instead of sailing straight to America. While at port, Lafayette was informed he was to return immediately to Marseilles and under no circumstances travel to America. The King, Lafayette's military superiors and his family remained enraged at Lafayette's conduct. Lafayette became unsure of his defiant actions. De Kalb insisted that Lafayette had to make a decision. Lafayette could carry on the expedition or cancel the excursion.

Lafayette believed everyone would support his actions if he personally pleaded his case. Lafayette left *La Victoire* and went by coach to Bordeaux. His next stop was to be Paris. The night Lafayette departed, de Kalb wrote his wife that he believed Lafayette would not return and the American adventure was at an end before it began.

Confusion reigned in France and England during this period. Was Lafayette proceeding to America? Was Lafayette returning to France as ordered by the King? Did Lafayette receive permission to go to America? Was Lafayette's venture sanctioned by the King? Was Lafayette in chains and bound for a French dungeon?

While English and French officials fretted over Lafayette's departure, the French public favored Lafayette's bold action. Lafayette was supporting a noble causes, freedom and individual liberties.

Back in Paris, d'Ayen demanded that Deane write to Washington and revoke Lafayette's commission. In an effort to repair relations with France, Deane agreed to do so. Later, d'Ayen rescinded the request and the letter to Washington was never issued. Deane did author an apologetic letter to the French prime minister.

Lafayette remained at Bordeaux and seemed to comply with the King's directive. Lafayette eluded a military escort taking him to Marseilles and hurriedly rode towards Spain. The military escort discovered Lafayette's escape and chased the fleeing Lafayette. At Saint-Jean de Luz, Lafayette was almost captured. An innkeeper's daughter recognized Lafayette through his disguise, but she saved Lafayette by misdirecting the escort.[17]

La Victoire, with Lafayette on board, finally set sail for America on April 20, 1777.

---

[17] Unger, p. 28.

Some of Lafayette's parting words, as de Kalb wrote his wife, were, "I am an outlaw. I prefer to fight for the liberty of America rather than lose my own liberty and languish in a French prison."[18]

[18] Leckie, p. 341.

The Victoire

·4·

Voyage of la Victoire

Setting sail from the Spanish coast, Lafayette overcame his first major barrier to becoming an American hero; he successfully eluded his King and his family to make the voyage to the British colonies.

While a free adventurer, Lafayette's brashness placed his return to France, his home and his family in question. Would the young Marquis be welcomed as a daring idealistic defender of freedom, or be placed in irons in a grungy French prison and be shunned by his family? His success or failure during his adventure in America would determine his personal fate in his home country.

The seven-week voyage began with Lafayette suffering from seasickness. He was not alone as many of his shipmates also were ill. Lafayette claimed in his memoirs that he recovered quicker than other travelers.

After gaining his sea legs, Lafayette worried about the safety of his ship and his crew. In his memoir, Lafayette wrote this slow and lightly armed ship would be easy prey for the "smallest privateer," let alone a menacing English warship. One sighting of a naval vessel caused angst among the crew, Lafayette wrote, but the ship turned out to be American. Luckily, *La Victoire* avoided armed conflict during the voyage.

Johann deKalb was a Franconian-French military officer who served as a major general

The weeks at sea weren't wasted by Lafayette. With the help of his fellow travelers, Lafayette studied the English language, of which he knew little, and discussed military tactics. Lafayette had packed books on martial strategies for his voyage. One of his tutors was de Kalb, who had spent time in the American colonies during the Seven Years and had come to respect America and its inhabitants.

De Kalb and the other officers sent by Broglie and authorized by Deane weren't intent on just being Lafayette's tutors. Their mission was to protect and promote French interests in the American Revolution.

Another French military officer on board the *La Victoire* destined to be an integral member of Lafayette's French officers' cadre was Jean-Joseph Sourbader de Gimat. Born in Gascony, Gimat was the son of a French military officer. He followed in his father's footsteps and became an ensign in the Regiment of Guyenne in 1761. By the time Gimat met Lafayette, he had only achieved the rank of first lieutenant. Gimat decided his future was brighter as a member of Lafayette's staff than as a lower grade officer in the downsizing French army.

Lafayette would be thankful for Gimat's personal service. At Brandywine, Gimat noticed Lafayette's loss of blood after Lafayette received his leg wound. Gimat helped Lafayette to his horse and away from the advancing British army. Gimat guided Lafayette to safety in a wooded lot and then assisted Lafayette in receiving medical treatment.

Gimat returned to France after serving in the American Revolution. In the spring of 1782, Gimat made colonel of the regiment of Martinique in the French Antilles. He also served as governor of the island of Saint Lucia, a post which he held from 1789 until early June 1792. Almost exactly one year later, Gimat was mortally wounded while commanding a corps against an invading force backed by a squadron of English warships,

At Brandywine with Lafayette and Gimat was another Frenchman who sailed on the *La Victoire,* Le Chevalier Du Buysson, who has been identified as Lafayette's cousin. Du Buysson chronicled Lafayette's heroic actions during the Brandywine engagement. During the American Revolution, du Buysson also served on the staff of de Kalb and was with de Kalb when he was killed at the Battle of Camden on August 16, 1780. Du Buysson was reported to have been wounded and captured during the encounter that claimed de Kalb's life.

Colonel du Buysson married a South Carolina woman, Huldah Russ, after he met her while de Kalb's aide de camp. The couple returned to France. After du Buysson's death in France, his wife and children returned to claim land granted to du Buysson by the United States Congress for his service in the American Revolution.

Another one of Lafayette's aides-de-camp was not a Frenchman but an American. Edmund Brice was born in Annapolis, Maryland, and met Lafayette while studying art in Europe. Brice's father died when Brice was a teenager and provided an inheritance that allowed him to study with famed Maryland artist Charles Willson Peale. Peale believed Brice had talent. In 1772,

Peale wrote a letter of introduction for Brice to another famous American painter, Benjamin West, who was in London.[19]

After doing some painting, Brice returned to Annapolis in 1775 but almost immediately set sail for London with his sister Betty and her loyalist husband Lloyd Delany. While in London, Brice was contacted by another Marylander, William Carmichael, Deane's aide in Paris. Carmichael wrote Brice that a job was waiting for him in Paris. The employment was with Lafayette. Carmichael figured Brice could help Lafayette learn English and assist him while in America. The letter was intercepted by British intelligence, but Brice successfully eluded the British and crossed the channel to France.[20]

All of the French officers on *La Victoire* suffered not only from the effects of the sea voyage, but also from the food served them. The cuisine wasn't fit for a French noble or cadre of military officers. They subsisted on fish, salt pork and hard biscuits.

After recovering from his seasickness and finding time between his English and military studies, Lafayette turned to a most troubling personal concern. Lafayette had reservations about his decision to abandon his young family and to launch his personal crusade for American freedom. Such a worrisome burden could easily affect Lafayette's performance in Washington's army. Lafayette had to find personal peace with his actions.

In an effort to remain connected, Lafayette wrote a long and remorseful letter to his pregnant wife Adrienne. On May 30, 1777, more than a month after departing France, Lafayette took up his pen and attempted to explain his sudden and unexplained

[19] Interview with Glenn E. Campbell, senior historian of the James Brice House of Historic Annapolis, Inc.

[20] Campbell interview.

absence and to assure her that he would be in no danger while fighting in America.

As for his motivation, he wrote, "Whilst defending the liberty I adore, I shall enjoy perfect freedom myself: I but offer my service to that interesting republic from motives of the purest kind, unmixed with ambition or private views; her happiness and my glory are my one incentive to the task. I hope that, for my sake, you will become a good American, for that feeling is worthy of every noble heart. The happiness of America is intimately connected with the happiness of all mankind; she will become the safe and respected asylum of virtue, integrity, toleration, equality, and tranquil happiness."

Obviously, Lafayette was worried about Adrienne's reaction to his departure and if she would forgive him. Did she still love him?

> *It is from afar that I write to you, my Dear Heart, and to this cruel separation I have to add the even more horrible doubt of when I can receive news from you. However, I hope to get some soon. Among the many reasons which make me wish to arrive, none give me more impatience than this one. So many fears and troubles need to be added to the already intense sorrow to be separated from everything which is dearest to me. How did you deal with my second departure? Do you love me less for it? Have you forgiven me? Did you consider that in any case I had to be separated from you, to roam in Italy and to live without glory among people most opposed to my plans and to my way of thinking? These thoughts did not stop me from feeling an awful emotion during the terrible moments which separated me from the shore. Missing you, my friends, Henriette, everything flashed in front of my soul in a tearing manner. It is then that I could no longer find any excuses for this trip. If you knew all I suffered; the forlorn days which I spent sailing away from all that I love most*

in the world. Will I have to add to these sorrows the knowledge that you do not forgive me! Truly, my Love, I would then be worthy of pity. But I have not given you any news of myself, my health; I know that these details interest you.

Since I last wrote I have been in the most boring country. The sea looks so morose that I believe we make each other sad. I should have already arrived, but the winds have cruelly betrayed me. I will not reach Charles town for another 8 to 10 days. It is in this city that I will disembark. What a great pleasure it will be! Once ashore, I will everyday hope to get news from France. I will learn so many interesting things on what is to be discovered and more importantly on what I have so regretfully left behind. May I learn that you are well, that you still love me and that many of my friends do also, I will then accept the rest with utter philosophy whatever it is and whichever country it comes from. But if my heart were attacked in its most vulnerable spot, if you no longer loved me, I would be utterly miserable. But I do not have to fear this, do I my Dear Heart? I was rather sick during the first part of the trip and, as mean people do, I could have consoled myself with the fact that I was not the only one. I took care of myself in my own way and got better sooner than the others. I now feel about the same as if I were on land.

Once ashore, I am convinced that my health will remain perfect for a long time. Please do not imagine that I will run any risk in my future activities. The position of general officer has always been considered as an assurance of immortality. It is a service so different from what I would have done in France, as a colonel for example. The post of general officer is one of counseling only. Ask all the French general officers whose number is all the larger because they do not run any risk; as a consequence they are not eager to let others in as they do in other branches. The proof that I am not trying to deceive you is that at present we are in some danger for we could be attacked by British vessels and mine is not equipped to defend itself. But once we have arrived I will be perfectly safe. You see, my Dear Heart, that I am telling you everything. Trust me and do not worry without cause. I will not journal my voyage for you. Here days follow one another and even worse look alike. Always the sky, always the water, and the following day it is the same. Truly, people who write volumes about a sea passage must be cruel prattlers. For, like others, I did have contrary winds, I did make a long journey, I did put up with thunderstorms; I also saw vessels and they were a lot more interesting to me than to any other travelers, but I noticed nothing worth writing or that anyone could have written.

But let's now talk about more important topics. Let's talk about you, about dear Henriette and her brother or sister. Henriette is so lovable that she makes me fond of girls. Whatever the sex of our new child, I will welcome it with much joy. Do not delay one instant to hasten my happiness by informing me of the birth. I do not know if it is because I now am a father twice that I feel more a father than ever. Mr. . . . and my friend Carmichael will avail you of ways to reach me and I am convinced that they will do everything in their power to make me happy as soon as possible. Do write; you could even send a trustworthy man; it would be such a pleasure to ask questions to someone who would have seen you. Landrin, for example; well, do as you think best. You do not know the strength or tenderness of my feelings for you if you think that you can neglect anything that concerns you.

> *This first letter will take a long time to reach you, but as soon as I have settled down, you will often receive news and fresher ones. There is not much difference between letters from America or Sicily. Let me tell you that Sicily is still very dear to my heart. I thought that I was so close to seeing you. But let's drop the subject of Sicily. Farewell my Dear Heart, I will write you from Charles town; I will write you before getting there. Good night for now.*[21]

Adrienne would not receive Lafayette's letter for another three months. Lafayette's doubts would remain within him for many more months. The sea voyage did nothing to lift Lafayette's spirits. He called the North Atlantic a tedious region of the world and the "sea so sad. I believe we sadden each other, she and I."[22]

Finally, *La Victoire* neared the South Carolina port of Charleston on June 12, 1777. Danger lurked before the American port. Two British frigates blocked the entrance. An American warship communicated with Lafayette's ship before *La Victoire* sailed into the hands of Lafayette's foe.

La Victoire altered course and turned north for 60 miles to avoid the British warships. On the afternoon of June 13, almost two months after setting sail from Spain, *La* Victoire anchored at the entrance to Georgetown Bay near North Island. Lafayette was ready to step ashore on American soil, the country destined to be his adopted home.

---

[21] Christine Valadon translation.

[22] Auricchio p. 39.

5

Conquer or Perish

The fledgling country Lafayette envisioned as he set foot in South Carolina was vastly different than the one he saw through his rose-colored glasses.

"The countryside is open and there is no fighting, at least not much," Lafayette wrote Adrienne shortly after his arrival in Charleston. "Manners in this world are simple, honest and, in all things, worthy of the country where the beautiful word liberty resonates."[23] Lafayette concluded that all Americans considered each other as brothers and the county contained no paupers, or peasants as they were called in France.

In reality, the new United States Lafayette encountered was a divided nation in so many ways.

Not every citizen desired to be independent of England. Many Americans fought with the British army in loyalist units throughout the long war. The British army, at least the officers, were honored guests in many homes of American cities during the long winter months of inactive campaigning. Philadelphia and New York were especially welcoming.

---

[23] Lafayette's Memoirs: From Correspondence and Manuscripts of General Lafayette published by his family in London in 1837. A letter dated June 15, 1777, to Adrienne. Christine Valadon, translator.

Morellet's quip that more Parisians supported American independence than those in the entire province of New York might not have been entirely accurate, but the sentiment had an essence of truth. Of course, the exact division isn't known, but an often stated belief was that a third of Americans wanted freedom, another third wanted to stay under the reign of England and the third just wanted to be left alone.

Two other groups, the displaced American Indians and imported African slaves, would vehemently dispute the notion that freedom and independence were at the heart of the conflict with England. They did not see freedom or independence in their future. To his credit, Lafayette established positive relationships with members of both groups during his time in America.

The first task in America was finding a pilot to safely guide *La Victoire* through the narrow mouth of the bay. Seven sailors rowed Lafayette and five other officers, including de Kalb, in search of a pilot during mid-afternoon of Friday, June 13, 1777. No able pilot was immediately found, and the quest continued into the night. The contingent came upon some slaves combing for oysters. The slaves offered transportation to their master's home, a North Island rice plantation owned by Major Benjamin Huger, a militia officer. Lafayette's party arrived about midnight.

Lafayette described his first physical contact with America in his memoirs. "I made it safely to Georgetown and took a canoe to American soil where I swore I would conquer or perish in aiding America. Landing at midnight, a light guided us to the home of Major Huger. Dogs barked and we were taken for a band of marauders landing from an enemy's ship. De Kalb told the owners who we were and suspicion abated."

The first comments by Lafayette on his impressions of America came in a letter he wrote on June 15, 1777, to Adrienne. Lafayette continued to be worried about his standing with his wife. "I have arrived my Dear Heart, and in very good health, at the house of an American officer and, by sheer good luck, a French vessel is setting sails. Imagine my joy! I am going tonight to Charles town. I will write you from there. There is yet no interesting news to report. The countryside is open and there is no fighting, at least not much. Manners in this world are simple, honest and, in all things, worthy of the country where the beautiful word liberty resonates. I meant to write to Mr. d'Ayen, but it is not possible. Farewell, farewell, my Dear Heart. From Charles town I will go to Philadelphia by land and then join the army. Isn't it so my Heart that you still love me?"

Huger proved to be an agreeable host and invited the French contingent to stay the night. Lafayette described Huger as a "kind and friendly man." Huger advised Lafayette to head for Charleston on land to avoid being captured by British forces. Having avoided being detained in France, the British replaced his countrymen as his hunters. Lafayette was destined to be a wanted man throughout his life.

In his memoirs, Lafayette reflected on his first few days in America. The experience had a "magical effect" on him. Lafayette awoke, "my room covered with mosquito nets, black servants asking what I needed" and vegetation all around." The next day Lafayette and his party hastened to Charleston, "a beautiful city offering comfort and luxury."[24] De Kalb complained that the three-day trip from North Island to Charleston was an unpleasant journey made in extreme heat. Du Buysson related that the trip had to be taken by foot as no horses were available. At Charleston, du Buysson recalled that the trip's hardships turned them into looking like "beggars" and they were greeted as such. Du Buysson was sensitive to the anti-French sentiment in Charleston even though Lafayette seemed immune to the slights du Buysson perceived.[25]

At Charleston, Lafayette met some of the American militia, including Generals Robert Howe and William Moultrie. State assembly President John Rutledge also stopped to see Lafayette.

---

[24] Lafayette memoirs, p 14.

[25] Auricchio, p. 43.

Lafayette's Masonic ties aided in his acceptance, as Freemasons were among the city's leaders.

Lafayette was given a tour of the town's fortifications. Charleston, according to Lafayette, was among the "best-built and handsomest and most agreeable cities I've seen." As was to become routine in America, Lafayette was an honored guest at meals. In his memoirs Lafayette wrote he found the customs in America to be about the same as those he found in England, "but simpler."[26]

One American was skeptical of Lafayette and the French officers. Captain Charles Biddle, a merchant mariner from Philadelphia, was in Georgetown at the time and agreed to be an interpreter for the group. Biddle was reluctant because he had heard horrid tales of French officers volunteering for the American army. Biddle had "conceived a very unfavorable opinion of them."[27]

On June 26, 1777, Lafayette purchased horses and four "light carriages" for the trek. Lafayette and some of his officers set off to Philadelphia, more than 550 miles—as the crow flies—to the north.

As Lafayette headed to Philadelphia, *La Victoire*, Lafayette's ship, was lost as it became lodged on a sand bar. The ship was bound for Saint Dominque and contained a cargo of rice.

Lafayette's journey to Philadelphia was long, tiring, and arduous. The light carriages didn't last long on the rough trails traveled by Lafayette and his compatriots. After less than a week, reportedly somewhere in North Carolina, the axles on the carriages failed and the transportation was abandoned. Some nights the party camped in the woods. Horses became fatigued and had to be replaced. Men became sick. The journey from South Carolina to Philadelphia became a challenge to the health and welfare of the Marquis and his colleagues.

Lafayette wrote a letter dated July 17 from Petersburg, Vir-

---

[26] Lafayette memoirs, p 15.

[27] Auricchio, p. 39.

ginia, to his wife stating that all of the members of his party were on horseback. He estimated he was still eight days away from Philadelphia. Lafayette confided to Adrienne that he heard a rumor that British General William Howe had departed New York City with an army and "martial duties" might soon commence.[28]

Those rumors were true. Howe was preparing his troops for an invasion of Pennsylvania and the capture of Philadelphia and members of the rebel Congress. In less than two months, General Washington made his major defense of Philadelphia by challenging the forces of General Howe at Chadds Ford, along the Brandywine River.

Lafayette's moment of destiny, a moment that would define Lafayette as an American hero, was approaching.

Lafayette recorded that he rode on horseback almost 900 miles as he traveled through North and South Carolina, Virginia, Maryland, Delaware and Pennsylvania. During the month-long fatiguing journey Lafayette reported encountering vast rivers and forests. "While studying the language and customs of the inhabitants, I observed also new productions of nature and new methods of cultivation. Vast forests and immense rivers combine to give to that country an appearance of youth and majesty."[29]

A report of Lafayette's progress was made to his wife in a letter on July 23. He was on board a boat in Annapolis and about ready to sail to Philadelphia. Lafayette had more bad news of the war for Adrienne. British General John Burgoyne had driven American forces from Ticonderoga. Gentleman Johnny, as Burgoyne was known, was marching towards his disastrous defeat at Saratoga, which took place only a few weeks after the Battle of Brandywine. Lafayette might have privately discussed disheartening news with his wife, but outwardly he was full of optimism. Du Buysson related that Lafayette's enthusiasm was inspiring.

---

[28] Lafayette memoirs, p 97.

[29] Lafayette memoirs.

A Lafayette aide accompanying him on the journey to Philadelphia was American-born Edmund Brice. During the stop in Annapolis, Brice's hometown, Brice conferred with his brother, James Brice. The two decided to assist Lafayette; they would purchase a slave for Lafayette's use. A receipt in the Maryland Historical Society dated August 4, 1777, indicates such a purchase was made and 180 pounds was given to a Dr. Murray by James Brice. The endorsement was for a "negro boy for Lafayette."[30]

There is no indication that Lafayette knew or endorsed the purchase of the slave. In fact, such a deed would be contrary to Lafayette's actions throughout his life.

Brice remained connected with Lafayette for more than a year. After Brice was made a lieutenant colonel in Washington's army, records indicate Brice went to Europe, possibly to generate support for the United States. In the spring of 1783, Brice returned to the United States and married but died the next year.[31]

On July 27, 1777, Lafayette entered Philadelphia. Lafayette was impressed with the town to be called the City of Brotherly Love. Lafayette wrote that founder William Penn must have imagined the city's grandeur when he "laid the first stone of its foundation."

While Lafayette found the city agreeable, his greeting by the Continental Congress was not hospitable. Lafayette encountered a crucial obstacle in his journey to becoming an American hero. The obstacle almost ended his American experience by sending the young Frenchman home without even meeting his father figure, General George Washington.

Washington himself was partially responsible for Lafayette's close call with a premature exit from America. The majority of the blame for the dire situation belonged to Lafayette's countrymen.

In the year following the Declaration of Independence, Washington's army was flooded with officers from France and other

[30] Campbell interview.

[31] Campbell interview.

parts of Europe. They all wanted to support the American cause. They came covered with glory and military acumen, or so they claimed. America could employ them—no unpaid volunteers—at a hefty salary.

Washington discovered to his dismay, and the detriment of the conduct of the war effort, that, for the most part, the European opportunists weren't worth the hefty investment poor America was making. In the weeks before Lafayette arrived in Philadelphia, Washington demanded that Congress stop handing out commissions to every fortune-seeking European.

In one angry letter to Congress on February 20, 1777, Washington wrote of foreign officers, "They seldom bring more than a commission and a passport, which we know, may belong to a bad as well as a good officer. Their ignorance of our language and their inability to recruit men are insurmountable obstacles . . . for our officers who have raised their men, and have served through the war upon pay that has hitherto not borne their expenses, would be disgusted if foreigners were put over their heads."

The anger Washington expressed in his letter wasn't enough to dissuade Congress from handing out the commissions. Washington followed up his letter with a private note, equally terse, to his friend and fellow Virginian Richard Henry Lee on May 17, 1777. The note to Lee, a member of Congress, was blunt and to the point.

What does Congress expect him to do with the many foreigners they have at different times promoted to the rank of field officers? Washington asked Lee. These men have no attachment nor ties to the country, don't know the language and thus can't give or receive orders, Washington wrote. Washington's officer corps was also upset about having "strangers put over them, whose merit perhaps is not equal to their own." Washington concluded by saying he was "disgusted" with Congress "giving rank to people of no reputation or service."[32]

---

[32] Unger, p 33.

Congress received Washington's message loud and clear this time. No more military commissions were to be given to foreigners unless Washington specifically requested. And, Washington had not pre-approved Lafayette and his colleagues.

So, no royal Congressional welcome awaited Lafayette.

In his memoirs, Lafayette acknowledged that the root of Washington's anger was justified. He wrote, "The Americans were displeased with the pretentions and disgusted with the conduct of many Frenchmen; the imprudent selections they had in some cases made, the extreme boldness of some foreign adventurers, the jealousy of the army, and strong national prejudices, all contributed to confound disinterested zeal with private ambition and talents with quackery."[33]

Immediately after arriving in Philadelphia and refreshing their appearances, the Frenchmen called on John Hancock, President of the Second Continental Congress. Hancock wasn't expecting Lafayette and dismissed the Marquis by telling him he needed to see Robert Morris, the Philadelphia representative in Congress. Lafayette and his troupe trudged to Morris. Morris listened to Lafayette and agreed to meet with him the next day at Independence Hall.

Thirteen French officers, including Lafayette, arrived in the morning for their scheduled meeting with Morris. They waited and waited until Morris finally made his way to the group with another member of Congress, James Lovell of Massachusetts. Lovell, who spoke French, was assigned to handle issues with representatives from France. Morris immediately excused himself from the meeting and disappeared.

Lovell served in Congress for five years and was the Secretary for the Committee for Foreign Affairs. One of 13 children, Lovell earned a scholarship to Harvard. Lovell was associated with the Sons of Liberty, the aggressive New England group that protested unfair British laws before the revolution began.

---

[33] Lafayette memoirs, p 16.

The British arrested Lovell on suspicion of spying on them during the Battle of Bunker Hill. Lovell was held in prison without being charged during the long winter. Washington was contacted about arranging an exchange of prisoners including Lovell. Washington in turn contacted Congress. An exchange was eventually arranged for a British colonel, and Lovell gained his freedom 18 months after his arrest. Soon after, Lovell was asked to join Congress.

Lovell, after this experience in prison, was not receptive to a bunch of foreigners looking, he believed, to make their fortune at America's expense.

Lovell's language skills were impressive, according to du Buysson. The Frenchman recalled Lovell called them "adventurers" in very good French. Lovell then launched into a harangue against Deane. Lovell accused Deane of sending inferior officers, including Major General Philippe Charles Tronson du Coudray. Deane had authorized du Coudray to be in charge of all American artillery, a commission that was not at all acceptable to Washington and Congress.

"Lafayette and his companions," Lovell concluded, "should feel free to head home."[34] At that moment, Lafayette's dedication to the American cause for independence was severely tested. Would Lafayette return to France and his young wife and family and abandon this promise to fight for the cause of freedom?

Lafayette, in his memoirs, wrote, "The coldness with which I was received might have been taken as a dismissal."

[34] Auricchio, p. 45.

·6·

Congressional Approval

Standing in front of the closed doors of Independence Hall, Lafayette wasn't deterred by the curt dismissal by Congressman James Lovell. Lafayette, alarmed and shocked by the unwelcoming welcome he received in Philadelphia, retained his determination to serve with General George Washington.

Lafayette wasn't alone in supporting his quest to become an American officer. Influential Americans recognized the importance of having a rich, noble Frenchman supporting the United States. France was desperately needed as an ally in the war with England. Without a European power siding with America, King George III's forces would be almost impossible to defeat. Lafayette became a key player in America's plan to win independence.

For the moment, Lafayette made little progress dealing with Lovell, although letters of introduction and support for Lafayette were delivered to him. The documents had no effect on Congress. Lafayette wasn't sure if the letters were read by members of Congress. Lovell maintained that Lafayette's chances of receiving a commission were slim. The time had come for Lafayette to take direct action.

On Lafayette's next trip to Independence Hall, he delivered a note stating his case. "After the sacrifices I have made, I have the right to extract two favors: one is to serve at my own expense,—the other to serve at first, as a volunteer."[35]

Besides Lafayette's persistent pleadings, Franklin and Deane beseeched Congress to make an exception and grant Lafayette's request for a military commission without Washington's approval. On May 25, 1777, the two American patriots wrote a letter on Lafayette's behalf to the Committee of Secret Correspondence. Congress authorized the committee to interact with those in Europe, including in England, sympathetic to the American cause. At the time, Franklin and Deane were under the impression Lafayette had royal permission for his trip.

> The Marquis de La Fayette, a young nobleman of great family connections here and great wealth is gone to America in a ship of his own, accompanied by some officers of distinction, in order to serve in our armies. He is exceedingly beloved and everybody's good wishes attend him; we cannot but hope he may meet with such a reception as will make the country and his expedition agreeable to him . . . we are satisfied the civilities and respect that may be shown him will be serviceable to our affairs here, as pleasing not only to his powerful relations and to the court but to the whole French nation. He has left a beautiful young wife big with child and for her sake particularly we hope that his bravery and ardent desire to distinguish himself will be a little restrained by the Generals prudence, as not to permit his being hazard much, but on some important occasion.[36]

---

[35] Lafayette memoirs, p. 17.

[36] Franklin and Deane to Committee of Secret Correspondence, Paris, May 25, 1777, Wharton, II: 324.

Lafayette's persistence, with the help of his friends, induced Congress to review the Frenchman's request. Lovell, to Lafayette's surprise, personally invited Lafayette to appear before Congress. Mistakes had been made. Congress wanted to offer new terms for Lafayette's service.[37] Lafayette's start date would be July and not when Lafayette signed his agreement with Deane, thus placating some aggrieved officers in Washington's army. Seniority was based on when commissions were issued.

On July 31, 1777, Congress gave Lafayette approval, though qualified, to become an American officer. Congress decided to accept the young Frenchman's request to serve because of Lafayette's "great zeal in the cause of liberty in which the United States are engaged, has quitted his family and country, and has come to offer his services to the United States, without demanding either pay or private indemnity, and he desires to expose his life in our cause, resolved that his services be accepted, and that on account of his zeal and commission of major-general in the army of the United States."[38]

Congress intended to have Washington decide how Lafayette was to serve in the army. Congress did not direct Washington to give Lafayette command of any troops. One belief in Congress was that Lafayette would spend little time in America and then retire to France to be an agent for America. Lafayette always saw his role differently; he was to lead troops in combat and win glory.

George Washington, if he desired one or not, had a full-fledged French freedom fighter on his hands. Lafayette wasted little time in purchasing a uniform and equipment for his use as a new member of the American army.

After being informed by Congress of Lafayette's appointment, Washington had the impression the rank was honorary. After meeting Lafayette, Washington knew Lafayette intended

---

[37] Auricchio, p. 47.

[38] Lafayette memoirs, p. 17.

to be an active member of his army. While camped along Neshaminy Creek, just outside of Philadelphia, Washington wrote of the confusion over Lafayette's status in a letter dated August 19, 1777, to Benjamin Harrison V. A member of Congress from Virginia, Harrison was a signer of the Declaration of Independence.

Washington insisted that Lafayette either didn't understand the "design of his appointment," or Congress failed to understand Lafayette's intent. The letter to Harrison stated:[39]

> If I understand *him*, that he does not conceive his Commission is merely honorary; but given with a view to command a division of this Army. True, he has said that he is young, & inexperienced, but at the same time has always accompanied it with a hint, that so soon as *I* shall think *him* fit for the Command of a division, he shall be ready to enter upon the duties of it; & in the meantime, has offer'd his service for a smaller Command; to which I may add, that he has actually applied to me for Commissions for his Two Aide, de, Camps.

Washington maintained he knew "no more than an unborn child," as to the intent of Congress and asked for instructions on how to handle Lafayette. Washington requested Congress to inform Lafayette that he was not intended to command troops. If Congress intended Lafayette to be an active general, Washington contended that he was misled. The flood of foreign officers and interference by Congress and state officials has caused "chaos" in his army, according to Washington.

Washington concluded his letter to Harrison by writing that he was going to personally address Congress for instructions

[39] National Archives.

but decided to write to a member of Congress, Harrison. Thus, Washington placed the Lafayette dilemma on the shoulders of his fellow Virginian, Harrison.

De Kalb, another member of Lafayette's officer's cadre, decided that Lovell's rebuff was a personal affront and began making plans to return to France. Lafayette championed Baron de Kalb with Washington and Congress, and on September 5, 1777, de Kalb was appointed a major general of the American army.

Congress also agreed to Deane's recommendation for Gimat, another one of Lafayette's aides. Gimat was commissioned a major and received retroactive pay. His rank dated to December 1, 1776. Brice, the American-born aide to Lafayette, was commissioned a major.

While Lafayette was battling Congress for his commission, General Washington was making preparations to battle the British Howe brothers. General William Howe and Admiral Richard Howe were on the move from New York City. When the British fleet was spotted around the Capes of the Delaware River, Washington made his way to Philadelphia.

Almost immediately after Lafayette received his commission from Congress, he attended a dinner in honor of Washington at City Tavern in Philadelphia. Lafayette "beheld for the first time the great man. Although he was surrounded by officers and citizens, it was impossible to mistake for a moment his majestic figure and deportment; nor was he less distinguished by the noble affability of his manner."[40]

Washington, who didn't hold a high opinion of the French, was initially skeptical of Lafayette. That distrust didn't stop Washington from inviting Lafayette to "establish himself in his house," that is to share meals and lodging. Lafayette had gained an honored position on Washington's staff. Washington wasted no time in introducing Lafayette to his army. Lafayette was

---

[40] Lafayette memoirs, p 18.

invited by Washington to join him in reviewing Philadelphia's defensive positions along the Delaware River.

Lafayette also had an opportunity to review Washington's troops on August 8. The young French general was not impressed. He wrote in his memoirs:

> About 11,000 men, ill armed, and still worse clothed, presented a strange spectacle to the eye of the young Frenchman. Their clothes were particolored, and many of them were almost naked. The best clad wore hunting shirts, large gray linen coats which were much used in Carolina. As to their military tactics, it will be sufficient to say that, for a regiment ranged in order of battle to move forward on the right of its line, it was necessary for the left to make a continued countermarch. They were always arranged in two lines, the smallest men in the first line: no other distinction as to height was ever observed. In spite of these disadvantages, the soldiers were fine, and the officers zealous; virtue stood in place of science, and each day added both to experience and discipline. Lord Stirling, more courageous than judicious, another general, who was often intoxicated, and Greene, whose talents were only then known to his immediate friends, commanded as majors-general. General Knox, who had changed the profession of bookseller to that of artillery officer, was there also, and had himself formed other officers, and created an artillery. 'We must feel embarrassed,' said General Washington, on his arrival, 'to exhibit ourselves before an officer who has just quitted French troops.' 'It is to learn, and not to teach, that I come hither,'

> replied M. de Lafayette; and that modest tone, which was not common in Europeans, produced a very good effect.

For the moment Lafayette curbed his assaults on Washington to obtain a fighting command. Lafayette waited for an opportunity to prove his bravery and military acumen. That moment was just a month in the future.

As the British fleet disappeared from New York City and then reappeared on the Chesapeake Bay, Washington's army awaited orders to move. For weeks, Washington and his officers weren't in agreement as to the British fleet's final destination. The options for the enemy included a return to New York and a march to reinforce Burgoyne in upstate New York, an inland landing and march on Philadelphia, or a voyage to the rebel stronghold of Charleston, where Lafayette had landed.

Once the fleet was spotted on the Chesapeake, Washington ordered his army to move from Philadelphia towards Wilmington, Delaware. In the early morning hours of August 24, 1777, the American army began parading through Philadelphia with Lafayette joining Washington at the head of the troops. Washington's army didn't completely pass through Philadelphia until 8:00 p.m.

Lafayette noted in his memoirs that the soldiers placed green branches in their caps during the parade and marched to the sound of drums and fifes. The green sprigs were meant to be a symbol of hope. "These soldiers, in spite of their state of nudity, offered an agreeable spectacle to the eyes of all the citizens," Lafayette observed.[41] Congressman and future President John Adams was also impressed with the soldiers but with qualifications. He wrote, "I find the army to be extremely well armed, pretty well clothed, and tolerably disciplined. . . . Much remains to be done. Our soldiers have not yet quite the air of soldiers.

---

[41] Lafayette memoirs, p. 19.

Hale-Byrnes House, front and rear

They don't step exactly in time. They don't hold up their heads quite erect, nor turn out their toes so exactly as they ought. They don't all of them cock their hats; and such as do, don't wear them in the same way."[42]

On August 26, Washington decided to see for himself the status of the British army. Washington rode off with a small escort of horse soldiers and three other generals, Nathanael Greene, George Weedon and Lafayette. The small force made its way from Wilmington down the King's Highway to Newport and then Iron Hill. Efforts to observe the enemy failed, so Washington's command continued to Grey's Hill, Maryland, overlooking the Head of the Elk River. A few enemy tents were noted but no great military intelligence gleaned.

As Washington returned to his army, a severe rainstorm overtook the group, and Washington decided to stay the night at a farmhouse near Iron Hill. Lafayette considered the stay a serious mistake. "General Washington exposed himself to danger in the most imprudent manner. After having reconnoitered for a long time the enemy's position, he was overtaken by a storm during a very dark night, entered a farm-house close to the hostile army, and, from a reluctance to change his own opinion, remained there with General Greene, M. de Lafayette, and their aides-de-camp; but, when at daybreak he quitted the farm, he acknowledged that any one traitor might have caused his ruin."[43]

Washington was searching for a defensive position that would enable him to protect Philadelphia and Congress. The Brandywine River was on his radar on August 31, 1777, as indicated by his general orders for the day. "Genl Potter will order two battalions of Militia (each to be 250 strong, rather more than fewer) to march, one to Richling's Ford and the

---

[42] George F. Scheer and Hugh F. Randin, *Rebels and Redcoats*, New York: Da Capo Press, 1994, p 233.

[43] Lafayette memoirs, p. 20.

other to Gibson's Ford, to take post on the east side of the Brandywine, and fix upon the best ground for defending those passes." The ford references came from a manuscript map by Jacob Broom dated August 27, 1777. The map displayed four fords, two in Delaware and two in Pennsylvania. Washington's notation for Chandler Ford was "very good but very broken ground and narrow defiles on the East Side." The other ford mentioned was Pyle's Ford.[44]

Maneuvering in Delaware continued and segments of the two armies met in a skirmish at Cooch's Bridge on September 3, 1777. The engagement was the only military engagement in Delaware and resulted in casualties of less than 50 in each army. Lafayette mentioned the battle in his memoirs. "After having advanced as far as Wilmington, the general had detached 1,000 men under (General William) Maxwell, the most ancient brigadier in the army. At the first march of the English, he was beaten by their advance guard near Christiana Bridge."[45]

British General Lord Cornwallis then commandeered the home of Thomas Cooch as his headquarters.

Washington knew he had to stop the British from reaching Philadelphia and capturing the Continental Congress. The new country, and also all of Europe, expected Washington to challenge Howe and the British army. Philadelphia wouldn't be abandoned without a fight. Three days after Cooch's Bridge, Washington held a council of war at the Daniel Byrnes home, now known as the historic Hale-Byrnes house, just outside of Newark, Delaware. Included in the council was Lafayette. He joined Washington, Greene, Henry Knox and other officers. The day also marked Lafayette's 20th birthday.

The results of the council of war at the Hale-Byrnes house didn't sit well with Lafayette. Lafayette criticized the tactics suggested by American leaders to defend Philadelphia. Public

---

[44] Washington's Papers, p. 99.

[45] Lafayette memoirs, p 22.

opinion forced Washington to challenge Howe in an open battle. Lafayette also couldn't understand why the Americans didn't challenge the British landing in Maryland. Lafayette was full of criticism as he also questioned Howe's desire to take Philadelphia and abandon Burgoyne in New York.

> During that time Howe was only thinking of Philadelphia, and it was at the expense of the northern expedition that he was repairing thither by an enormous circuit. But, on the other side, why were the English permitted to land so tranquilly? Why was the moment allowed to pass when their army was divided by the river Elk? Why in the South were so many false movements and so much hesitation displayed? Because the Americans had hitherto had combats, but not battles; because, instead of harassing an army and disputing hollows, they were obliged to protect an open city, and maneuver in a plain, close to a hostile army, who, by attacking them from behind, might completely ruin them. General Washington, had he followed the advice of the people, would have enclosed his army in a city, and thus have entrusted to one hazard the fate of America; but, while refusing to commit such an act of folly, he was obliged to make some sacrifice, and gratify the nation by a battle. Europe even expected it; and, although he had been created a dictator for six months, the general thought he ought to submit everything to the orders of Congress and to the deliberations of a council of war.[46]

[46] Lafayette memoirs, p. 21.

The planning at the Byrnes home went for naught as British General Howe marched his army to the north and east away from Delaware and into Pennsylvania towards Philadelphia. At first Washington believed his army would be attacked near Newport, Delaware, but then detected the British movement that would evade a direct conflict in Delaware and send the British army past his army. A dawdling race between the two armies was on to Philadelphia.

Washington explained the situation to Congress in a letter to John Hancock on September 9, 1777. Washington stated he was eight miles from Wilmington at the time.

> The enemy advanced yesterday with a seeming intention of attacking us upon our post near Newport. We waited for them the whole day, but they halted in the evening at a place called Mill Town about two miles from us. Upon reconnoitering their situation, it appeared probable that they only meant to amuse us in front, while their real intent was to march by our right and by suddenly passing the Brandywine and gaining the heights upon the North side of that river, get between us and Philada and cut us off from that city. To prevent this it was judged expedient to change our position immediately, the Army accordingly marched at two o'clock this morning and will take post this evening upon the high grounds near Chad's Ford. We have heard nothing circumstantial from the enemy this day, when I do I shall immediately transmit you an account. I have the honor to be (your most obedient servant, George) Washington.[47]

---

[47] National Archives.

Washington's scouts sent him reports about the British camping near Kennett Square, just a few miles west of Chadds Ford. Washington wanted confirmation. Washington would be plagued by the lack of accurate intelligence during the Brandywine campaign. Tench Tilghman, Washington's aide-de-camp, wrote to Captain David Hopkins of the 4th Continental Dragoons on September 9 that Washington required written reports and not verbal communications from Hopkins' representatives because the "messengers often are confused and unintelligible." Later in the day, Tilghman reminded Hopkins how important it was for Washington to receive accurate information. Hopkins was told to do whatever was necessary to file precise reports.

The next day Tilghman sent off a letter to Major General William Heath with a telling postscript of impending action at Brandywine. "Chad's Ford (Pa.) 10th Sepr 1777: His Excellency prevented from signing as he is called out to form the troops, the enemy being on the approach."[48] The day before, September 9, Washington established headquarters nearly a mile east of Chadd's Ford at the house of Benjamin Ring. He would remain at the Ring house until September 11.[49]

As the two armies slowly made progress towards the Brandywine River, Lafayette was a young,—he celebrated his 20th birthday on September 6—and little-known foreign officer on Washington's staff with no battle experience and no troops under his command. He wasn't even a paid professional army officer, just an unpaid foreign volunteer. In a matter of hours, Brandywine would result in a dreadful defeat for Washington, a battle he was loathe to recount in later years. As for Lafayette, at the end the day he emerged as an aspiring American hero.

---

[48] Washington Papers, p. 161.

[49] Washington's Papers, p 174.

·7·

A Brandywine Morning

Lafayette's place on Washington's staff allowed the young Frenchman to observe the events leading up to the largest land battle of the American Revolution, Brandywine. As Howe and the British headed north, past Washington's right flank, Washington quickly switched locations and raced to the eastern shore of the Brandywine River.

A "nocturnal council of war," as Lafayette described the meeting of Washington's generals, resulted in the decision to defend the capital city at Brandywine, even though the site was more than 30 miles from Philadelphia. The river, Washington believed, provided an advantageous position for his American army. The central point of the American defense was the area around Chadds Ford. Washington amply defended the location by placement of his artillery, Lafayette wrote in his memoirs.

Lafayette's memoirs contained a telling statement about Brandywine: "It was that hardly examined station." By not scouting the area surrounding the Brandywine and the river's fords, Washington handed the British an opportunity to destroy the American army. British General Howe exploited Washington's gaffe and came close to destroying the American army and crippling the American quest for freedom that day. Several British officers wrote that if another few hours of daylight had been available, no American army would have remained after September 11, 1777.

Washington's mistake and the British success resulted in Brandywine being relegated to a historical footnote, an undeserved fate. Washington and the American army, the losers, weren't keen on reminding the world of a major defeat. The battle's victors, the British, lost the war. Thus, a major triumph at Brandywine became but a faint notation in British history, as England doesn't dwell on the war that lost the American colonies.

Howe's taking advantage of Washington's faulty tactics did result in an opportunity for Lafayette to show his valor and dedication to the American cause of freedom. Lafayette didn't pass on the chance; Lafayette embraced the opportunity. Lafayette fearlessly rushed into a dangerous and desperate situation to help Washington's faltering troops. On the fields of Birmingham Hill, Lafayette shed his own blood in defense of America.

Brandywine shouldn't be remembered as a disastrous American loss, as it is now. Brandywine should be remembered as marking the creation of a much needed American hero, the Marquis de Lafayette.

Brandywine was a key component of the loss of Philadelphia, Congress fleeing to York and the harsh winter at Valley Forge for Washington and his troops. In hindsight, those negative outcomes are minor when compared with Lafayette's contributions to winning American freedom.

Credible intelligence received by the British and a lack of reliable information given to Washington set the stage for Lafayette's moment of destiny on Birmingham Hill.

On initial viewing, the Brandywine seemed a reasonable, but not perfect, defensive position for Washington's army. The Brandywine is by no means a roaring river. Lafayette named the

Brandywine a stream, and at times the body of water has been called a creek. Heavy rains in the late summer of 1777 swelled the Brandywine. At fords on the river on the day of the battle, the water was reported to be at a man's waist. The Brandywine wouldn't stop a British soldier from crossing, but the water hazard would slow him down a bit.

The hills and tree lines on the east bank of the Brandywine shielded Washington's artillery and troops from the sight of the British. Any attempt of a forced crossing by Howe's troops into the midst of the whole American army would cost the British numerous causalities. Washington longed for a chance to catch Howe's troops in mid-stream.

If General Howe wanted to take Philadelphia and capture the Continental Congress, he would have to go through Washington's army in front of the Brandywine. At least, that was Washington's hope and belief. Washington promised a city official that he would vigorously defend Philadelphia, saying, "I shall take ever measure in my power to defend it."[50]

The night before the battle, decisions were made that proved fatal for Washington's defense at Brandywine. Faulty information was utilized, either from uninformed local citizens or reliance on the sketchy Jacob Broom map, to anchor Washington's right flank at Brinton's Ford. Washington was assured that the British army would have to march days to ford the Brandywine north of his right flank.

General John Sullivan, who was entrusted with the defense of the all-important right flank, wrote that at the meeting he was informed, along with Washington, no fords were within 12 miles of Buffington's Ford, just north of Brinton's Ford. Sullivan sent troops to protect Buffington's Ford. If a flanking movement was attempted, Washington and Sullivan believed the British would be in for a long hike on a bad road.

---

[50] Joseph J. Ellis, *His Excellency George Washington*, Vintage Books, New York, 2004, p. 102.

As night fell on September 10, Washington's deployment of troops was nearly complete. The left flank was manned by troops of General John Armstrong. Armstrong's brigades of Pennsylvania militia were stationed at Pyle's Ford, south of Chadds Ford. Washington didn't expect an attack at Pyle's Ford. Washington deemed the militia to be the least reliable brigades in his army.

General Greene's troops were just east of Chadds Ford and just to his right were the forces of General Anthony Wayne, fighting in his home county of Chester. Colonel Thomas Proctor commanded the artillery on the heights next to Wayne.

Sullivan was ordered to protect Brinton's Ford, about a mile north of Chadds Ford. As a reserve for Sullivan, General William Alexander Stirling, known as Lord Stirling, held his men to the east of Sullivan. In the vicinity was General Adam Stephen's division. Stephen's men were available to support either Sullivan or Wayne and Greene.

Washington expected September 11 to be a grand day in the fledgling country's history. He gathered his staff, including Lafayette and Alexander Hamilton, early in the hot and foggy morning. Washington was ready to avenge his earlier defeats by the British. He greatly relied upon the dutiful assistance of aides-de-camp and his scouts. Washington actively reviewed American positions early in the morning. He gave orders and he moved his troops. As Washington ably performed his duties, Lafayette was by his side.

A large contingent of British troops under the command of Hessian General Wilhelm Knyphausen marched early in the morning from its camp at nearby Kennett Square towards the Brandywine. Washington hoped all of Howe's forces were taking part in the assault. American General William Maxwell and his light infantry were positioned on the west side of the Brandywine to challenge the British advance and then withdraw to the east shore of the Brandywine. Maxwell was not to make a stand against the British.

Maxwell's men did as ordered. They fired volleys and gradually fell back to the Brandywine. One of Maxwell's soldiers contesting Knyphausen's force was future United States Supreme Court Justice John Marshall. Washington didn't want Maxwell to become involved in a major clash on the west side of the Brandywine. Washington wanted the Brandywine to be between his troops and the British army when the main fighting took place.

Knyphausen also didn't want a major engagement with Washington that morning. His orders were to contain the Americans at Chadds Ford and then force a crossing of the Brandywine when he heard Howe's troops attacking the rear of Washington's forces. Washington's army would be trapped between the two segments of Howe's army. By 10:30 a.m. Knyphausen had driven the Americans off the heights on the west side of the Brandywine. The Hessian general halted, lightly engaged Washington's forces and waited for Howe's expected surprise assault on Washington.

As the morning progressed, Washington deftly handled the duties of a commanding officer. Washington, Lafayette and other members of Washington's staff spent part of the battle at the John Chad house, near where the artillery was placed, observing the battle. Washington encouraged his men and he issued orders. His engagement of the British was unfolding as planned, Washington believed. To ensure that his army was following orders, Washington bravely exposed himself to British marksmen.

During late morning, while Lafayette was with Washington, British Captain Patrick Ferguson, a Scottish-born marksman and inventor, took aim on a high-ranking American officer in the vicinity of the Brandywine River. Ferguson wrote that a brave American was twice in his range and the rifle range of several of his marksmen. The American officer was doing his duty, so Ferguson withheld his fire and wouldn't allow his troops, a unit designated Ferguson's Rifles, to open fire on the American officer.

The identity of that high-ranking American officer has not been confirmed. By the description given by Ferguson, some historians believed the officer was either Washington or a European officer. The horse Ferguson described fit the markings of the horse Washington rode that morning. The next day an unidentified wounded American officer was said to have told Ferguson that Washington was the target. Ferguson's meeting with the wounded American has not been documented.

Ferguson was recognized as one of the best marksmen in the British army. Ferguson wrote that he could have shot the American officer multiple times before the officer could have escaped. If the American officer was Washington and Ferguson had fired, American history would have been drastically altered. If the foreign officer was Lafayette, the American hero would have been shot before having a chance to prove his bravery and assist America in winning its independence.

The rifle Ferguson was using was one he designed. The Ferguson rifle was the first British weapon that could be reloaded from a prone position, thus not exposing a British soldier to enemy fire while standing and reloading. The Battle of Brandywine was the first time the weapon had been used. Few of the originals exist. One is showcased at Edinburgh Castle in Scotland.

Ferguson was wounded in his right arm at Brandywine. He was being treated for his injury when he is reported to have talked to the unidentified wounded American officer. After recovering from his wound, Ferguson led British loyalists at Kings Mountain, North Carolina, and was killed at the battle on October 7, 1780.

In his memoirs, Lafayette recalled the morning events before Chadds Ford. The British appeared on the western banks of the Brandywine about 9:00 a.m., according to Lafayette. "The enemy was so near the skirts of the wood that it was impossible to judge the size of his force: some time was lost in a mutual cannonading. General Washington walked along his two lines and was received with acclamations which seemed to promise him success," Lafayette noted.

Lafayette's memoirs contained another bit of information

not known, of course, to Washington or Lafayette on the day of the battle. Lafayette recorded that Howe had split his force into two columns and sent one—Lafayette estimated the column to include about 8,000 men—to the fords of Birmingham, about three miles to the right of Washington's flank.

Even though he lacked specific intelligence as to the position of the British army, Washington was well aware of the danger a flanking attack posed to his army. The loss at Long Island the year before was etched in his mind. There, Howe utilized the flanking maneuver to gain the British victory.

Sullivan, in charge of the American right flank, expanded his area to include three fords north of Brinton's Ford to Buffington's Ford. Delaware forces under Colonel David Hall and Colonel Moses Hazen's Canadian regiment were ordered to defend this vulnerable position. Colonel Theodorick Bland's dragoons had the responsibility of patrolling the area. Bland was ordered to report directly to Washington. The results of the scouting forays by Bland's men were essential to Washington. Washington needed accurate information on the British movements if he had a chance to defeat the professional army fielded by England.

Washington was not receiving the solid information he needed. By noon, staff members reported that Washington was complaining about not having reliable reports on the exact whereabouts of the British army. Lafayette and Washington's other aides were trying to make sense of conflicting information. Colonel Thomas Pickering, Washington's adjutant, wrote that as late as "11 or 12 o'clock (Washington) bitterly lamented that Col. Bland had not sent him any information at all, and that accounts he had received from others were of a very contradictory nature."[51]

Washington sent an urgent note to Bland. "I earnestly entreat a continuance of your vigilant attention to the movements of the enemy, and the earliest report not only of their movements, but of their numbers and the course they are pursuing. In a particular

[51] Papers of George Washington, p. 190.

matter, I wish to gain satisfactory information of a body confidently reported to have gone up a ford seven or eight miles above this. It is said the fact is certain. You will send up an intelligent, sensible officer immediately with a part to find out the truth, what number it consists of, and the road they are now on. Be particular in these matter."[52]

A credible report was received by Washington about noon. Lieutenant Colonel James Ross, son of a signer of the Declaration of Independence, reported from the Great Valley Road at 11:00 a.m. "Dear General, A large body of the enemy from every account 5,000, with 16 or 18 field pieces, marched along this road just now. . . . We are close to their rear with 70 men." Ross reported that his men fired several shots at the British.[53]

During the long morning hours, Bland and his men desperately attempted to satisfy Washington's need for proper intelligence on the British army's movements. One of the first messages Washington received, about 9:30 a.m., from Sullivan was a report from Major John Jamison of Bland's dragoons. Jamison scouted north of Washington's right flank and discovered no enemy troops. The exact location and the exact time of Jamison's expedition north of the fords were not noted. Lafayette and the rest of Washington's staff needed those crucial elements of time and place to make sense of the seemingly contradictory reports.

Sullivan realized the need for additional intelligence and ordered Jamison to send another dragoon north of Buffington's Ford. That officer reported back that the enemy "had passed that way." As the afternoon of September 11 approached, additional reports indicated that Howe was on the march and attempting a flanking movement. Sullivan relayed a message from Hazen that reported that Howe indeed was on the march. Hazen had seen British troops near the forks of the Brandywine, where the two branches of the Brandywine join into one waterway.

[52] Papers of George Washington, p. 190.

[53] Papers of George Washington, p 196.

Which of the reports should Washington believe? Washington faced a dilemma, and also an opportunity. If Howe had taken a large portion of his army north, the British force immediately in front of him was vulnerable. Washington could leave his formidable defensive position, charge across the Brandywine and fight what seemed to be an inferior force commanded by the Hessian Knyphausen. The plan would end in disaster for Washington if Howe was in the vicinity and could quickly bring his whole army to fight the Americans in the open.

Lafayette witnessed Washington agonizing over the decision to attack or hold his defensive position. "The intelligence that was received of the movements of Cornwallis was both confused and contradictory. Owing to the conformity of name between two roads that were of equal length and parallel to each other, the best officers were mistaken in their reports. The only musket-shots that had been fired were from Maxwell, who killed several of the enemy, but was driven back upon the left of the American army, across a ford by which he had before advanced," Lafayette wrote in his memoirs.

In one moment, Washington authorized an advance and attack on the remaining British forces he faced west of the Brandywine. In the next moment, Washington called off the attack and remained behind his secure position. Pickering reported that Washington became convinced Howe was rejoining Knyphausen at Chadds Ford. At least Washington believed his army was safe with the waters of the Brandywine separating him from Knyphausen's command.

One historian believed "Washington conducted the Brandywine operation as if he was in a daze. The general who always had stressed the necessity of procuring the fullest intelligence and of analyzing it correctly had failed to do either or to employ his light horse adequately when the price of error might be the loss of Philadelphia."[54]

---

[54] Douglas S. Freeman, *George Washington—Leader of the Revolution,* Vol. IV, New York, Charles Scribner's Sons, 1951, p. 489.

By the time Bland discovered the British, the British army was well on its way to successfully executing another flanking movement against Washington. Bland didn't discover the main body of the British army, under the command of generals Howe and Cornwallis, until about 1:00 p.m., ninety long minutes after Washington sent his urgent request to Bland.

Lafayette recorded this observation on the status of the American troops. He wrote, "The left of the army tranquil while the right was poised to receive the heavy blows."

Since Washington couldn't ascertain solid information from those under his command, he wasn't about to take the word of civilian. Patriot Thomas Cheyney, later to become a squire, saw Howe and his troops crossing the Brandywine. Cheyney and his relative, Colonel John Hannum of the Pennsylvania militia, left Martin's Tavern in nearby Marshallton in the morning and observed the enemy soldiers. As Hannum rode to rejoin his unit, Cheyney rode to warn Washington. Neither Sullivan nor Washington immediately believed Cheyney. How could a civilian obtain credible information on Howe's movements when Washington's dragoons failed? Cheyney was arguing with Washington when Bland's report finally reached Washington confirming Howe's flanking movement. The civilian Cheyney was correct. Howe had indeed outflanked Washington, again.

Washington was still plagued by inaccurate information. One report had only two brigades, and not more than half of the British army, taking part in the British flanking march. After consulting with Hazen, Sullivan corrected Washington's misimpression about the size of Howe's army forming in the vicinity of Osborne's Hill and the Quaker Birmingham Meeting House.

How were Howe and Cornwallis able to elude the Americans on the morning of September 11, 1777? First, Cornwallis made sure that the farmers and civilians he passed on his march were not able to alert Washington's forces. Also, the dense morning fog shielded early movements of the British army. The most important element was that Howe had better intelligence from area loyalists then Washington received from his local supporters.

The most important loyalist was Joseph Galloway, a Philadelphia lawyer and politician. Galloway declined an invitation to be a member of the second Continental Congress as he resisted the persuasive efforts of Benjamin Franklin to join the cause of freedom. Galloway united with Howe in 1776 and was with the British army at Brandywine.

Galloway was familiar with the terrain of the battle's area. Howe used Galloway's knowledge to formulate his winning tactics. Other loyalists were guides, including Curtis Lewis of East Caln Township, a central Chester County municipality. Captain Johann Ewald called Lewis a "veritable geographical Chart . . . I was often amazed at the knowledge that this man possessed of the country."[55]

Following the expert guidance offered by Lewis, Howe's column crossed the west branch of the Brandywine at Trimble's Ford, about two miles above the forks of the Brandywine, at approximately 11:00 a.m. Howe didn't want to string out his command and halted the lead troops to allow the whole column to cross the west branch of the Brandywine before marching three miles farther to cross the east branch at Jefferis Ford at about 2:00 p.m.

While Washington was slowly coming to the conclusion that he was outflanked, the British army made its way to Osborne's Hill, an elevated mount just north of Birmingham Hill. The long and grueling march covering more than 14 miles came to an end about 2:30 p.m. One soldier reported the British army "refreshed" itself for an hour and watched the rebel army form on the opposite height, Birmingham Hill.

---

[55] Samuel Smith, *Battle of Brandywine*, p. 13.

The Birmingham Friends Meeting House today.
Registered in "Historic Places in the U.S.A."

·8·

A Hero is Born

Lafayette was in the midst of chaos.

Washington's army was in danger of being routed, maybe even destroyed, by British General Howe's risky, but successful, flanking movement. For the second time in a little more than a year, the first being at Long Island, Howe unexpectedly appeared in the rear of Washington's army by evading American scouts.

Howe was on the verge of ending the American rebellion. The proverb—fool me once, shame on you; fool me twice, shame on me—that was memorialized a century before the Battle of Brandywine certainly could be applied to Washington.

As soon as Washington received confirmation that the troops of British generals Howe and Cornwallis were massed on Osborne's Hill, the American general undertook drastic measures to avert a defeat and save his precious army. The first order of business was to get American troops in front of Howe and stop, or at least slow down, the British assault. The closest forces belonged to the reserve divisions of generals Stirling and Stephen. The men were to immediately depart from the Brandywine River and form near the Birmingham Meeting House, just to the east of Birmingham Hill.

Washington then ordered Sullivan's troops to join Stirling

and Stephen and take overall command of the American forces at Birmingham Hill. Within five minutes of receiving Washington's directive, Sullivan was making his way to block the British advance. Soon after starting his advance, Sullivan came into contact with Hazen. Hazen gave Sullivan some unwanted but expected news. Sullivan was about to face a large number of British soldiers. Hazen reported that the bulk of the British army was upon his heels.

Hazen's report was confirmation that the Americans were in a desperate struggle for survival.

While Sullivan was attempting to place his troops into a defensive line on Birmingham Hill to the west of the position of Stirling and Stephen's troops, the British launched a major assault from Osborne's Hill. One witness called the assault the most grand and noble sight imaginable. The long line of British and Hessian soldiers in colorful uniforms stretched along Osborne's Hill. The time was close to 4:00 p.m. when Cornwallis ordered his three columns, with the light infantry and German jaegers on the left, the British and Hessian grenadiers in the center and British troops to the right, to advance.

A deadly gap existed between Stirling and Stephen's divisions, an opening that the British could use to divide and conquer the fragile American defense on Birmingham Hill. When Sullivan arrived, he ordered the two generals to move their troops to the right near Birmingham Meeting House. Sullivan's force would be placed to the left, about 400 yards west of the Birmingham Meeting House, on Birmingham Hill, in front of a tree line. Sullivan's troops would fill the dangerous gap.

A disastrous delay in deployment took place when General Preudhomme de Borre, one of the French generals commanding American forces, insisted that his troops hold the strategic far right of the American line. De Borre's troops would be among the first to flee the coming British onslaught. For his actions at Brandywine, de Borre was threatened with a court martial. De Borre, instead, resigned and departed America in 1779.

The shift caused additional confusion among the American troops as the British advanced closer to the rebels. The fighting intensified as the British descended upon the Americans. A British officer mentioned in his diary that the Americans fired cannons and then small arms when the British were within 40 paces of them. The British responded with a ferocious volley. The English grenadiers then furiously attacked the Americans with their fixed bayonets.[56]

Sullivan's report stated that for more than an hour and a half his troops fought for control of Birmingham Hill. Five times the British drove his troops from the hill, and five times his troops reclaimed the hill, according to Sullivan. The hill was depicted as being contested muzzle-to-muzzle a large part of the time. Sullivan added that General Thomas Conway, who has seen much service, said he never saw so close and severe a fire.[57]

At Brandywine, Conway commanded the 3rd Pennsylvania Brigade in Stirling's division. Conway was in charge of the 3rd, 6th, 9th and 12th Pennsylvania regiments and also Spencer's Continental regiment.

Among those fighting with General Conway that afternoon was a young Frenchman, Lafayette.

Lafayette realized the seriousness of the situation once he became aware of the march made by the troops of Howe and Cornwallis. Lafayette besieged Washington with a request to be allowed to join Sullivan's forces. Lafayette was determined to assist in stemming the British advancement. Washington looked at his youthful French officer and gave his assent.

Lafayette with his aides, Gimat and Chevaler La Colombe,

[56] National Archives.

[57] National Archives.

rode their horses as fast as possible to cover the more than a mile of distance from Washington's staff to Birmingham Hill.

Upon arriving on Birmingham Hill, Lafayette observed that both flanks of Sullivan's forces were crumbling under the British onslaught. Lafayette wrote that he joined Sullivan's central division and witnessed Conway commanding 800 men "in a most brilliant manner." Lafayette recalled that his joining the fray "seemed to inspirit the (American) troops."[58]

This was the first time that Lafayette was under fire, though he behaved like a seasoned veteran.[59]

Harlow Giles Unger in his book *Lafayette* described the scene:

> Americans fled in panic. Lafayette tried to halt their retreat. He reared his horse into the air, wheeled to the right, to the left, galloping back and forth to block the fleeing troops. Finally he jumped off and grabbed at men's shoulders and arms, ordering them to turn about, stand and fight—a major general in full uniform; a madman refusing to face defeat.
>
> Stirling and his men rallied and his brigade formed on a slight rise behind Lafayette and gave him covering fire. British troops overwhelmed them. Lafayette ordered his men to fall back beside Sullivan and Stirling's men, and they stood their ground until the British were within 20 yards and forced them to flee to the safety of the woods behind them. It was then that Gimat looked down and saw blood seeping from Lafayette's boot. Musket ball through calf of his left leg. Gimat and La Colombe lifted

[58] Lafayette memoirs, p 23.

[59] Colonialwilliamsburg.org.

> Lafayette onto his horse and joined the retreat toward Chester.[60]

Chevalier du Buysson recalled that Lafayette and his French aides were eager to join the fighting, arriving on Birmingham Hill as the action was at its hottest. The contingent rode towards the north on Birmingham Road and turned to the left, coming in behind General Conway's Pennsylvania brigade.

Du Buysson described the heroic action of Lafayette. His account stated that Lafayette did his utmost to make Conway's men charge with fixed bayonets. Some of the Americans were faltering and withdrawing when Lafayette dismounted from his horse and rallied Conway's troops to turn and face the enemy. The British army advanced through an open field and concentrated its full fire upon the American center. The assault resulted in great confusion among the Americans. During this period, Lafayette was wounded with a ball passing through his left leg.

Colonel McClellan of the 9th Pennsylvania, under Conway's command, told a reporter of a local newspaper, the *Village Record*, that he was near Lafayette when the Frenchman was wounded.

As Lafayette's blood mingled with the American soil on Birmingham Hill, the Americans gave way and retreated towards Sandy Hallow and beyond. Lafayette wrote in his memoirs that he owed a debt to his aide-de-camp Gimat, as his fellow Frenchman assisted Lafayette back on his horse and escorted him to the momentary shelter of the nearby woods.

As Lafayette was assessing the seriousness of his wound, he saw Washington arriving in the distance with fresh troops. Lafayette wrote that he was determined to join Washington to continue fighting the British. Lafayette's loss of blood was too great. He stopped to have the wound bandaged. Washington's personal physician, Dr. John Cochran, was said to have applied a quick

---

[60] Unger, pages 44–45.

field dressing to stop the blood. While receiving medical attention, Lafayette reported that he was almost captured by his foes.

Another similar account of Lafayette's actions depicted Lafayette dismounting his horse during the crisis, running forward with his sword up to cheer on the troops and rally the faltering soldiers. "While thus engaged, in the thick and fury of it, he was hit by a musket ball, which passed clear through his leg below the knee, but luckily severed no artery and broke no bone. Gimat helped him to get to the rear. By great good fortune, Major de Gimat piloted Lafayette out of range. The boot was full of blood, and running over with it, when a surgeon was found."[61]

For sure, "Lafayette performed his first military service in the cause of American independence, displaying a personal devotion in the heat of battle which won distinction for him at once as a soldier, and left him, when the action was ended, one of the heroes of the day."[62] The description continued by stating that Lafayette saw the panic in Sullivan's troops and threw himself from his horse, plunged among the hurrying masses and strove to renew confidence by his voice and by his example. Lafayette stayed and fought until the British were within 20 yards of them and then escaped into the woods with a musket ball in his left leg below the knee.[63]

Lafayette described his action at Brandywine in an interview to the *Poulson's Advertiser*, a Philadelphia newspaper, on February 25, 1825, during his grand tour of the United States.

> The ball went through and through; I was on foot when I received my wound; a part of our line had given way but a part still held its ground. To these I repaired. To encourage my comrades, and

---

[61] George Morgan, The *True La Fayette*, J. B. Lippincott Co., Philadelphia, 1919, p. 111.

[62] Charlemagne Tower, *The Marquis de La Fayette in the American Revolution*, J. B. Lippincott, Philadelphia, 1926, p. 229.

[63] Tower, p 230.

> to show them I had no better chance to flight than they, I ordered my horse to the rear. The news of my being hurt was conveyed to the commander-in-chief, with the usual exaggerations in such cases. The good General Washington freely expressed his grief that one so young, and a volunteer in the holy cause of freedom, should so early have fallen; but he was soon relieved by an assurance that my wound would stop short of life, when he sent me his love and gratulation that matters were no worse. On the field of battle the surgeon prepared his dressings, but the shot fell so thick around us, that in a very little time, if we had remained, we should both have been past all surgery. Being mounted on my horse I left the field.

Lafayette earned Washington's respect during the afternoon of September 11, 1777 and was unquestionably on the road to becoming America's first international hero. Also, in his memoir, Lafayette wrote that Washington wanted his medical staff to care for Lafayette as if he were Washington's own son.

While the wounded Lafayette was being escorted off the field, Washington was occupied with serious concerns about the welfare of his entire army. British generals Howe, Cornwallis and Knyphausen were circling for the kill. Knyphausen faithfully executed his orders, as he had done all day, and forced his way across the Brandywine and past the defense of American General Anthony Wayne. Howe and Cornwallis pressed Washington and the Americans to retreat from Birmingham Hill and the Birmingham Meeting House, past Sandy Hallow and through the village of Dilworthtown.

Knyphausen successfully attacked Wayne, who was supported by the light infantry of Maxwell and Proctor's artillery. The British crossed the Brandywine without stopping to fire a shot even though being assaulted by the American artillery and small arms. The British forces successfully used the bayonet to subdue the Americans resistance and capture valuable American artillery pieces.

Washington needed assistance from the remaining troops at Chadds Ford and ordered General Nathanael Greene to quickly reinforce Sullivan's retreating men. Greene reported that he hurriedly marched a division almost four miles in less than hour. When arriving on the field, Greene found his comrades routed and withdrawing in a "most broken and confused manner."[64] Greene ably covered the retreat and with Washington's consent set a trap for the British just west of Dilworthtown. There General George Weeden's brigade suffered almost 100 casualties but held off the British for more than an hour.[65]

The rearguard action by Greene's forces allowed the remaining portion of Washington's battered army to retreat towards Chester, Pennsylvania.

Lafayette described the disheartening withdrawal in his memoirs.

> Fugitives, cannon, and baggage now crowded without order into the road leading to Chester. The general employed the remaining daylight in checking the enemy: some regiments behaved extremely well, but the disorder was complete.

[64] National Archives.

[65] National Archives.

> During that time the ford of Chad was forced, the cannon taken, and the Chester road became the common retreat of the whole army. In the midst of that dreadful confusion, and during the darkness of the night, it was impossible to recover; but at Chester, 12 miles from the field of battle, they met with a bridge which it was necessary to cross. I occupied myself in arresting the fugitives. Some degree of order was re-established; the generals and the commander-in-chief arrived; and I had leisure to have my wound dressed.

Lafayette reported that he couldn't recognize anyone along the road because of the darkness. Washington had the same issue. "Washington was asking for Lafayette. After seeing Lafayette, Washington ordered Surgeon William Magaw of the First Pennsylvania to dress (Lafayette's leg wound). (General) Knox, upon seeing Lafayette, said, "The boy we thought lost is found."[66]

In his newspaper interview for the *Poulson's Advertiser*, Lafayette gave additional information on the retreat. "Being mounted on my horse I left the field, and repaired to the bridge near Chester, where I halted and placed a guard, to stop fugitive soldiers, and direct them to join their respective regiments. I could do no more; becoming faint, I was carried into a house in Chester and laid on a table, when my wound received its first dressing. The general officers soon arrived, when I saluted them by begging that they would not eat me up, as they appeared to be very hungry, and I was the only dish upon the table in the house.

"The good general-in-chief was much gratified on finding me in such spirits, and caused a litter to be made, on which I was

---

[66] Morgan, p. 113.

conveyed to the Indian Queen (a tavern/hotel) in Philadelphia, and was there waited upon by the members of Congress, who were all booted, spurred and on the wing for a place of greater safety to hold their sessions."

A future American President assisted Lafayette the night after the battle. Captain James Monroe, a French-speaking Virginian on Stirling's staff, spent the day carrying messages to Washington from Stirling. At Chester, while Lafayette rested on a makeshift litter, Monroe commiserated with him and attended to his needs.[67] Monroe, who was seven months younger than Lafayette, had suffered a severe wound the year before at Trenton. Monroe was shot through his upper chest and shoulder. Dr. John Cochran, who first attended to Lafayette's wound on the Brandywine battlefield, also treated Monroe at Trenton.

While the British army was victorious at Brandywine, the victors made an egregious error the night of the battle, according to Lafayette, that could have ended the war. "If the enemy had marched to (Chester), the (American) army would have been cut up and destroyed. They lost an all—important night; and this was perhaps their greatest fault during a war in which they committed so many errors."[68]

Washington's aide, Colonel Timothy Pickering, agreed with Lafayette. Pickering wrote in his diary, "It was fortunate for us that the night came on, for under its cover the fatigued, stragglers, and some wounded made their escape." A month after the battle, Howe admitted in a letter to Lord George Germain, who was in charge of the American conflict for England, that "the enemy's army escaped a total overthrow that must have been the consequence of an hour's more daylight."[69]

Howe's army inflicted a severe beating on Washington's army. The Americans suffered more than 1,200 casualties—no definite

[67] Unger, p 46.
[68] Lafayette memoirs, p 23.
[69] National Archives.

number can be obtained because the American army didn't keep accurate records—while the British reported less than 600 men killed, wounded and missing.

Washington believed that it was his duty to inform Congress of the defeat at Brandywine. By the time he reached Chester and took shelter in a home, he was exhausted from the day's fighting and stresses. A letter was sent to John Hancock that evening and signed by Washington. The letter was in Pickering's handwriting.

Pickering's son, Octavius Pickering, wrote a biography of his father. In that work, the author wrote that Colonel Harrison of Washington's staff was asked to write the report but declined because of fatigue. The duty then fell to Pickering. Washington approved the draft but wanted some "words of encouragement to be added" to take some of the sting out of the defeat.[70] Lafayette was only one of a few officers named in the report sent to Congress.

The letter to Hancock was marked from Chester at midnight.

> Sir,
>
> I am sorry to inform you that in this day's engagement we have been obliged to leave the enemy masters of the field. Unfortunately the intelligence received of the enemy's advancing up the Brandywine, & crossing at a ford about six miles above us, was uncertain & contradictory, notwithstanding all my pains to get the best. This prevented my making disposition adequate to the force with which the enemy attacked us on our right; in consequence of which the troops first engaged were obliged to retire before they could be reinforced. In the midst of the attack on the right, that body of the enemy

[70] Washington's Papers, p. 201

> which remained on the other side of Chad's ford, crossed it, & attacked the division there under the command of General Wayne & the light troops under General Maxwell, who after a severe conflict also retired. The militia under the command of General Armstrong, being posted at a ford about two miles below Chad's, had no opportunity of engaging. But though we fought under many disadvantages, and were from the causes above mentioned, obliged to retire; yet our loss of men is not, I am persuaded, very considerable . . . We have also lost seven or eight pieces of cannon. . . .
>
> I have directed all the troops to assemble behind Chester, where they are now arranging for this night. Notwithstanding the misfortune of the day, I am happy to find the troops in good spirits; and I hope another time we shall compensate for the losses now sustained.
>
> The Marquis La Fayette was wounded in the leg & General Woodford in the hand. Divers other officers were wounded, & some slain; but the numbers of either cannot now be ascertained. I have the honor to be, Sir, your obedient h'ble servant.
>
> Go. Washington

The dark and desolate night following a disastrous day had one brilliant ray of light; Lafayette departed the fields of Brandywine an American hero.

9.

Bethlehem Recovery

While Brandywine marked the beginning of Lafayette's ascent as an American hero, the young Frenchman's future included many crucial challenges that impacted history in the United States and France. Lafayette earned his triumphant tour of the United States that took place more than four decades after Brandywine.

Washington's defeat at Chadds Ford immediately made Philadelphia a dangerous place for those supporting the revolution and opposing King George III. Three days after the battle, John Adams wrote to his wife Abigail that his departure was imminent as Howe's advancing army was about 15 miles distant.

"How much longer Congress will stay here is uncertain," Adams's letter stated. "I hope we shall not move until the last necessity that is until it shall be rendered certain, that Mr. Howe will get the city. If we should move it will be to Reading, Lancaster, York, Easton or Bethlehem, some town in this state. It is the determination not to leave this state. Don't be anxious about me—nor about our great and sacred cause—it is the cause of truth and will prevail."[71]

---

[71] National Archives.

Also, Lafayette wrote to his wife Adrienne. The day after the battle Lafayette reassured her that he wasn't seriously injured.

"I must begin by telling you that I am perfectly well because I must end by telling you that we fought a difficult battle last night, and that we were not the strongest. Our Americans, after having stood their ground for some time, ended at length by being routed; while I was trying to rally the troops, the gentlemen of England did me the honor of shooting me, which hurt my leg a little, but it is nothing, my sweetheart; the ball touched neither a bone nor a nerve, and I will have to stay in bed for only a little while, which has left me in a bad mood. I hope, sweetheart, that you won't be anxious; you should not be: I shall be hors de combat for some time, and you can be sure that I will take good care of myself. This defeat, I fear, will have harsh consequences for America."[72]

The encroaching British army made Lafayette's lingering in Philadelphia impossible. The convalescence of the young Frenchman took place in the Moravian town of Bethlehem where other wounded members of Washington's army were treated by the religious Brethren. Lafayette was first transported by boat from Philadelphia to Bristol, Pennsylvania, on September 16. From Bristol to Bethlehem Lafayette rode in the coach of Congressman Henry Laurens of South Carolina. Laurens cushioned Lafayette's leg for the two-day trip. A warm friendship developed between the two men during the journey. Lafayette wrote a letter to Laurens thanking him for his kindness and stating that his physical condition would have been worse without Lauren's assistance.[73]

Laurens would later become President of the Congress and an important ally for Lafayette. Also, Lafayette was an important ally for Laurens. Lafayette and his wife didn't forget the kindness Laurens showed him. After Laurens was captured by the British on his way to Europe and imprisoned in the Tower of

[72] Lafayette memoirs, p. 102.

[73] Unger, p 48.

London, Adrienne asked the British to give Laurens "all possible consideration."[74]

When Lafayette arrived at Bethlehem, he found the Moravian conclave overrun with suffering soldiers. Food was scare, as well as public accommodations for the injured. Lafayette was initially taken to the Sun Inn and placed in a second-floor room. The room was so crowded that Lafayette only stayed one night. He was transferred to a private home on Main Street near the Sun Inn. A Pennsylvania Historical marker was erected at 534 Main Street at the home of George Frederick Beckel and indicated that Lafayette was treated in the home. Moravian and Bethlehem histories list several different versions of persons responsible for the care Lafayette received.

"Finally the family of George Frederick Beckel agreed to take Lafayette into their home. Beckel was the superintendent of Bethlehem's farms. This was a highly important post as at that time Bethlehem's farms provided food for the town's inhabitants. The chief task of caring for Lafayette would be borne by the women of the family, his wife Barbara and daughter Liesel."[75]

In the Bethlehem Diary for September and October 1777 in the Moravian's Archive, Lafayette's care is credited to Beckel's second wife and her 21 year-old step-daughter, Elisabeth. The Bethlehem diarist twice described Lafayette as a "handsome young man," who toured the Single Sisters' house and read reports of the Moravian missionaries from Greenland "with much pleasure."

In his memoirs, Lafayette wrote that he "was conducted to Bethlehem, a Moravian establishment, where the mild religion of the brotherhood, the community of fortune, education and interests, amongst that large and simple family, formed a striking contrast to scenes of blood and the convulsions occasioned by a civil war."

---

[74] Morgan, p. 115.

[75] *Moravian Diary*. There is also an entry in the Moravians Archive that indicates Lafayette stayed at the Inn.

Lafayette was much more than a tourist biding his time while healing. Lafayette wanted revenge on the British for the drubbing of Washington at Brandywine and his wounding. Lafayette vowed to set Europe and Asia aflame.[76] Lafayette wrote letters intended to inflame the passions of his countrymen and influence French policy. Lafayette's urging his country's leaders to officially join the United States in fighting England was a bold move for a soldier who escaped France under the threat of arrest and was considered a fugitive.

Lafayette's letters were sent to Foreign Minister Vergennes, Prime Minister Count Maurepas and others. Lafayette wasn't satisfied with targeting Howe and the British forces in the United States. Lafayette wanted an all-out war with campaigns in the Caribbean, Canada, India and the China Sea. Lafayette's costly suggestions were dismissed in Versailles. Maurepas did comment of Lafayette, "When he has taken anything in his head, it is impossible to resist him."[77] Maurepas also commented that Lafayette would sell every last stick of furniture in Versailles to financially support the American cause of independence.

Letters were also sent letters to the French commander of Martinique, his cousin Marquis de Bouille, and urged an attack on British islands under the flag of America. Lafayette wrote to the governor of the Windward Islands and urged him to do the same.

> Confined to my bed for six weeks I suffered from my wound, but still more severely from my inactivity. The good Moravian brothers loved me, and deplored my warlike folly. Whilst listening to their sermons, I planned setting Europe and Asia in a flame.[78]

---

[76] Unger, p. 49.
[77] Lafayette memoirs, p. 27.
[78] Lafayette memoirs, p. 27.

Despite having his grandiose plans rebuffed, Lafayette's standing in the French court was rising. Lafayette became the leading representative of France in America just after having fled France a few months before his wounding.

Lafayette's wellbeing became an ongoing concern for all of France. After the Battle of Brandywine, a rumor circulated in Paris that Lafayette had died. That rumor distressed the government and, of course, Lafayette's family.

Finally, on October 1 Lafayette penned a letter to his wife about this health. To not worry Adrienne that he was taking risky chances with his life, Lafayette downplayed his actions at Brandywine and the bravery he displayed before the British army. He described his injury to Adrienne as "the slight wound I met with I know not how, for I did not expose myself to peril. It was the first engagement I was present, so you see how rare engagements are." Lafayette added that surgeons were astonished at his recovery. Lafayette did confide the wound "is most disagreeable, painful and wearisome. If a man wished to be wounded for his amusement only, he should come and examine how I was struck, that he may be struck in precisely that manner."[79]

> Do not be concerned, sweetheart, about the care of my wound. All the physicians in America are paying close attention to me. I have a friend who has spoken to them in such a way that I can be assured of the best care. That friend is General Washington. This estimable man, whom I at first admired for his talents and qualities and whom I have come to venerate as I know him better, has become my intimate friend. His affectionate interest in me soon won my heart. I am a member of his household and we live together like two brothers in mutual intimacy and

[79] Lafayette memoirs, p. 102.

> confidence. This close friendship makes me as happy as I could possibly be in this country. When he sent his chief surgeon to care for me, he told him to care for me as though I were his son, for he loved me in the same way.[80]

On October 2, General William Woodford reported to Washington from Bethlehem that "The Marquis is much better, & in high spirits."[81] In the same letter, Woodford informed Washington that he receives daily complaints from the community of robberies being perpetrated by soldiers, the "Scum of the Army." Woodford, who was also recuperating from a wound, was doing his best to bring the criminal soldiers to justice. The incidents didn't help the relationship between the Moravians and the army. Lafayette indicated that he discussed with the Moravians their anti-war sentiments. The Moravians didn't take to Lafayette's hostile ways.[82]

On October 14, Lafayette wrote to Washington saying he hoped to be back with the army within a week. Lafayette spoke of his upcoming role in Washington's army. He wanted to command troops. Lafayette also wrote endorsements for de Kalb and La Colombe and praised Conway as a "brave, intelligent and active officer." Lafayette fought with Conway at Brandywine but would soon oppose Conway, who was born in Ireland and became a nationalized Frenchman, because of Conway's participation in a group—known as the Conway Cabal—supporting the ouster of Washington. Conway turned against Washington after Washington opposed his promotion to major general.

Lafayette's recovery was seconded by Woodford. On October 16, Woodford informed Washington in a letter that he would be returning to camp with Lafayette in a "few days."

---

[80] Lafayette memoirs, p. 105.
[81] Washington's Papers, p. 371.
[82] Morgan, p. 118.

Indeed, Lafayette departed on October 18 and left on good terms with the Moravians. A Moravian diarist noted, "The French Marquis de La Fayette left us today for the army in company with Gen. Woodford. We found him a very intelligent and pleasant young man. He occupied much of his time in reading, and, among other matter read an English translation of the history of the (Moravian) Greenland Mission. Before bidding us adieu, he requested to be shown the Sisters' House, a request which we were pleased to grant, and his admiration of the institution was unbounded." [83]

Lafayette was in a hurry to rejoin Washington's army. The American victory at Saratoga instilled hope that the British could be defeated. Alas, the departure from Bethlehem was premature. Lafayette's Brandywine wound had not fully healed. After his five weeks of convalescence, Lafayette was able to wear only one boot and limped off to rejoin Washington. In his memoirs, he noted, "Without waiting for my wound to be closed, I returned to the headquarters, 25 miles from Philadelphia."

On October 20, Washington ordered his troops to draw and cook one day's provisions and be ready to march the next morning to his new headquarters near Whitemarsh. The camp was close to Germantown, a site of another defeat for Washington's army. While Lafayette was at Bethlehem, Washington's forces under the command of General Anthony Wayne were also defeated at Paoli.

The British army strengthened its hold on Philadelphia by capturing forts along the Delaware River. Generals Howe and Cornwallis were intent on making Philadelphia a British stronghold, the same as New York City. The British needed control of the forts to receive provisions from the British navy.

Washington needed intelligence on the deployment of the British army to plan future actions against his foe. Washington selected General Greene to execute a reconnaissance mission. To

---

[83] Washington's Papers, p. 535.

no one's surprise, Lafayette volunteered to join Greene for the November 20 military operation. Lafayette had been in Washington's camp about a month after departing Bethlehem.

Greene, who had been on the same part of the field at Brandywine where Lafayette was wounded, developed a strong relationship with the Frenchman. Greene wrote his wife of Lafayette, "He is one of the sweetest-tempered young gentleman. He has left a young wife and a fine fortune . . . to come and engage in the cause of liberty—this is a noble enthusiasm."[84]

To gain a look at the British forces, Greene led his troops across the Delaware River and into New Jersey. At Gloucester, the Americans were a little north of the British troops. Greene then entrusted Lafayette with a command—Lafayette's first—of about 400 riflemen. On November 24, Lafayette was ordered to advance to the British, observe and report back to Greene. Greene urged Lafayette to take precautions so as not to be encircled by the much larger British force.

Lafayette wanted a first-hand view of the enemy and ventured within rifle range of some of the British sentries. Lafayette acted upon his own intelligence and launched an attack against an estimated 400 Hessians. The Hessians were caught by surprise and fled camp. Lafayette and his troops chased the Hessians for about an hour and inflicted as many as 60 casualties. "We made them run very fast."[85] Cornwallis sent reinforcements to the Hessians, and Lafayette smartly withdrew to Greene's location. Lafayette reported a loss of one dead and five wounded.

On November 26, Greene gave Washington a glowing report on Lafayette's leadership. "The Marquis is determined to be in the way of danger."[86] In his memoirs, Lafayette described the action.

---

[84] Unger, p 54.
[85] Lafayette memoirs, p. 120.
[86] National Archives

> At Gloucester I advanced to a strip of land called Sandy Point. For my imprudence I would have paid dearly, (as almost captured or killed). I found myself about two miles from the English camp of 400 Hessians and their cannon at 4 p.m. With only 350 men, mostly militia, I attacked the Hessians and drove them away. Cornwallis came to the field but was driven back to Gloucester. Greene arrived during the evening but wouldn't attack. The British retreated over the river and Greene and I returned to Whitemarsh and Washington. The slight success at Gloucester gratified the army, especially the militia.

Lafayette wrote to Washington that he hoped his little expedition gave the general some pleasure.

Washington was pleased, especially with Lafayette's initiative and leadership. Washington sent a letter to the new president of Congress beseeching them to give Lafayette a vacant command of a division. The new head of Congress was Henry Laurens, the same man who befriended Lafayette on his trip to Bethlehem. "I am convinced he possesses a large share of that military ardor, which generally characterizes the nobility of his country," Washington wrote of Lafayette to Laurens.[87]

Congress, convinced by Washington's support, authorized Lafayette to be a full-fledged fighting commander of American troops on December 1, 1777. Washington gave Lafayette the choice of several divisions, and Lafayette chose troops from Washington's home state, Virginia.

On Christmas Day, Lafayette was invited to share a sparse dinner with Washington and five other officers, including de Kalb.

[87] Unger, p. 54

"The meal was as plain and rough as the surrounding landscape: unadorned mutton, veal, potatoes, and cabbage, washed down by water."[88]

Lafayette had additional glad tidings bestowed upon him in December. He received a packet of letters. One of the letters informed Lafayette of the birth of his daughter, Anastasie.

[88] Thomas Flemming, *Washington's Secret War: The Hidden History of Valley Forge*, Smithsonian Books, NY, NY, 2005, p. 33.

·10·

Canadian Invasion

Lafayette, a newly minted American general with a minor military victory at Gloucester to his credit, had achieved some of his immediate American goals of fighting for freedom and being a commander of fighting soldiers. As he joined Washington at Valley Forge for the 1777–1778 winter, Lafayette's military standing was escalating. Also, Lafayette was quickly becoming Washington's trusted confidant.

The promotion and military successes gave Lafayette time to turn his attention to a troublesome matter in France, his relationship with his family.

The last contact he had with his father-in-law, Duc d'Ayen, was hostile, as Lafayette fled France against the express wishes of his father-in-law and the king. A letter, at times contrite, sent from Valley Forge to Duc d'Ayen, spoke of Lafayette's military accomplishments and the important contacts he was making, including John Adams who was on his way to France to replace Silas Deane. The American excursion would make Lafayette a better officer in France's army, Lafayette reasoned. Lafayette, somewhat, apologized for his rash actions upon his departing France and wrote of his maturity. "I read, I study, I examine, I listen, I reflect and I try to develop a reasonable common-sense opinion. I do not talk too much—to avoid saying foolish things—nor risk acting in a foolhardy way."[89]

Adrienne was the main family member Lafayette was trying to appease for his unexpected and unannounced departure from his home. On January 6, 1778, Lafayette sent a long missive to Adrienne asking for forgiveness, expressing his love and assuring her that he was in good health. The letter stated in part:

> What a date, My Dear Heart, and what a country from which to write in the month of January! It is in a camp in the middle of woods; it is fifteen hundred leagues from you that I find myself buried in midwinter. Not too long ago, we were separated from the enemy by a small river; now we are seven leagues away from them and it is here that the American army will spend the winter in small barracks hardly more cheerful than a jail. . . . In all sincerity, My Dear Heart, don't you think that strong reasons forced me to this sacrifice? Everyone has been encouraging me to leave; honor told me to stay, and indeed when you learn in details my circumstances, that of the army, my friend who leads it, My Dear Heart, I trust that you will excuse me and I dare almost say that you will approve my decision. It would give me such pleasure to tell you all the reasons myself, and, as I embraced you, to ask your forgiveness that I am sure to obtain. Please do not condemn me before you hear me.
>
> Beside the reason I gave you, there is another one that I do not want to tell everyone because I would seem to attribute to myself a ridiculous

[89] Unger, p. 55.

importance. At the present time, my presence is more necessary to the American cause than you would imagine. Many foreigners, whose help was turned down and whose ambition was not served, created powerful intrigues and, with all sorts of tricks, they tried to turn me away from this revolution and its leader; they relentlessly spread word that I had left the continent. For their part, the British affirmed it. In all conscience, I cannot make these people be right. If I leave, many Frenchmen, who are useful here, would follow my example. General Washington would really be unhappy if I told him that I was leaving. His trust in me is deeper than I dare say because of . . . In the place he occupies, he is surrounded by flatterers and secret enemies. He finds in me a trustworthy friend in whom he can confide and who will always tell him the truth. Not a day goes by without his talking to me at length or writing long letters to me. And he is willing to consult me on most interesting points. There is presently a particular circumstance where my presence is not useless to him; so it would not be appropriate to talk to him about departing.

At present, I also have an interesting correspondence with the president of Congress. The abasement of England, service to my homeland, the happiness of Humanity whose interest it is to have a completely free country in the world, all these reasons contributed to my not leaving, precisely when my absence could have been harmful. In addition, after a small success in Jersey, the General, following the unanimous wish of the Congress, asked me to take an army division and to train it as I saw fit, as well as my mediocre means would allow. Was I to answer his proofs of trust by asking him to take his messages to Europe? Such are, My Dear Heart, part of my reasons which I entrust to you. I could add many others, but cannot risk writing them in a letter.

This letter will be brought to you by a French gentleman who traveled one hundred miles to take my messages. A few days ago, I gave a letter for you to the famous Mr. Adams. He will make it easier for you to send news to me. You must have received a letter which I sent as soon as I heard of your delivery. How happy this event made me, My Dear Heart; I like to talk to you about it in all my letters because I like to think about it all the time. What pleasure I will have to kiss my two poor little daughters and to have them ask their mother's forgiveness. Do not believe me insensitive or ridiculous enough to think that the sex of our new child has diminished in the least the joy of her birth. Our . . . is not so to stop us from having another one without a miracle. The next one will absolutely need to be a boy. By the way, if it is because of the name that one should be annoyed, I declare that I have taken the resolution to live long enough to bear it myself for many years to come before having to pass it on to a new being.

It is the Maréchal de Noailles who brought me the news. I am very impatient to receive some from you. . . . I beg you, Dear Heart, when you write to me, do give me news from all those I

> love and of the whole society . . . (those) who do not know the reasons which force me to remain here, must think that I am rather ridiculous, when they see, My Dear Heart, from what lovely woman I stay away; nevertheless, this very idea should make them feel that I have invincible reasons to do so.
>
> The bearer of this letter will tell you that I am in good health, that my wound has healed and that the change of country has not harmed me. Don't you think, Dear Heart, that when I return we will be . . . enough to settle in our house, to live together, receive our friends, establish a sweet freedom and read newspapers from foreign countries without having the curiosity to go there and see for ourselves what is happening. I enjoy building castles in France (air castles) of happiness and pleasures. You are always half of all these plans, My Dear Heart, and once we are reunited—not to be separated again—what will stop us from savoring together, one by the other, the sweetness of love, the most delicious and quiet tranquility.
>
> A thousand kisses to the Vicomtesse and to my sisters. Farewell, farewell. Love me always and do not forget the unhappy exile who thinks of you with renewed tenderness. [90]

The pleading letter revealed some troubling matters taking place at Valley Forge. Lafayette's surrogate father, George Washington, was being criticized by foreigners and others in the

---

[90] Lafayette memoirs, translated by Christine Valadon.

American military and government. Lafayette stood staunchly beside Washington throughout the attacks on the commanding general. For backing Washington, Lafayette and other officers supporting Washington were included in the unjust criticism.

Washington responded to Lafayette's loyalty by sponsoring Lafayette into the American military branch of the Masons, an organization that contained numerous American officers. "His fellow officers dubbed him 'Our Marquis,' and by winter's end, every Patriot soldier and, soon after, every Patriot in America called him 'Our Marquis,' a title he retained for the rest of his life."[91]

While standing with Washington, Lafayette suffered along with Washington's troops during the long and cold winter at Valley Forge. Lafayette rejected having accommodations in a private home and lived in one of the huts built by soldiers. He supplied his own troops with food and clothing as both were in short supply at Valley Forge and many suffered and perished by the lack of necessities. "The unfortunate soldier was in want of everything. Their feet and legs froze until they became black and it was often necessary to amputate them."[92] In his memoirs, Lafayette summed up the condition by writing "the soldiers lived in misery."

At Valley Forge, Lafayette witnessed Washington jousting with Congress on several fronts, including the failure of Congress to provide proper support of the army and undermining Washington's authority. Congress injected Lafayette into the fray by naming him an independent commander of the army's northern group with an aim to invade Canada.

The Canadian venture turned into a crisis threatening relations between France and the United States and came close to causing Lafayette to return to France.

The Canadian invasion was a horrendous idea from the start.

---

[91] Unger, p. 59.

[92] Lafayette memoirs, p. 35.

A political maneuver and not a military one, the plan's goal was a way to lessen Washington's control and Lafayette's ascending stature in Congress.

Generals Horatio Gates, Thomas Conway and others—part of the Conway Cabal—pressed Congress to replace Washington. Conway had previously written to Gates and called Washington a "weak general" for Washington's failed campaigns against British General Howe. The letter was intercepted and given to Washington. Gates, British born, claimed credit for the American victory at Saratoga.

When Washington became aware of Conway's missive to Congress, Washington responded by complaining to Richard Henry Lee. Washington believed Conway's importance to Washington's army existed more in Conway's mind than in reality. Washington opposed any promotion for Conway, contending such a move could possibly cause more deserving officers to resign. Congress didn't immediately promote Conway and Conway threatened to resign from the army but didn't do so.

Some members of Congress wanted to replace Washington with Gates. One of the anti-Washington Congressional members was James Lovell, the same man who dismissed Lafayette when the young Frenchman appeared before Congress.

Congress didn't oust Washington, but it did create a new entity, the Board of War, which had power over Washington and the army. Upon learning of the Board of War, Washington's cadre of generals and aides, including Lafayette, Greene, Hamilton and John Laurens, the son of the President of Congress, all wrote letters to Congress supporting Washington.

Gates and Conway won approval from Congress to launch the Canadian invasion with Lafayette in command. The official sanction from Congress came on January 22, 1778.The cabal leaders reasoned Lafayette would surely leap at the opportunity for personal glory and revenge on England. After all, England had taken Canada from the French. Why not have a Frenchman lead an invasion against the English in Canada? When the invasion failed, Lafayette's standing with Congress would plummet and thus, one of Washington's supporters neutralized. To persuade Congress to approve the Canadian invasion, the cabal argued a victory by Lafayette would cement relations with France and ensure the aid needed from France to defeat England. The opposite almost took place.

To some extent, the cabal's reasoning was sound. Lafayette relished the idea of a major command and wrote to his wife and father-in-law of the honor of leading a large force of Americans. Freeing the oppressed Frenchmen of New France from the rule of the British was a glorious thought in Lafayette's head, one he admitted he shouldn't have dwelled upon. Lafayette was intrigued by the prospect of the Canadian invasion.

Washington was not consulted about the invasion or Lafayette's appointment. The Board of War made Lafayette the commander with a rank equal to Washington and had him report directly to Congress and the war board. Conway, a major player in the cabal, was appointed Lafayette's second in command. Lafayette was ordered to appear before Congress, then sitting in York, Pennsylvania.

Immediately, Lafayette protested. He would not accept a position equal to Washington. Lafayette said he preferred the duty of aide-de-camp to Washington. Washington calmed down Lafayette's fervor and urged him to go to York and accept the assignment. Lafayette did so, but first received valuable advice from his commander. At Washington's urging, Lafayette requested from Congress a list of conditions of his service, including written details of the Canadian operation. One of the conditions insisted upon by Lafayette was that he would remain subordinate to Washington and all orders would come through Washington.

The negotiations amounted to a major crisis in American-French relations and for Lafayette.

If the war board failed to accede to Lafayette's demands, Lafayette could return to France and undermine French aid to America. The war board had no choice but to agree to Lafayette's wishes. One of the demands by Lafayette was that he would appoint his own officers. Lafayette reached out to a number of French military men, including his aides Gimat and La Colombe. Another officer was Captain Pierre Charles L'Enfant. An engineer, L'Enfant designed the city of Washington, D.C., and determined the location for Fort Delaware, a major fortification during the American Civil War.

Lafayette had another surprise for Conway, his cabal and the war board. Conway was dismissed as second in command and replaced by de Kalb, a long-time associate of Lafayette and a staunch supporter of Washington.

The war board promised Lafayette 2,500 men and supplies would be ready when he arrived in New York state to begin the Canadian expedition. An issue with the pledged provisions was evident. The man in charge of supplying Lafayette's force was Quartermaster Thomas Mifflin, a vocal critic of Washington. Lafayette was suspicious—later proved correct—of the war board's promise of men and supplies.

The goal of the mission was the taking of Montreal and the capture of all of the military arms in the city. If the Canadians wanted to join the Americans in the quest for freedom, Lafayette was to inform them they were welcome.

Lafayette questioned the sanity of attacking Canada in winter. Gates replied that the British wouldn't expect such a tactic and would be surprised. Gates' explanation didn't convince Lafayette. Taking steps to protect his reputation, Lafayette sent a letter to Congress placing the responsibility—or more likely the blame—for the operation on Gates. Lafayette didn't want Gates to be able to point the finger at him if the expedition failed.

Before departing York on February 3, 1778, Lafayette was invited to a dinner at Gates's home. In his memoirs, Lafayette gleefully described making a toast to Washington and forcing a red-faced Gates to raise his glass in honor of Washington.

Brutal weather, rain and snow, took its toll on Lafayette and his band of French officers during their trip to New York state.

For 10 days, Lafayette's party of officers traveled by horseback and sometimes sleds to reach Albany. After making the arduous trek, Lafayette discovered his suspicions about Gates, Conway and Mifflin were sound. Half of the men promised Lafayette were awaiting him. No supplies had been gathered for his ghost troops. The $2 million promised him to pay the troops was nowhere in sight.

No invasion.

"I have been deceived by the Board of War," Lafayette emphatically declared. The local commissary wasn't even informed of the operation. Also, Lafayette discovered three American generals in the area, including Benedict Arnold, had previously advised Conway that such an invasion in winter was impossible. Lafayette informed Washington of the situation and wrote that he could find no supporters for the Canadian operation.

Besides his report to Washington, Lafayette took steps to protect his reputation in France and before Congress. Knowing that Duc d'Ayen would show his letter to the royal court, Lafayette detailed Gates's treachery in a dispatch to his father-in-law. Lafayette then turned his ire on Congress and wrote a scathing letter to President Laurens. In his memoirs, Lafayette said the failed plan of the war board was full of "blunders, madness and deception." Lafayette went as far as to state he never wished he had set foot on American soil. He threatened to expose to the public the sad and treacherous tale.

Stymied from proceeding to Montreal, Lafayette was unsure of his next action. On March 11, Lafayette challenged the Board of War to give him additional instructions. "There has been a good deal of deception and neglect," Lafayette added.

While waiting for a reply, Lafayette accepted a request from General Philip Schuyler to assist Schuyler in negotiating a peace treaty with local Indian tribes. Lately, the Indians were fighting with the British, accepting bribes and conducting brutal raids on Americans. Since the Indians fought with the French in the

French and Indian Wars, Schuyler reasoned Lafayette could help him in getting the Indians to switch allegiances.

Lafayette joined Schuyler on a 40-mile trip to Johnson's Town near the Mohawk River to meet with the leaders of the Indian's Six Nations. Lafayette described in his memoirs a gathering of 500 tribe members. Lafayette mingled with the Indians and his sociable manner generated trust among the Indians. When the session was completed, the Indians agreed to make peace with the colonists.

Lafayette was adopted by the Indians and departed with a new name. The Indians called Lafayette Kayewla, the name of a legendary warrior.

When Lafayette returned from Johnson's Town to Albany, orders were waiting from Congress and the Board of War. The Canadian mission was terminated. Congress thanked Lafayette for his "high sense of prudence, activity and zeal." Laurens sent Lafayette a personal note assuring him that the praise in the Congressional resolution was 'genuine, not merely complimentary.'"[93]

Lafayette returned to Valley Forge and General Washington with both his honor and relations with France intact.

---

[93] Unger, p. 68.

· 11 ·

French Alliance

Lafayette was not a happy general when he returned to Valley Forge from his Canadian venture. Even though Lafayette retained his unsullied reputation in the halls of Congress and the French royal court, he sensed that a crisis of American military leadership was about to erupt anew.

Time and again through actions on the battlefield and by his written words in his many letters to friends and family and national and international leaders, Lafayette demonstrated his unquestionable loyalty to General George Washington. Without Washington, Lafayette opined, there would be no American Revolution.

Lafayette noted that he remained faithful to Washington, even at times when Washington seemed to be ruined. Washington assured Lafayette that he was not about to succumb to jealousy and lies. Washington informed Lafayette, "If I am displeasing this nation, then I will retire. Until then, I will oppose all intrigues."[94]

Washington, the man he likened to a father, continued to be threatened by the leaders of the Conway Cabal, even after the failed Canadian invasion scheme. Lafayette took the insults hurled at Washington as personal insults.

---

[94] Lafayette memoirs, p. 38.

The duplicity of the Conway Cabal was exposed by Lafayette during the Canadian fiasco, but the cabal leaders still controlled the war board. After having dispatched Lafayette and de Kalb back to Washington at Valley Forge, the war board named Conway to replace Lafayette as commander of the American northern army.

Not so fast, Lafayette fumed.

Lafayette lashed out at Congress once again and threatened to poison America's relationship with France if Conway was allowed to keep his lofty new position in the American army. Lafayette's letters had the desired result as Congress overruled Conway's promotion by the war board. Conway, the Irish-born Frenchman, was demoted.

Even though demoted, Conway continued insulting Washington whenever he had a chance. Conway's slurs resulted in a challenge to a duel by Washington loyalist General John Cadwalader. Cadwalader severely wounded Conway in a duel on July 4. Conway recovered, apologized to Washington, resigned from the American army and returned to France.

The Conway Cabal was on life support as another key member, Quartermaster Thomas Mifflin, resigned his post under a cloud of suspicion. Mifflin, a former member of Washington's staff, was criticized for not doing his duty by failing to properly supply the army at Valley Forge. Washington confronted Mifflin after being told Mifflin had diverted supplies intended for the troops at Valley Forge to his own business and selling the items for profit. Mifflin denied any wrongdoing but resigned after the confrontation. Mifflin later returned to the army as quartermaster.

Washington was not idle as his detractors sniped at him from afar. Washington strengthened his command at Valley Forge by giving loyal officers additional responsibilities and rooting out those undermining him. General Nathanael Greene, whose troops saved Washington's army at Brandywine, was named to replace Mifflin as quartermaster. Greene's leadership led to supplies flowing into Valley Forge and the suffering of the soldiers lessening.

In November, Washington ordered two brigades to be formed into a division under the leadership of de Kalb. De Kalb, who arrived in America with Lafayette, detested the "incessant intrigues" taking place in the American camp, especially among the French officers. De Kalb made an exception for Lafayette. "He is an excellent young man, and we are good friends," de Kalb wrote. De Kalb added that Lafayette is much liked and on the best of terms with Washington.

Lafayette also impressed an influential member of Congress, Gouverneur Morris. Morris wrote to Washington in July, "I do most devoutly wish that we had not a single Foreigner among us, except the Marquis de la Fayette, who acts upon very different principles than those which govern the rest."[95]

Congress appointed Morris to a committee in charge of coordinating reforms of the military. Morris was appalled by the conditions at Valley Forge and became a Congressional champion of the troops. Morris had an ally in a new member of Washington's staff, Friedrich von Steuben. A Prussian, Major General Baron von Steuben became Washington's Inspector General and taught the troops the essentials of the military, including drills, tactics and discipline. Later, von Steuben, who had many years of military experience in Europe, served as Washington's chief of staff.

Previously, Benjamin Franklin had attempted to recruit von Steuben for service in America, but von Steuben refused as Congress declined to offer rank and pay for foreign officers. Later, Franklin authored a letter of introduction to Washington for von Steuben and advanced travel funds. Von Steuben set sail for America in September 1777 and arrived in New Hampshire in

[95] Washington's Papers

December. By May 1778, von Steuben had shown his worth and was made a major general with pay.

Lafayette wasn't left out by Washington in his reorganization. Washington gave Lafayette responsibility over the organization of foreign soldiers in his ranks. Lafayette was a logical choice for the duty. One of the new cavalry ranks Lafayette created was led by Marquis de La Rouerie. Also, Lafayette persuaded Count Casimir Pulaski, who fought with Lafayette at Brandywine, to command another unit of foreign troops, both cavalry and light infantry.

In his memoirs, Lafayette wrote that Washington never placed complete confidence in any one person except for Lafayette. Following the leads of Washington and von Steuben, Lafayette noted he "broke" some negligent officers in his command. In another honor while at Valley Forge, especially for a foreign-born officer, Lafayette was selected to administer to Washington's officers an oath of allegiance to the United States.

For more than a year, Lafayette had been a champion in France in all things American. He was a key component in the budding relationship between America and France. Lafayette played a significant part in France's decision to sign a formal alliance with America. Franklin fashioned treaties in which France recognized American independence, gave America most favored nations status and a military alliance. The treaties were signed in Paris on February 6, 1778. After the French notified the British of the alliance, England declared war on France.

France and the United States were indeed allies. Congressman Robert Morris, known as financier of the American Revolution, believed the French alliance guaranteed America's victory over England.

Washington was notified of the French treaty by Simeon Deane, brother of Silas Deane, who rode into Valley Forge on May 1, 1778. As Washington read details of the alliance, Lafayette teared up and embraced Washington. The celebration turned somber for Lafayette, as another letter brought by Deane notified Lafayette that his daughter Henriette had died. Lafayette's grief didn't show to his fellow soldiers. That night Lafayette wrote to Adrienne about the cruelty of separation and his pain and inability to comfort his wife. "The loss of our poor child is almost always on my mind," Lafayette wrote.[96]

Lafayette turned away from personal tragedy to the good news from Paris. Lafayette sent a congratulatory letter to his good friend, who had transported him to Bethlehem some eight months previously, Henry Laurens, president of Congress.

Five days after receiving the news of the treaty, Washington ordered his men to assemble and grandly celebrate the French alliance. Lafayette commanded the left division of a Valley Forge parade. De Kalb proudly recalled that he commanded the second line on the left. Stirling commanded the right division. The artillery fired 13 times.

A false rumor at the time was circulating that Lafayette was going to depart Washington's army and become France's ambassador to the United States. Henry Laurens was especially relieved to find that it wasn't true, as he believed Lafayette was a better soldier than diplomat. Lafayette did confide to a French diplomat that he would join the French army if needed to fight for his home country.

Washington couldn't spare Lafayette to be a French ambassador or a French army officer. He needed Lafayette as an officer in his American army. Washington selected Lafayette for an important assignment, gathering information about the movements of the British army at Philadelphia. Washington needed every scrap of information Lafayette could accumulate on British plans. Was Howe keeping his troops in Philadelphia, retreating to New York City or planning to attack Washington's forces?

Lafayette led more than 2,000 men, including 600 militia

---

[96] Unger, p. 72.

and 47 members of the Oneida Indian tribe whom he recruited, across the Schuylkill River on the mission. Washington's directive was direct, gather information on the location and movement of the British army and do not engage them. An added bit of advice came from Washington: Lafayette was to not stay too long at any one location as the mighty enemy might discover his position.

Lafayette marched his men 11 miles, crossed the river and found an excellent observation post on Barren Hill. The location was about midway between Valley Forge and Washington and Philadelphia and Howe. Instead of moving his command to a new location the next day as Washington had suggested, Lafayette stayed anchored at Barren Hill. Lafayette did take precautions in case the British attacked by securing his flanks. To protect his left flank, Lafayette stationed militia at Whitemarsh.

The British discovered Lafayette's detachment when a British spy, who was embedded in Lafayette's command, delivered detailed information. Howe, who had been recalled to England, delayed his planned departure to act upon the opportunity to capture the boy general, Lafayette. Before leaving Philadelphia for New York and then home to England, Howe vowed to make Lafayette a prisoner of war. Howe dispatched a massive force, a majority of the men under his command at Philadelphia, to hunt down Lafayette.

The British, under General James Grant, moved on Whitemarsh. The militia that Lafayette sent earlier to guard his left flank at Whitemarsh fled. Lafayette was in danger of being encircled as British troops converged on him from three directions. The British seemed to be everywhere Lafayette looked, but the young general didn't panic. Lafayette deftly withdrew his men while misdirecting the British army. In a surprise, and risky move, Lafayette traveled a road situated much lower than the heights occupied by the British, crossed the Schuylkill and returned to Valley Forge. Lafayette lost only nine men on the mission.

Lafayette wrote about the mission in his memoirs: On May 18 at Barron Hill, Lafayette found a hill with a good elevation. His right flank rested on rocks and the river. To the left, Lafayette reported, were fine stone houses and a small wood. For protection, Lafayette placed five cannons.

When Lafayette received word of the British advance, "I discovered a British column was on my left and changed positions. I was then cut off on the Swedes Ford road by Grant. I was told I was surrounded and was forced to smile at that unpleasant piece of news. Several officers said they failed to find a path back to Valley Forge. Every moment was precious and I proceeded on the road to Matson Ford. The enemy was closer to his objective than I. General (James Potter) was in charge (at Whitemarsh) and I sent Gimat, my personal aide-de-camp, to aid him. I placed myself as rear guard and marched on the road. Grant had the heights and my path was below him."

Lafayette wrote that he deceived Grant by giving the illusion that his force was larger than it was. Lafayette's forces then crossed Matson's Ford before Howe's main division arrived. "I formed on the opposite side of the shore but the enemy dared not attack. Howe returned without capturing even one man."[97] Lafayette reported that cannons were fired in celebration at Valley Forge when he arrived and he was well received by Washington. Lafayette added that members of the Oneida confronted British dragoons at one point but both parties withdrew without an engagement.

While Washington lauded Lafayette's cunning daring, Lafayette received mixed reviews from military men and the press. Lafayette was depicted as either a crafty leader or a bumbling boy general lucky to have escaped Howe's clutches.

---

[97] Lafayette memoirs, p. 48.

The negative reviews of Lafayette's generalship didn't deter Washington from placing Lafayette in a key position in one of Washington's major victories of the American Revolution, the Battle of Monmouth.

Sir Henry Clinton, the new commander of England's forces, decided to consolidate the British army in New York City. Clinton sent part of his command away on ships. The rest of the soldiers, with a baggage and artillery train that stretched 12 miles, headed off on a march through New Jersey on June 18, 1778. The strung-out British command offered Washington plenty of opportunities to inflict losses on his enemy without directly engaging a large portion of the British army.

Washington's new tactic amounted to quick hits and withdrawals. The quick-hitting gambit was not universally accepted within his officers' corps. At one council of war, General Charles Lee said he was "passionately opposed" to such tactics. Lee, who previously served in the British army, had some support for his position. Washington's staunch supporters, Greene, Wayne, Cadwalader and Lafayette, opposed Lee and approved Washington's new strategy.

Tactics were not the only disagreement between Lee and Washington. Lee believed himself to be a better officer than Washington and that Congress made a mistake in appointing Washington instead of him as commander-in-chief of the American army. Washington didn't trust Lee, thinking Lee might still favor his former employer, King George III of England. Washington's suspicion increased after Lee, who was captured on December 12, 1777, at White's Tavern in Basking Ridge, New Jersey, was paroled in April 1778.

After the council of war, Washington decided to follow Clinton's forces and not engage the British. Trying to move men and many carriages is difficult at best. The summer weather—heat, rain and humidity—added to the slow going of the British. On June 26, the British camped at Monmouth Courthouse.

During a second council of war, Lee urged Washington to

allow Clinton safe passage to New York City. There was a suspicion among Washington's officers that a negotiated end to the war was at hand. Again, Greene, Wayne, Cadwalader, Hamilton and Lafayette opposed Lee. Greene, Wayne and Cadwalader told Washington to "fight, sir." Lafayette added, "It would be disgraceful for the army command and humiliating for our troops to permit them to travel the length of New Jersey with impunity."[98]

Lafayette's words and the support of the other three generals swayed Washington. The American army would fight the British. Washington devised a plan where two smaller segments of the American army would attack the British. If they were successful, additional troops would be committed by Washington. If a large segment of the British army turned and fought, Washington could easily disengage his troops.

Washington turned to his senior officer, General Lee, and placed him in command. Lee refused, pronouncing the plan a disaster. Washington didn't argue with Lee. Washington gave the command to Lafayette, the next highest-ranking officer. With Wayne as his second in command, Lafayette made ready to engage the British.

On June 26, Washington sent orders to Lafayette concerning supplies for his troops and urged Lafayette to be prudent. "Though giving the enemy a stroke is a very desirable event, yet I would not wish you to be too precipitate in the measure or to distress your men by an over hasty march."[99] A second part of the order was dated at 9:45 a.m. from Cranbury, New Jersey, after Washington arrived at the head of the army. He again urged caution and to wait for the supplies.

As Washington camped about six miles from Clinton's force, he had a surprise visitor to his tent, Lee. Lee had reconsidered his hasty refusal of the command and asked Washington to reinstate

[98] Lafayette memoirs, p. 51.

[99] Founders.archives.gov.

him. Lee claimed his honor was at stake. Washington refused to do so unless Lafayette acquiesced to Lee's request. Lafayette did so. Lee was to command the attack with Lafayette as his subordinate.

When Lee was informed at 5:00 a.m. on June 28 that the British army was breaking camp, he ordered Wayne to take his men and assault the British rear guard. Lee intended on circling Clinton's forces but didn't convey his plans to all unit commanders. Clinton, apprised of Wayne's movements, sent reinforcements back to Monmouth Courthouse to assist the British rear guard. Lee countered by placing Lafayette's forces on his right flank.

Lee's plan fell apart as the officers commanding the left flank, the ones not informed of Lee's orders, fell back as did some of Wayne's outnumbered troops. When Lafayette's attempt to silence British artillery failed, some of Lafayette's troops joined the retreat. Lee recognized his desire to envelop the British had failed and ordered a withdrawal. Lee issued the retreat without consulting or informing Washington.

The main body of the army, with Washington leading, encountered Lee's retreating command at about noon. Within an hour Washington found Lee and demanded to know why his men were leaving the battlefield. Washington pointed out to Lee that his command was in disorder and confused. Lee attempted to blame his subordinates and to remind Washington that he was not in favor of Washington's plan in the first place.

Washington was furious with Lee. His ire was evident as Washington rode off to take command. In what may have been Washington's finest hour as a commander, Washington rallied the troops and eventually blocked the advancing British. Lee was told to command the rearguard where he also engaged the British.

In his memoirs, Lafayette wrote about Monmouth. He penned when the British fired cannons, Lee halted his attack on the British rearguard. Then, Lee ordered Lafayette to cross the field and attack the left of the British army, thus opening Lafayette's troops to cannon fire. While executing the command, Lee ordered Lafayette to retire to a village where Lee had gathered the rest of his troops. There, Lee ordered a fallback changing his attack into a retreat. Cornwallis had time to form the British army. Lafayette wrote he sent word to Washington of the retrograde movement. Washington hurried his command to support Lee and found Lee's ranks in confusion and retreating. Washington gave Greene command of the right and Stirling to the left and placed Lafayette in command of the second line. When the British army exposed its flank, Washington attacked and drove them back. Americans continued to gain ground, and Clinton retired during the night.[100]

The Battle of Monmouth Courthouse was inconclusive, and both commanding generals had reasons to claim victory. As he had planned, Clinton made his way to New York City. Washington commanded the field at the end of the battle.

Lafayette wrote, "During this affair, which ended so well, although began so ill, General Washington appeared to arrest fortune by one glance, and his presence of mind, valor, and decision of character, were never displayed to greater advantage than at this moment."[101] Washington spent the evening after the battle resting under a tree with Lafayette, and discussing Lee's conduct.

The clear loser was Lee. Lee wrote a letter to Washington claiming he had saved the army at Monmouth and that Washington was guilty of cruel injustice towards him. Lee should have apologized or remained silent. Lee was arrested and faced a court martial on charges of disobeying orders to attack, conducting a shameful retreat and being disrespectful towards Washington. The trial took more than a month with both Wayne and Lafayette testifying against Lee. Congress confirmed Lee's guilt on all three charges.

---

[100] Lafayette memoirs, p. 53.

[101] Lafayette memoirs, p. 54.

Lee was suspended from the army and continued to claim Washington was the villain in the Monmouth engagement. Two of Washington's aides, John Laurens and von Steuben, challenged Lee to duels. Laurens wounded Lee in the one duel that was fought. Lee was dismissed from the army and returned to his Virginia home. During a visit to Philadelphia on October 2, 1782, Lee was stricken with a fever and died.

General Charles Lee

·12·

Return to France

Next for the emerging American hero was an unexpected challenge, one Lafayette would not face on a battlefield. Lafayette's engaging personality and diplomatic skills were desperately needed to rectify a rocky start with America's newest ally, France.

On July 4, 1778, while camped at Brunswick, New Jersey, Washington's army celebrated the second anniversary of the founding of the United States. The Americans had reasons to celebrate. First, a rare victory was won a few days earlier. The second celebratory item was more important; Washington had received notification that the French army and navy were in the Delaware Bay, near Philadelphia.

On April 13, France dispatched General and Vice Admiral Jean Baptiste Charles Henri Hector, Comte d'Estaing to America with 17 ships, including 12 battleships, then called ships of the line, and about 4,000 soldiers. For the next two years, d'Estaing fought on behalf of the United States without distinction. D'Estaing's forces were involved in two unsuccessful sieges, one in Newport, Rhode Island, in 1778 and the other in 1779 at Savannah, Georgia. After departing America, d'Estaing returned to France and was executed by guillotine during the Reign of Terror of the French Revolution.

D'Estaing's inability to work with Washington's army greatly contributed to the failed siege operations. Washington turned to Lafayette to mollify d'Estaing. Lafayette was to be the buffer between the two armies. Lafayette rode to Rhode Island to fulfill his directive. Also, Washington sent General Greene, a Rhode Island native, to assist Lafayette.

Lafayette wrote in his memoirs that on July 22 he was ordered to lead 2,000 Americans from Washington's base near White Plains, New York, to Providence, Rhode Island, where General Sullivan was to unite with d'Estaing to attack British forces.

Lafayette had previously reversed the unfavorable impression held by Washington and other American officers towards the French military. Lafayette's new assignment would prove to be just as challenging. Lafayette was placed in an almost impossible situation as he was forced to defend France's honor against American slights while making peace between the Americans and the French.

D'Estaing's initial efforts to assist Washington's army came in July 1778 near Sandy Hook, New Jersey, where his ships blockaded a small British force under the command of Admiral Howe. D'Estaing refused to advance and enter New York harbor as he believed his larger ships couldn't clear the bar at the harbor's mouth. Washington desperately wanted to liberate New York, the main American city occupied by the British.

The French problem began with d'Estaing's abandoning the New York City operation.

D'Estaing reengaged with the American forces under the command of General Sullivan and planned a joint attack on August 10 at Newport, Rhode Island. Bickering took place as to whose troops would lead the attack. Lafayette brokered a compromise that included a simultaneous advance by the two armies.

Since d'Estaing's appearance in America, Lafayette had been corresponding with the admiral, letting him know that if a chance existed, he would rather fight under the French flag than under the American command. In a two-week period, Lafayette wrote six letters to the admiral. D'Estaing was impressed with Lafayette and reported to the French Ministry of the Marine that no one was better situated to serve as a link between France and America than Lafayette.[102] On July 30, d'Estaing expressed his gratitude to Lafayette for the assistance Lafayette had provided.

All seemed well between the French and American forces.

Sullivan received word that the British were withdrawing and ordered an attack a day early, August 9, without informing d'Estaing. D'Estaing took Sullivan's independent action as an affront to the French honor and withdrew from the operation.

All was not so well between the French and American forces.

When the opportunity arose, d'Estaing decided to put to sea to battle Admiral Howe's fleet. The British sent Howe with 36 ships to reinforce its New England command and battle the French fleet. The French and British ships endured a violent three-day storm, beginning on August 12. The two navies briefly engaged each other before the storm forced a cessation of the naval battle. While the British navy did little damage to d'Estaing's fleet, the storm caused considerable damage.

D'Estaing returned to Rhode Island and offered to help evacuate Sullivan's battered and shrinking forces. When Sullivan declined the offer, d'Estaing sailed to Boston for much-needed repairs to his ships on August 22.

Relations deteriorated between American and French forces as Boston officials threatened to not allow the French to dock and make much needed repairs. Lafayette hurriedly rode to Boston on the night of August 26 to save the weakening alliance. While doing so, relations between Lafayette and Sullivan were strained to the breaking point.

In Lafayette's memoirs, he noted a "great discontent and embarrassment" was prevalent. Americans in Boston proposed not allowing the French fleet to dock for repairs. American officers drew up a protest letter against the French that Lafayette

[102] Auricchio, p. 72.

refused to sign. Sullivan stated, "Our allies have abandoned us."[103] Sullivan intimated America would be better off without the assistance of the French. Lafayette took offense to Sullivan's statement and insisted his fellow American general retract his words. Lafayette wasn't about to let the scurrilous slights against his homeland to go unchallenged.

A rift between Sullivan and Lafayette was deepening, and a duel was not out of the realm of possibilities. Letters flew from Sullivan, Lafayette and Greene to Washington about the escalating crisis. Washington responded with letters of his own to calm and quell the pending disaster.

Lafayette regained his composure and for the most part hid his anger at both Sullivan for his slight of France and at d'Estaing for sailing off from Rhode Island and abandoning Sullivan. Sullivan didn't pursue the matter and even offered an apology to Lafayette. Lafayette believed Sullivan took note of Lafayette's close friendship with Washington.

Sullivan had little choice but to recognize Lafayette's standing and Washington's wishes to end the argument. In a letter on September 1, Washington informed Sullivan that the dispute made him uneasy. Sullivan was reminded that Europe was keeping a close eye on the French-American alliance. Washington told Sullivan to keep the disagreement private and not to discuss the matter with the public, or his troops. Sullivan was to "cultivate good harmony and agreement."[104]

Washington also implored Greene to work with Lafayette and Sullivan and the French. On the same day he wrote to Sullivan, Washington wrote Greene stating he (Washington) "feared seeds of distrust will be sown with American's new allies. Greene was asked to take prudent measures to suppress the feuds and jealousies that have arisen." Washington assured Greene that Lafayette would be receptive to any advice Greene had to offer.

---

[103] Lafayette memoirs, p. 58.

[104] Lafayette memoirs, pp. 196–197.

D'Estaing also received soothing letters from Washington. Washington was well aware that without France's aid the war with England would end in a defeat.

Lafayette partnered with Greene and John Hancock to save the French partnership from tearing asunder. Hancock, who spoke excellent French, dined and entertained d'Estaing at his elegant Boston home. Congress and Washington congratulated Lafayette for his diplomatic services in Boston.

Washington lauded Lafayette's actions in a letter. Washington assured the young Frenchman that his devotion to the United States was appreciated and that he considered Lafayette a close friend. "Let me beseech you, (Washington wrote) therefore, my good sir to afford a healing hand to the wound that unintentionally has been made. America esteems your virtues and your services and admires the principles upon which you act. Your countrymen, in our army, look up to you as their patron. . . . And I, your friend, have no doubt but that you will use your utmost endeavors to restore harmony, that the honor, glory and mutual interest of the two nations may be promoted and cemented in the firmest manner."[105]

Indeed, without Lafayette's diplomacy, d'Estaing may have fled Rhode Island in disgust and sailed to French holdings in the West Indies. If d'Estaing had done so, French aid would have stopped. Lafayette saved the alliance and kept America's dream of independence alive.

Lafayette's duties in New England didn't conclude with his conflict mediation in Boston. Lafayette rejoined Sullivan's shrinking force, which had retreated to northern Rhode Island. As Sullivan's men were retreating before a superior British force, Lafayette took command of 1,000 men acting as Sullivan's rear guard and led them to safety. Lafayette, in his memoirs, wrote that he rode 80 miles in less than eight hours to Howland's Ferry where he took command of American soldiers

---

[105] Lafayette memoirs, p. 58.

and withdrew them from the clutches of the British without losing a man.[106]

With the withdrawal of Sullivan's troops from Rhode Island, the campaign of 1778 was rapidly drawing to a close. Britain held New York City and a small portion of New England and parts of the southern United States but had abandoned Philadelphia. The year was a positive one for the Americans, especially with the French joining the cause of independence.

Lafayette had spent the late summer of 1778 developing grandiose schemes in which he would lead invasions of far-flung English possessions as well as another foray into Canada. He sought and failed to receive permission and support to enact his plans. Washington advised Lafayette that the winter would be better spent by Lafayette with his family in France. Washington believed that little chance existed that Congress or France would approve Lafayette's proposed military expeditions. France did decline, citing the exorbitant cost of a Canadian invasion. Washington later revealed grave concerns about France's ultimate intentions and wrote "no nation is to be trusted farther than it is bound by its interests."[107]

For Lafayette, the time had arrived to seriously plan a return home, even for a limited period of time. Lafayette's father-in-law wrote him a letter saying that Lafayette would be forgiven for departing without the King's blessing. He then wrote to Adrienne, saying he loved her and hoped to be soon reunited with her.

Before staring out on his journey to France, Lafayette spent three weeks in Philadelphia. Lafayette wisely made friends and strengthened alliances with members of Congress. A French official in Philadelphia wrote to French foreign minister Vergennes, "I cannot refrain from saying that the prudent, courageous and amiable conduct of the Marquis de Lafayette has made him the idol of the Congress, the army and the people of America. They

[106] Lafayette memoirs, p 59.

[107] Washington's Papers.

all hold a high opinion of his military talents. . . . The Americans strongly want him to return with the troops which the king may send."[108]

Lafayette was appointed American liaison to the Court of Versailles. Congress then arranged transportation for Lafayette to return on the ship *Alliance*. In a grand gesture, Congress ordered Franklin, the American ambassador, to arrange for an "elegant sword" to be prepared in Paris and presented to Lafayette.

Congress, as had Washington, totally embraced Lafayette. The base of Lafayette's rise to position of an American hero had been accomplished in little more than a year. Congress even sent a formal notice to King Louis XVI of the accomplishments of Lafayette and the high-regard Lafayette held in the United States.

Lafayette planned to travel to Boston to confer with d'Estaing before departing to France. A portion of his trip was by horseback and through a horrid rainstorm. The combination of a long military campaign, the many celebrations and the bad weather caused Lafayette to collapse when he reached Fishkill, New York. He was only a few miles from Washington's camp.

When Washington learned of Lafayette's illness, Washington sent his personal physician, Dr. John Cochran, to administer to Lafayette. Cochran was the same doctor who had treated Lafayette at Brandywine. Lafayette's temperature was high, and he suffered severe headaches. Lafayette feared for his life. Washington was also concerned for the health of his young general and close friend. Lafayette wrote that Washington visited him every day and "showed the most tender and paternal anxiety."[109]

Concern for Lafayette's well-being spread throughout the colonies, and some newspapers reported that Lafayette's death was near. For three weeks Lafayette convalesced as his health slowly returned.

On December 2, Lafayette departed Fishkill for Boston and

[108] Unger, p. 89.
[109] Lafayette memoirs, p. 64.

his return to France. Before embarking on the *Alliance* on January 11, 1779, Lafayette received a friendly letter from Washington. Washington wished Lafayette well, and reinforced his sincere friendship for Lafayette and mentioned Lafayette's military talents and merit. Washington then desired that Lafayette would have a safe trip and a joyful reunion with Adrienne and his family.

Lafayette responded by writing several notes to his "most beloved general" and promising to return.

·13·

HOME

As the return trip to France from America began, Lafayette was full of thoughts about a reunion with his wife Adrienne, daughter Anastasie and the other members of his family. During his stay in America, Lafayette wrote many endearing letters to Adrienne professing his love for her and other missives to relatives but received scant few letters in return. Would Lafayette receive a warm family reception?

Another kind of warm reception gave Lafayette pause. He was unsure about the greeting he would receive from King Louis XVI. After all, Lafayette violated direct military and royal orders in making his midnight escape from France. Was the arrest order still in effect? Was a jail cell in the Bastille and not the family estate to be his residence?

The answers to Lafayette's future would have to wait. First, he would have to survive the sea voyage of the *Alliance*.

As the ship neared Newfoundland, a mighty storm tossed the ship about and tore away its top mast and vital navigating equipment. The heavy seas that dark night, Lafayette wrote, came near to capsizing the defenseless vessel. Lafayette spent the harrowing night sick in his bed. Even a brief dip in the cold Atlantic in the dead of winter would have been fatal. One passenger reportedly readied his pistol and vowed to commit suicide rather than freeze in the icy water.

The *Alliance* and Lafayette weathered the destructive storm.

A second danger, one not of nature but of man, threatened the lives of those on board the ship, including Lafayette. A portion of the *Alliance*'s crew planned a mutiny.

England encouraged crews on American ships to mutiny and steer the commandeered ships into British ports. There, the mutinous crew members would be amply rewarded for their criminal and murderous conduct by sharing in the value of the contents of the ship. Members of the crew and passengers opposing the takeover of a ship were killed.

The *Alliance's* crew was comprised of a mixture of Americans, French volunteers seeking passage home, and deserters from the British army. Since ship Captain Peter Landais was unable to find the needed 220 American sailors, the Frenchmen volunteered to secure a quick return to France. At the conclusion of the voyage, some of the British planned to then escape France and return to England. The diverse lot of crewmembers didn't share a strong bond. In fact, they had little in common.

Once underway, the British crew members began plotting the capture of the *Alliance*. A successful venture would quicken their return to their homeland and bring them some riches. That payoff might be enhanced as one of the Alliance's passengers himself was the rich and famous, Lafayette. King George III would certainly pardon the mutineers for their transgressions in exchange for Lafayette.

As the *Alliance* was about 500 miles from France, the mutineers were ready to put their plan into action. The mutiny, as Lafayette described in his memoirs, was to be launched at 4:00 a.m. as the ship's officers and passengers came on deck. The British crew would control four cannons loaded with grapeshot. An English sergeant attempted to secure other weapons for the mutineers. When the cry of "sail" from one of the plotters was given, the mutiny would begin. The British crew planned to fire the cannons and blow their opposition to pieces.[110]

The plot was discovered and foiled with a great assist from Lafayette. In his memoirs, Lafayette wrote that no Americans or French took part in the mutiny. "An American, who lived in Ireland and had an Irish accent, discovered the plot and alerted the crew one hour before it was to take place. The man had been offered command of the frigate. Armed officers seized 31 men (some sources say 38) involved in the plot. The prisoners were placed in irons."[111]

A more detailed recount of the incident stated, "An hour before the plot, and an hour before the scheduled mutiny, Lafayette led a team of forty officers and passengers to the crew's quarters, sliced the hammock cords of the four sleeping ringleaders, and when they dropped on the floor, bound them and clapped them into irons."[112]

The remainder of the voyage was without incident as the mutineers were restrained in shackles. The *Alliance* docked at Brest, France, on February 6, 1779.

As he set foot on French soil, Lafayette's future was questionable as he noted in his memoirs. Some royal advisers suggested confining Lafayette in the Bastille, the Paris fortress used as a prison by French kings. Within days of landing, Lafayette ventured to Versailles to plead his case and ask forgiveness of King Louis XVI. Lafayette came armed with letters of support from American officials and missives he had written to the King.

Lafayette arrived at the palace in the early morning hours, too late for an audience with the King, and called upon his cousin, who was nearby and hosting a ball. The appearance of a young officer dressed in an American uniform caused a great stir when

[110] Lafayette memoirs, p. 66.
[111] Lafayette memoirs, p. 66.
[112] Unger, p. 93.

Lafayette was recognized. He was hailed as a hero and not a traitor to France. Lafayette was welcomed throughout France and embraced by ministers in Paris and even Queen Marie Antoinette. "I had left as a rebel and fugitive and returned in triumph as an idol," Lafayette declared in his memoirs. In his memoirs, Lafayette made references to reveling in the "celebrity status" in Paris and throughout France.

Lafayette couldn't escape unscathed for disobeying the King. King Louis XVI refused to grant a personal audience, as per Lafayette's request, but the King considered Lafayette's case. The King and his ministers conferred on a just punishment for Lafayette, keeping in mind Lafayette's growing stature in America and in France. Lafayette was confined to the family residence in Paris, the Hôtel de Noailles, for a week. Lafayette was also advised to avoid areas of France where such a slight to the King might be considered more egregious. "I was interrogated, complimented, and exiled but to Paris. Instead of honoring me with a cell in the Bastille, as some of the King's advisors proposed, the king chose the precincts of the Hôtel de Noailles as my prison for the next week."[113] The house arrest was lifted after Lafayette wrote a letter of apology to King Louis XVI.

Presently, Lafayette was offered and purchased the rank of colonel in the French cavalry. He also spent time answering questions about America posed by the King and even hunting with the King. King Louis XVI was impressed with Lafayette's exploits, and Lafayette became a celebrated member of court.

The reception Adrienne gave her husband was adoring and loving. Adrienne told relatives of her extreme joy in anticipating Lafayette's return. When Lafayette arrived, Adrienne wrote to her husband's relatives in Chavaniac that her joy was impossible to describe. Unlike most arranged marriages of the time, the couple was in love and devoted to each other. Adrienne offered enduring support to Lafayette during many future crises.

---

[113] Unger, p. 95.

Adrienne's letter to Chavaniac stated, "My happiness is easy to believe, impossible to express. . . . Monsieur de Lafayette has returned as modest and charming as when you last saw him. . . . The most distinguished and gracious person in the world, this is whom God has preserved for us in the midst of the most enormous dangers. For me, when I reflect on my place in life to be his wife, I am truly grateful to God. I find myself so far from being gracious like he, that I am distressed about it, and then I hope that my affection makes up for my shortcomings."[114]

With a warm reception from Adrianne and the issue with King Louis XVI settled, Lafayette turned his attention to promoting American interests in France. The schemes Lafayette presented to French and American officials always included a central role for Lafayette. American envoys Benjamin Franklin and John Adams quickly visited Lafayette and consented to work with him on plans to attack English strongholds in America.

As the planning sessions progressed, Lafayette detected a shift in the Royal Court's attitude supporting the American Revolution. Helping America was draining the French treasury and the first foray under d'Estaing was troubled and provided few positive results. There might be a better way to achieve France's goal of crippling its hated foe. Instead of supplying America with goods and soldiers across the vast Atlantic Ocean, why not launch a direct attack on England, a mere 20 miles distant from France's shores?

Lafayette and Franklin—a formidable pair with twin dynamic personalities—began plotting against England. The pair had worked on producing a series of prints to describe atrocities, some real and some fabricated, committed by England in America. The print propaganda scheme was abandoned.

A more serious plan authored by Lafayette and Franklin involved direct attacks on England. Any damage done to England would help the American cause, especially if England was forced

---

[114] Lane, p. 53.

Benjamin Franklin

John Adams

John Paul Jones

to withdraw some of King George III's army from the colonies. Franklin, with his knowledge of England from his time there as an American representative, identified towns to be raided. Franklin wrote a long letter to Lafayette on March 22 outlining possible targets to raid. Lafayette, trusted by both the United States and France, was the essential connection between the two allied countries that gave hope to the joint attack. Lafayette and Franklin needed a naval captain of daring and cunning to lead the expedition. Their pick was John Paul Jones.

Jones, who was born in Scotland, had been a sailor most of his life and had joined the American Navy about the time America declared independence from England. Jones, who conducted successful raids on British towns, was the logical choice to be in command of the Lafayette/Franklin plan.

The attack on England was deemed to be an American endeavor, and Lafayette, the American general, was to be in charge of the army involved in the raids. France promised to provide five ships and 2,000 men for the operation. Unlike d'Estaing and Sullivan, Lafayette and Jones vowed to work together to defeat any English forces they faced.

The attack on England's coastal towns was apparently abandoned when Lafayette was ordered to join French military forces far from Jones's fleet. The order taking him away from Paris had a negative personal side—Adrienne was pregnant. In December, Adrienne gave birth to their son, named after George Washington.

Both Lafayette and Jones were livid over the apparent action of the French court to end the planned operation. Neither received an explanation. In fact, the French Court had no plans to mothball plans to strike England. France was preparing a full-scale invasion. Lafayette's mission was to prepare troops for the upcoming fight. Lafayette was to lead a 30,000-to-40,000 man invasion force. France needed additional sea power to succeed and enticed Spain to join in the assault. When the French and Spanish fleets were combined, an expected 100 ships would set sail.

When informed of the expanded invasion plan, Lafayette was excited about the venture and wrote a letter to Franklin on July 12. Lafayette indicated he was expecting to depart for England in a few days and believed the expedition would go "very well" on the part of the army. He did caution Franklin that word was being received that the British fleet was gaining strength. In the letter, Lafayette asked for news from America and expressed a wish that Spain would declare openly its bond with France and send a frigate to Boston to aid Washington.[115]

A long delay took place in joining the invasion forces, caused in part by disease. A smallpox outbreak eventually spread to both the French and Spanish sailors. Lafayette became restless. He was unsure if the invasion would even take place. He fired off letters to Paris and America. In one, Lafayette suggested that if no action was to be taken from France, he should be sent to America with a large French army and navy to end the British reign in the colonies.

Finally, six weeks behind schedule, the French-Spanish forces were ready to launch the naval attack. The weather turned bad, and the invasion armada lost the element of surprise. The French/Spanish force failed to eliminate the British fleet. Without controlling the sea, Lafayette's men could not attempt a landing. The Lafayette/Franklin/French/Spanish invasion was in dire shape.

As the British fleet was preparing for battle, on September 3, 1779, the French commanders decided to end the operation. The navy was losing sailors to sickness at an alarming rate. The long delay meant that if the army could be landed, Lafayette's force would be forced to battle Britain's winter weather plus the British army. In the end, Lafayette's army didn't have a chance to fire a shot on England's soil.

Lafayette's attention returned to America. He exchanged letters with Washington, who again was struggling to keep his army

[115] To Benjamin Franklin from the Marquis de Lafayette, 12 July 1779," *Founders Online,* National Archives.

together and supplied to oppose the British. Winters were harsh on the American army. Lafayette's return to America would be welcomed, Washington assured Lafayette. D'Estaing continued to have difficulties working with American commanders. The siege of Savannah under the command of the French officer ended in failure. Washington desperately needed Lafayette's assistance.

In a letter dated October 7, 1779, to Washington, Lafayette indicated that he is well treated in France but is looking forward to his return to America. Lafayette indicated he wanted to finish the war under Washington's orders. When Lafayette sails, it will be "one of the most wished for and happiest days in my life." He closed by writing, "Oh, my dear general, how happy I shall be to embrace you again!"[116]

During the summer, Lafayette received a reminder of the esteem that Americans held for him. The promised ornate sword authorized by Congress was delivered to Lafayette by Benjamin Franklin's grandson, William Temple Franklin, as Franklin was ill. The sword had a gold handle and was carved with mottoes, coats of arm and engraved scenes from four of Lafayette's battles in America. They were Monmouth, Barren Hill, Gloucester and Rhode Island. On one side, Lafayette is shown slaying the British lion, and on the other, America is released from Britain's chains and offers Lafayette an olive branch.

During the Christmas season of 1779, Lafayette and Adrienne enjoyed their family life with Anastasie and newborn George Washington. General George Washington was exchanging long and endearing letters with Lafayette. Lafayette was admired in two worlds, America and France. All that was missing was the action that Lafayette constantly craved.

Lafayette began the year 1780 in a whirlwind of activity. He devised schemes to aid America and defeat Britain. He wrote numerous letters to French officials claiming that aid from France would ensure American victory. Lafayette was relentless.

---

[116] Lafayette memoirs, p. 312.

His spirit and enthusiasm for American independence never faltered. America's success was vital for France, Lafayette reminded France's ministers. Lafayette reasoned a victorious England might then attack the French West Indies. On January 10, 1780, Lafayette wrote to Franklin saying he believed his campaign was gaining traction.

The French ministers finally agreed to Lafayette's urging and agreed to send 6,000 troops, supplies, and weapons to America. France also discussed with Franklin the possibility of loans to the United States. One point of Lafayette's plan was rejected; Lafayette would not command the French troops. The ministers wanted a more experienced French general to be in charge of the land forces, and they selected Marshal Jean-Baptiste Donatien de Vimeur, Comte de Rochambeau. The fleet would sail under the command of Charles-Henri-Louis d'Arsac, chevalier de Ternay.

To avoid the issues encountered with d'Estaing, France placed Rochambeau under the command of Washington. The French fleet with six ships of the line was slated to sail to America. The naval contingent would also come under Washington's command. Lafayette's role was to be the liaison between Washington and the French military.

As France was gathering the men, munitions and navy to assist America, Lafayette was directed to immediately depart for America. He would carry the news of France's aid to Washington. Dressed in his American uniform, on February 29, 1780, Lafayette rode to Versailles to take formal leave of King Louis XVI and Queen Marie-Antoinette. This time Lafayette would not have to disobey his king to go to America as he had the King's sanction.

Before departing, Lafayette visited his friend Benjamin Franklin. Franklin penned letters to both Washington and Congress praising Lafayette's extreme efforts in assisting America. Without Lafayette's support, Franklin and the other American representatives had little chance in obtaining the vital French aid.

In turn, Lafayette wrote to Washington about his anticipated return. Lafayette wrote about his joy of finding himself again one of Washington's "loving soldiers . . . I have affairs of the utmost importance which I should at first communicate to you alone."[117]

Lafayette's relatively brief time in France was well spent.

- He strengthened ties with his wife and his family. In a move seldom done in France at the time, Lafayette turned over power of attorney of his wealth to his wife, Adrienne.
- He soothed his trouble with the monarchy and became the King's confident and a French champion.
- He became a well-known, honored and loved French nobleman throughout Paris and the French countryside.
- He established strong relationships with Franklin, Adams and other American diplomats.
- And Lafayette, heroically, returned to America with the French resources that would ultimately win independence for the United States.

Lafayette departed Paris on March 6, 1780. The separation from Lafayette depressed Adrienne. Lafayette did leave a letter declaring his love for her. He closed the missive by saying, "Love me, take care of yourself, and believe that I love you to distraction."[118]

---

[117] Chernow, p. 352.

[118] Unger, p. 110.

·14·

Benedict Arnold

For once, Lafayette experienced an uneventful crossing of the Atlantic. Unlike the previous two voyages, Lafayette was not the subject of a royal arrest warrant as he departed France; no life-threatening storms manifested during the cruise; the ship's crew was devoid of mutineers; and British warships didn't menace his host ship.

Lafayette returned to American soil after the frigate *Hermione* arrived at Marblehead, Massachusetts, on April 27, 1780. As expected, one of Lafayette's first letters was to Washington. Lafayette, always the effervescent writer, told his "dear general" that he felt joy in again being with Washington's loving command. Washington replied to Lafayette with similar sentiments and offered an escort through Tory territory so the two could be safely reunited.

A grand reception, including a 13-gun salute by the cannons protecting Boston, greeted Lafayette upon his arrival on April 28. On hand were many leaders of the young nation, including Samuel Adams and John Handcock. Lafayette was rightfully viewed as a possible savior of the faltering revolution. In a letter to Adrienne, he described his return sparked several days of celebrations, dinners and fireworks. When Lafayette arrived in

Washington's camp on May 10, the troops also gave Lafayette a rousing welcome home.

Stepping on American soil, Lafayette discovered that the state of the American army wasn't improved during his absence. Washington's soldiers had survived a cold and harsh 1779–1780 winter in New Jersey without proper clothing and food. The encampment was reminiscent of the one at Valley Forge, except more snow fell at Morristown, New Jersey.

The 1780 campaign began with major losses as the French military allies remained rooted in Rhode Island. One of Lafayette's entries mentioned that a major defeat of the war for the Americans, the loss of Charleston, South Carolina. American General Benjamin Lincoln surrendered more than 3,000 men to British generals Henry Clinton and Charles Cornwallis on May 12, 1780, at Charleston. The British, as part of a new southern strategy to end the colonial revolution, had laid siege to the city at the beginning of April.

A more than satisfied Clinton returned to New York City, leaving Cornwallis in charge.

Several other American outposts in South Carolina capitulated. A second major blow to American hopes of victory took place on August 16, 1780, when General Gates, the officer who wanted to replace Washington as commander, was routed at Camden, South Carolina, by Cornwallis. The Americans lost 2,000 men, either killed or captured.

The Camden disaster took place despite a warning by Baron de Kalb, Gates's second in command. The 3,000 untrained American soldiers could not stand up to the professional cavalry of Cornwallis, de Kalb told Gates. De Kalb's prediction was all too accurate. The British cavalry under Lieutenant Colonel Banastre Tarleton routed the Americans and took no prisoners, reportedly striking some dead as they surrendered. All of Gates' army, except the Delaware and Maryland troops led by de Kalb, fled in disarray. De Kalb, the German/French officer who landed in

America with Lafayette, received multiple stab wounds, and died in the service of the United States.

Within months, the British new and effective southern strategy, according to one report, cost the American army more than 5,000 soldiers, more than 300 artillery pieces, almost 6,000 muskets, ammunition, 49 ships and barrels of flour, rice and rum. The American losses in South Carolina were staggering. Needed supplies could not be replaced as Congress was bankrupt.

To save his battered American army and reinvigorate his French allies, Washington needed to take bold action and realign his command structure. A critical move was relieving Gates, who then retired, and appointing General Nathanael Greene as commander of the Continental army's southern division. Greene was one of Washington's most capable generals.

Another change was the appointment of General Benedict Arnold to defend West Point, New York. Arnold had won Washington's trust because of his military accomplishments during the early part of the war. Those accomplishments, Arnold believed, were not properly rewarded by the Continental Congress. Thus, an embittered Arnold was in charge of a major American post close to the British stronghold of New York City.

Arnold's discontentment with Congress was fueled by his association with Loyalist families in Philadelphia. Arnold married Peggy Shippen, a daughter of one of Philadelphia's Loyalist sympathizers. Peggy Arnold's close friend was British Major John André, who spent time in Philadelphia after the British victory at Brandywine.

Elements were in place for another American disaster, this time at West Point.

The crippling setbacks in South Carolina and the elevation of Arnold to command at West Point set the stage for Lafayette's upcoming decisive southern clash with Cornwallis.

Washington was elated to see Lafayette for personal and professional reasons. His surrogate son had returned. Lafayette brought much needed hope for Washington's beleaguered army. Lafayette took great pride in relaying to Washington the promise made by France for additional men, ships and resources. The good news of French aid spread quickly among Washington's men and soldiers. A grand reception for the French contingent was planned by Alexander Hamilton and Lafayette.

Without the French assistance, the American army's days were numbered as the individual states appeared unwilling to support the rebellion. Washington dispatched Lafayette to Congress to inform the governing body of the coming of additional French troops and ships and to request provisions. Congress was, of course, elated to see Lafayette. The members officially and warmly welcomed Lafayette back to America. The members also failed to approve any of Washington's requests for supplies. Washington did not give up hope that the individual states would assist his army. A letter-writing campaign by Lafayette was authorized by Washington. Lafayette's personal plea spurred some of the leaders to send much needed assistance.

As for his reluctant French allies, Washington then dispatched Lafayette to Newport after the French forces arrived on July 10. The Americans were disappointed to discover that fewer men and ships had been sent to America than had been promised to Franklin and Lafayette. The added strength was not enough for the Americans to strike New York City, as Washington had planned.

On his way to see the French officers, Lafayette stopped at Harford, Connecticut, and received assurances from Governor Jonathan Trumbull that his state would aid the American army. Before meeting with Rochambeau and de Ternay, Lafayette took pleasure in meeting with Vicomte de Noailles, his brother-in-law, and French officers whom he knew.

So far, the New England trip was a successful one for Lafayette. The tenor of Lafayette's mission was about to abruptly change.

The reluctant French allies turned out to be stubborn allies. Rochambeau and de Ternay told Lafayette that they would not fight the British until another division of French troops and additional ships arrived from France. Lafayette vehemently argued for immediate action, stating that a delay would be crippling to the American army and inaction by the French military was not helping America in the least.

Lafayette's well-known pleasant manner deserted the young French/American general. Veteran military man Rochambeau was not amused by young Lafayette's lecture. In fact, Rochambeau's refused to have any additional discussion with Lafayette and demanded an audience with Washington. Lafayette tried to make amends by apologizing to Rochambeau. Lafayette's apology seemed to soothe Rochambeau somewhat, but Rochambeau still insisted on conferring only with Washington, not Washington and Rochambeau's subordinate, Lafayette.

Washington acquiesced to Rochambeau's request and dealt directly with the French general. Also, Washington didn't oppose Rochambeau and de Ternay's insistence that they stay in Rhode Island and not engage the British until additional French forces arrived. Those forces were not soon in appearing. A British fleet blockaded a French fleet in a French home port while another British battle group reinforced New York City. The main British city in America was safe from attack in 1780.

While waiting for his next opportunity to strike the British, Washington continued reorganizing his army. Lafayette took command of a light infantry division of about 2,000 men. In typical Lafayette fashion, Lafayette paid to cloth his troops. Lafayette also drilled his new troops until they were fit for combat. One of his officers in his light infantry command was his former aide Gimat, the officer who helped Lafayette to his horse after Lafayette suffered his leg wound at Brandywine.

Both armies were content to rest, regroup and avoid engaging with their opponent. The American army, as Lafayette made clear to Rochambeau and de Ternay, was suffering by the inaction. Washington's army was decreasing in size as terms of service expired, desertions took place and disease claimed lives. Washington could not risk sitting and being a do-nothing leader. Washington gathered Lafayette, Hamilton, General Henry Knox and others and on September 17 set off for a meeting with Rochambeau at Hartford.

On their way, Washington and his contingent stopped at West Point to have lunch with Arnold. The meeting was cordial, no signs of any issues, and Washington promised to stop on his return from Hartford and inspect the defenses at West Point. Washington also planned to dine with Arnold and his Tory-leaning wife, Peggy.

Washington's confab with the French was productive. Washington and Rochambeau were in agreement that the French ministers had underestimated British strength in America and that additional support was needed. Ambassador Anne-César de La Luzerne, a royal representative, attended the meeting and forwarded to Versailles a document drafted by Washington and Rochambeau requesting immediate increased supplies, ships and soldiers. The allies, again, agreed to work with each other against England.

With the relationship with Rochambeau rebuilt, as promised Washington and Lafayette made their way to West Point to inspect the defenses on the banks of the Hudson River and meet with General Arnold and his wife. The day, September 25, 1780, would conclude with Arnold being unmasked as the most infamous traitor in American history. Arnold planned to sell West Point to the British.

Lafayette's version of the events was recorded in a letter written that night to Minister La Luzerne. "West Point was sold, and it was sold by Arnold! The same who had covered himself with glory and signal services to his country recently signed a despicable pact with the enemy, and but for our chance arrival at midday and a series of chance events that led to the fall of the adjutant-general of the British army into the hands of some farmers."[119] Arnold had planned to tell Washington he had been taken unaware by a surprise British attack and had been forced to surrender the fortification to the superior British force, according to Lafayette.

Lafayette gave additional observations and details:

While approaching West Point, Washington and Lafayette sent messengers to Arnold that they would join him for lunch. Arnold and his wife were at the breakfast table when word of the impending visit by Washington and Lafayette. The two generals would arrive within a few hours. Arnold also received notice that a British spy, André, had been captured by American militia. Arnold went "pale" at the news and excused himself from the room and beckoned his wife to meet him in their bedroom. Peggy Arnold "fainted" when told of André's arrest. Arnold then made a quick escape—a half hour before Washington's arrival—on an aide's horse, as it was saddled near his front door, calling out he would return in an hour. Arnold never returned.

Arnold rode to the Hudson River shore and rowed in a canoe to the British sloop *Vulture*. When Washington arrived at West Point, Lafayette wrote, Washington was astonished that he was not expected. After Washington returned to Arnold's home, Washington was told that Arnold was not there and the dinner was delayed. Then, the documents from the captured André were given to Washington. André was under arrest, Washington and Lafayette were informed. The papers found on André, written by Arnold, included details on the West Point defenses and a suggestion of how best the British could attack and capture the fortification.

"We chased after Arnold, but he escaped in a boat to the English frigate *Vulture*, and since no one suspected he was fleeing, none of the sentries thought to stop him. Colonel Hamilton, who chased after him, received soon after, under a flag of truce, a letter from Arnold to (Washington) giving no details to justify

---

[119] Lafayette memoirs, p. 349.

his treason, and an insolent letter from the English commander Robertson demanding release of (André), who had only acted with permission of General Arnold."[120]

Fearing an attack from the British, Washington and Lafayette took command of West Point, strengthened defensives along the Hudson River and summoned additional troops from Washington's main encampment.

The day included an award-winning dramatic performance by Peggy Shippen Arnold. When confronted with her husband's treachery, she acted surprised and feigned histrionics in an attempt to convince Washington that she knew nothing of her husband's betrayal. Later, a letter from André to Peggy was discovered with information that Peggy had been involved in the treason from the beginning of the plot.

A plea to have André returned to the British army was denied. André was convicted at a military trial of being a spy and sentenced to death. Greene convened the trial two days after Arnold's treachery was uncovered. Lafayette, Knox and Lord Stirling were among the generals sitting in judgement. Their decision was unanimous. No doubt existed that André, who was using an assumed name and was dressed in civilian clothes and not his uniform, was a spy. A death sentence was issued.

Lafayette wrote a letter to Adrienne about his impressions of André. Lafayette believed André conducted himself in a forthright manner at the trial. Lafayette admitted to his wife he developed a liking for the British officer.

André, 29 years old, was hanged at high noon at Tappan, New York, on October 2, 1780.

Lafayette realized that, without André's apprehension, he might well have been captured by the British at West Point, along with Washington and Hamilton. The revolution could very well have ended that day. Arnold sold out his country for money, a

---

[120] Lafayette memoirs, p. 351.

pension and a commission in the British army. Lafayette couldn't understand or condone André's conduct.

In a letter, Lafayette wrote that Arnold's action "confounds and distresses me." Arnold "humiliates me to a degree that I cannot express. I would give anything in the world if Arnold had not shared our labors with us, and if this man, whom it still pains me to call a scoundrel, had not shed his blood for the American cause. My knowledge of his personal courage led me to expect that he would decide to blow his brains out."[121]

Arnold had no plans to commit suicide. Arnold received a commission in the British army and prepared to do battle against his former comrades, including Lafayette. In the coming year, Lafayette was tasked with capturing Arnold, one of the most reviled men in American history.

Lafayette refused to remain inactive waiting for the 1781 campaign to begin. He devised a plan with fellow officer Colonel "Lighthouse Harry" Lee to attack the British on the Staten Island section of New York. Lafayette called off the attack after he failed to receive enough boats to ferry his men to the attack position. The abortive attack didn't deter Lafayette. He asked Washington's approval to launch an attack against Hessians in New York City before the conclusion of 1780. Lafayette argued that a victory would imbue confidence in America's allies in Europe. Washington countered that such an attack on well-entrenched British position could well lead to disaster and abandonment by those same allies.

The British were safe within the confines of New York City.

Since idleness was not in Lafayette's nature, he petitioned Washington to be allowed to join General Greene's new command in the South. A number of other French officers in Washington's army wanted to accompany Lafayette in transferring to Greene's division. Washington politely listened and then politely

[121] Unger, p. 125.

denied their request. The Frenchmen were staying in the North for the winter.

Those French officers received sad news from Newport concerning French Admiral de Ternay's death. On December 15, 1780, while aboard his flagship *Duc de Bourgogne*, de Ternay died of typhus.

To pass some of the months of inactivity, Lafayette made a journey to Philadelphia with his brother-in-law and other French officers. Besides seeing the sites of the big city, Lafayette toured two of his early battlefields, Barren Hill and Brandywine, where his leg wound marked the beginning of his American rise to fame.

The winter of 1780-1781 compounded the hardships suffered by Washington and his men. Lacking adequate supplies, Lafayette began a letter-writing campaign to friends in France to drum up support and financial contributions to the American cause of freedom. The situation was becoming desperate for the army.

Congress, Washington and Lafayette all fretted about the possibility that France would withdraw from the alliance because of the state of the American army. Congress was so worried that it sent former president Henry Laurens to France to discuss the state of America. The British intercepted the ship carrying Laurens to France, and Laurens was imprisoned in the Tower of London. Adrienne did her best to secure humane treatment for Laurens, who had kindly assisted her husband after the Battle of Brandywine.

Military matters deteriorated from critical to desperate on New Year's Day. All of the hardships suffered by the soldiers resulted in a mutiny by 1,500 men of the Pennsylvania Line, all under the command of General Anthony Wayne. Their complaints were myriad. Some maintained that their three-year enlistments had expired and they were no longer American soldiers. Others complained about the pay they received and in some instances didn't receive. Food was scarce and clothing and housing inadequate.

The soldiers threatened to take their complaints directly to

Congress in Philadelphia. The mutiny lasted a week before an agreement could be reached with members of the Pennsylvania Line. The agreement was ratified by Congress in late January but not before a similar uprising by New Jersey troops. In his memoirs, Lafayette noted that Washington sent him and his light infantry to help quell the revolt by the New Jersey Troops as Wayne was dealing with his Pennsylvania men.

The Pennsylvania Line mutiny, even though seemingly settled, adversely affected Lafayette's next assignment from General Washington.

The British General Lord Cornwallis
as painted by Thomas Gainsborough

·15·

CHASING CORNWALLIS

Lafayette's joyful return to America from France, even with his youthful enthusiasm, determination and political and military savvy, couldn't change the misfortune of Washington's army during 1780. Disastrous defeats in the southern United States, broken promises by allies, treachery and a mutiny combined to make a bleak outlook for 1781.

The year began in the same vein for Lafayette. The first six months of 1781 very well could have been Lafayette's most frustrating time in America. Lafayette, his men and Washington's army continued to suffer from lack of support from Congress. French military contributions didn't live up to Lafayette's expectations. Lafayette's troops deserted him at one point. And Washington failed to take Lafayette into his confidence concerning a grand plan to bag the British General Cornwallis. Not knowing Washington's intentions, caused Lafayette some anxiety.

Lafayette was dejected and felt misused and rejected at times in 1781.

By year's end, a miraculous change in fortune would take America to the verge of freedom and independence. Playing a major role in the events transforming defeat into victory was none other than Lafayette. Lafayette built upon his stature as an American hero.

A spark of hope was glimpsed by Washington at an unlikely area designated the Cowpens, a pastureland near Spartanburg, South Carolina. Successful officers of both armies faced each other during the cold and clear morning of January 17. American General Daniel Morgan, whose men helped win the battle of Saratoga in 1777, engaged forces under Colonel Banastre Tarleton, the ruthless British officer whose forces massacred de Kalb's men at Camden a year earlier and struck fear into communities throughout the South.

On the small Cowpens battlefield, measuring some 500 yards long and just as wide, Morgan out-maneuvered Tarleton and handed the hated British officer a stunning and overwhelming defeat. In less than an hour, Morgan inflicted more than 800 casualties, including 110 dead, on Tarleton's vaunted forces. Morgan's losses were reported to be less than 75 with only 12 deaths.

Cowpens emboldened Washington. With Greene and Morgan occupying the forces of Cornwallis in the Carolinas, Washington took aim at the reviled British General Benedict Arnold. After committing his treason at West Point and joining the British army, Arnold was ordered to Virginia in December 1780 by Clinton. Arnold was directed to raid military supply bases, rally loyalists to the cause of King George III and to cause havoc with Greene's forces.

Washington turned to one of his most trusted generals, Lafayette, to hunt down Arnold. If the despised turncoat was captured, Lafayette was ordered to hang Arnold on the spot. For several reasons, Lafayette relished the idea of the campaign against Arnold. The forthcoming engagements offered a second inducement for Lafayette. General William Phillips was sent to Virginia by Clinton to be Arnold's commanding officer. Phillips was the British officer in charge of the artillery that killed Lafayette's father in the 1759 battle of Minden in Prussia during the Seven Years War. Lafayette was handed a chance to avenge his father's death.

Lafayette began the expedition with his light infantry. The small command was supported by a small French fleet. Lafayette's immediate goal was to link up with the Virginia militia under the command of Baron von Steuben of Valley Forge fame. To provide cover for Lafayette's departure from camp and to hide Lafayette's destination, Washington feigned an attack on Clinton at New York City.

On March 1, Lafayette and his men were ferried from Trenton, New Jersey, past Philadelphia and on to Wilmington, Delaware. The men then marched to the Head of the Elk, the same location where the British disembarked to begin the Philadelphia campaign that included Brandywine. Lafayette expected a French fleet to be waiting for his men. The ships never arrived.

The French fleet battled a British contingent near the mouth of the Chesapeake Bay. After suffering a loss, the French retreated and eventually returned to Rhode Island, leaving the British navy in control of the Chesapeake Bay and Lafayette stranded.

Lafayette was not deterred. He wrote to Washington to request a larger French naval force to oppose the British flotilla. Lafayette was not about to sit around and wait for the French assistance. Too often, Lafayette wasted valuable time in camp while promises of support were broken. Lafayette rode to Baltimore seeking help for his troops from the city's merchants. He wanted boats, equipment and food for his men and money to pay them. Lafayette's mystique and charm proved to be magical. The merchants rendered the requested supplies.

Equipped and with transportation, Lafayette set off for his rendezvous with von Steuben. Again, the British fleet foiled his advance. Lafayette's ships were no match for the British and were forced to anchor at Annapolis. With the sea path blocked, Lafayette, supported by a small detachment of men, set off by land to link up with von Steuben. He did so at Yorktown, Virginia.

The operation seemed doomed as a second French fleet

returned to Rhode Island after being driven off by the British ships. The British navy ruled the ocean. Writing to Hamilton, Lafayette criticized the lack of effort of the ministers at Versailles. Washington was also disheartened by the events and decided the prudent move was to recall Lafayette and his troops to his main headquarters outside of New York City.

Before departing, Lafayette conferred with von Steuben. Von Steuben outlined a plan to attack Cornwallis that included forces of Greene, von Steuben and Lafayette. The British army would be assaulted from different directions. Lafayette thought the plan had merit and the two generals forwarded the scheme to Washington.

Again, Lafayette played a waiting game. After failing to receive word from Washington on von Steuben's plan, Lafayette decided Washington had rejected the idea. He and his men began the long trek back to Washington's camp. At the Head of the Elk, Lafayette received new directions from Washington. The direction Lafayette's troops were to march was south, where they had just been.

The counter march order was too much for Lafayette and his troops. After a month of marching back and forth, the troops were exhausted, hungry and ill-clothed. Some of Lafayette's men mutinied and threated not to budge and some others skedaddled. In his memoirs, Lafayette noted desertions increased as his northern troops "harbored prejudices against the South and the fear of an unhealthy climate." Lafayette scrambled to properly equip his men and take care of their needs. Lafayette noted he "gained more trust from soldiers by hiring a cart to transport an officer with a diseased leg."

Lafayette himself was not happy. He needed Congress to properly support his men and he needed the French officials to live up to their lofty promises of controlling the ocean. Lafayette's pen flew to paper, and his displeasure was made known in Versailles, Philadelphia and General Washington's camp.

What Lafayette didn't know, and Washington wasn't divulging, was Lafayette was designated to play a major part in a scheme to trap Cornwallis in Virginia. Washington was extremely cautious about sharing his plans as he was afraid British spies would discover his strategy was to concentrate his resources in Virginia against Cornwallis and not against Clinton in New York City. Washington didn't want Clinton to congregate his British army in Virginia and overwhelm Lafayette.

So, Washington kept mum. He didn't fully inform anyone, even Lafayette, of his intentions. A few weeks later, Washington fabricated a letter to Lafayette, one he knew would most likely be captured by the British, where he tricked Clinton into thinking New York City was the true goal of Washington's army in 1781. Clinton was deceived and withheld vital support from Cornwallis during the siege of Yorktown.

Washington was well aware of Lafayette's frustration and took steps to calm his young French general. Washington dispatched his nephew, George Augustine Washington, to see Lafayette with a message that included a promise to send General Wayne with 800 Pennsylvanians to assist Lafayette in the campaign. An immediate objective was a movement against Arnold at Portsmouth, Virginia, Lafayette was told.

Lafayette was more than ready to carry out Washington's directives. About face and march, that was Lafayette's order to his men on April 10. While Lafayette was proceeding south, many of his men decided to go north to their homes. The loss of men through desertion disheartened Lafayette, as he expressed in a letter written to Washington on April 13 from the home of Colonel James Rigbie in Harford County, Maryland.[122]

To stem the stream of deserters, Lafayette began arresting all he could identify. After crossing the Susquehanna River, harsher penalties were imposed by Lafayette. At least one

[122] *Lafayette in Harford County*, Memorial Monograph 1781–1931.

deserter was reportedly hung. The close scrutiny of his own troops unmasked Tory spies within Lafayette's ranks. One, upon Lafayette's order, was hung. Lafayette was loathe to rule with a ruthless iron fist. In his sincere and persuasive manner, Lafayette made an impassioned plea to his troops. Stay and fight with him in the upcoming mission, Lafayette implored. Lafayette's men abandoned their rebellious ways and followed their French leader on to Virginia.

Before seeking out Arnold, Lafayette first led his men to Baltimore where he secured a personal line of credit and used the money to fully clothe his army. Lafayette's caring ways enamored him to his troops. Lafayette's 2,000 men were fully prepared to faithfully follow Lafayette to the battlegrounds of Virginia.

For the next few days, Lafayette waited for Wayne's Pennsylvania troops to join him. Lafayette would have an interminable wait. Lafayette complained to Washington about Wayne's absence. Wayne was not being purposely obstructive as the Pennsylvania general was having issues of his own gathering troops, paying them and equipping and feeding them.

Wayne wanted the loyal members of his old command, the Pennsylvania Line, to join him in heading to Virginia. Only a few members were available for action with Wayne as many of the Pennsylvania Line left military service and many others were fighting with units in Washington's main army. Wayne traveled to York and Lebanon, Pennsylvania, to gather expected recruits. The recruitment drive was disappointing as only a few hundred joined Wayne's ranks.

Wayne's recruiting efforts were hampered in Pennsylvania as other states gave larger bonuses to those enlisting. Wayne pleaded with former soldiers and frontiersmen to swell his depleted command. Wayne, the respected general, slowly grew his ranks. Wayne wasn't moving fast enough for Lafayette and Greene as each general urged Wayne to quicken his pace. In one of his letters, Wayne could only promise a small detachment at first and maybe 1,200 by April 1.[123]

The April Fool's Day deadline was missed by more than two months. In May, Wayne was still in York attempting to quell additional mutiny threats and stem desertions. Some of Wayne's officers offered their resignations after executions were carried out to restore order among the troops. On May 26, 1781, Wayne was ready to march his 800 men, many poorly trained, to Lafayette's aid.

"Wayne, at last gave the signal to start for Virginia. Just at what point he would meet Lafayette, Wayne did not know; the Marquis, he was confident, would hurry north to meet the Pennsylvanians and the two forces would join somewhere in northern Virginia."[124] Rain, muddy roads and other impediments slowed Wayne's advance. He would not see Lafayette until June 10.

On April 20, almost three weeks after Wayne promised 1,200 men, Lafayette's patience was at an end. He knew he would have to press on if he would have any chance of capturing and dispatching Arnold. A march was ordered to Richmond, Virginia, about 150 miles distant. The trip was grueling. To quicken the pace, Lafayette decided to allow the slower moving artillery and supply wagons to proceed at their own pace and not impede the speed of the foot soldiers. The men arrived in 10 days in remarkably good shape. Lafayette used wagons to transport half of his army for an hour. Then he would have

---

[123] Harry Emerson Wildes, *Anthony Wayne: Trouble Shooter of the American Revolution*, Harcourt, Brace and Company, New York, 1941, p. 239.

[124] Wildes, p. 245.

those in the wagon march an hour as the other half of the army were transported by wagon.

Richmond was selected as the destination because the town was an important supply depot for the American army in the South. Lafayette's assessment that Richmond would be a target of the British was correct. Lafayette's rapid movement saved vital supplies. "Richmond was filled with munitions warehouses. Its pillage would have proved fatal. We marched here so rapidly that, when General Phillips neared Richmond and learned that we had arrived the day before, he would not believe it."[125]

Lafayette's appearance was in the nick of time. Phillips and Arnold with a force of about 2,500 men had successfully maneuvered along the James River and captured the town of Petersburg, about 25 miles south of Richmond. The British had vastly outnumbered von Steuben's small force of untrained militia. Von Steuben petitioned Governor Thomas Jefferson to supply men and equipment. None were forthcoming as von Steuben and Wayne were having the same lack of support from their state governments. In person, Lafayette tried to persuade Jefferson to supply the much-needed assistance. As the two great men of history met for the first time, Jefferson apologized and explained that as governor he didn't have the power to order provisions to be provided to the American army.

Lafayette and von Steuben would have to do the best with their limited resources. The American soldiers were put to the test on April 30 as a British detachment crossed the James River to capture Richmond, a town they believed to be undefended. They were wrong. Lafayette spread his soldiers on the high ground surrounding Richmond and held off the British advance. Using a tactic employed at Barren Hill, Lafayette constantly moved his men so the British would believe he had a much larger force under his command.

---

[125] Lafayette memoirs, p. 260.

Phillips fell for Lafayette's ruse and retreated to Petersburg to wait for reinforcements from Cornwallis.

The much-needed American victory, the first major triumph in Virginia, was celebrated. Lafayette ordered a parade to be held on May 1. Lafayette then took a few days to develop a strategy to do as much damage to the British as possible. Lafayette kept in mind admonitions he had been given not to engage the superior British forces in an open battle. To gather necessary information, Lafayette recruited spies, including slaves, to gain intelligence for him. Slaves were also being enticed by the British. England was offering freedom for help in defeating the rebels.

While at Richmond, Lafayette's slow-moving artillery and supply wagons arrived. He was prepared to engage the British and was more than ready to take revenge on Phillips. On May 10, Lafayette moved on Petersburg. At Lafayette's direction, a cannon ball was fired at Phillips' headquarters. Phillips was not there. Phillips had been stricken with a fever, possibly typhoid, and taken to a private residence where he died on May 13.

During Lafayette's encounter with British troops, Arnold offered a letter to Lafayette by means of a flag of truce. Arnold wanted to exchange prisoners. Lafayette refused to accept the correspondence from a traitor. The thought was repugnant, Lafayette confided. If any other British officer would have contacted him, Lafayette indicated he would have received the letter. "The refusal gave great pleasure to General Washington and the public."[126]

As summer 1781 approached, clearly Virginia was becoming the main battleground for the year's ongoing campaign and for the war. Cornwallis and Tarleton made their ways from the Carolinas to Virginia to join Arnold. General Greene's troops were closing to add to American strengths in Virginia. A major clash was looming. From the American perspective, all that was missing was support from the French army and navy and Washington, himself.

---

[126] Lafayette memoirs, p. 260.

In his memoirs, Lafayette wrote that Washington urged him to delay the British conquering of Virginia as long as possible as he knew the forces of Cornwallis were much stronger than Lafayette's small contingent. "(My) efforts were more successful than any person had hoped."[127] Lafayette maintained he was facing 4,000 British troops with 800 cavalry members.

"Lafayette, in fact, dared not fight, lest he be cut to pieces and his militia scattered. He played a waiting game, skirmishing a bit in order to keep up Virginia's confidence, but not risking a major battle. 'I am not strong enough,' Lafayette confessed, 'even to get beaten.' "[128]

Lafayette's troop strength desperately needed bolstered. Besides contacting Washington, Lafayette communicated with General George Weeden, who was recruiting troops in the Fredericksburg, Virginia, area. Being unaware of Wayne's situation, Lafayette sent another pleading letter to the Pennsylvania general. On May 20 the situation for Lafayette's Virginia command grew dire, Cornwallis linked up his command with Arnold. As additional troops, 1,800 from New York, arrived to bolster Cornwallis's command, Lafayette received word from Wayne that he had not yet departed Pennsylvania.

All seemed lost for Lafayette as he stood almost alone against the British's swelling army. Another disappointing development for Lafayette took place. Upon arrival, Cornwallis ordered the American traitor Arnold, who was not universally trusted within the British army, to return to Clinton at New York City. Thus, Lafayette and Washington missed the opportunity to capture and hang the most wanted traitor on American soil. Arnold fought in New England for a time before traveling to England. Arnold died in 1801.

As Lafayette regrouped at Richmond, he once again contacted von Steuben, Weeden and Jefferson in a desperate attempt to

---

[127] Lafayette memoirs, p. 261.
[128] Wildes, p. 245.

secure support. No help was forthcoming Lafayette's way. In a plaintive letter to Hamilton on May 23, Lafayette wrote, "We have 900 Continentals. Their infantry is near five to one; their cavalry ten to one."[129] Lafayette asked his good friend Hamilton to join him.

Lafayette was doing his best to annoy Cornwallis without risking the loss of his total force against the superior British forces. Even though he was not fully aware, his actions were exactly what Washington desired, denying Cornwallis total control of Virginia. Washington was using the time to persuade the French to join him in opposing Cornwallis in Virginia. Washington realized Cornwallis's army was much more vulnerable after a waging a hard campaign in the South than Clinton's army sitting in fortified New York City.

In a major development, Washington won over Rochambeau to his Virginia plan. Rochambeau joined with Washington in asking French admiral François Joseph Paul, Comte de Grasse for assistance. Rochambeau wrote de Grasse, "These people here are at the end of their resources. Washington has not half the troops he counted on; I believe, though he is hiding it, that he has not 6,000 men. Lafayette has not 1,000 regulars with the militia to defend Virginia . . . This is the state of affairs and the great crisis at which America finds itself."[130]

The joint appeal moved de Grasse into action. From his base in Saint-Domingue, his fleet set sail with 3,000 troops. Canons, dragoons and cash to pay the soldiers were also promised by de Grasse.

Help was on the way for Lafayette. Fearing he couldn't protect Richmond, Lafayette moved all of the munitions out of town, finding hiding places in the countryside. On May 26, the feared confrontation with Cornwallis was a possibility. The British

---

[129] Unger, p. 142

[130] Burke Davis, *The Campaign that Won America: The Story of Yorktown,* Eastern National, 1970, p. 17.

crossed the James River with Tarleton's feared dragoons in the van. Lafayette's available cavalry numbered less than 50, not nearly enough to stand against Tarleton's force estimated at 800. Cornwallis informed Clinton of his move against Lafayette. A stated goal was the capture of Lafayette. An oft quoted statement attributed to Cornwallis—"The boy cannot escape me"—has not been fully verified.

Lafayette did escape Cornwallis at Richmond. Cornwallis had difficulty in cornering American leaders. Jefferson and the Virginia state government decided to flee to Charlottesville, Jefferson's home, in light of the British advance. Lafayette conducted a strategic retreat. His next step was to find Wayne's troops somewhere in northern Virginia. Bad weather, lots of rain, hindered Lafayette's movements. The rain and mud also slowed down Cornwallis. Wayne was not spared as his march towards Lafayette was at times stuck in southern mire.

Cornwallis trailed Lafayette but couldn't bring the cunning Frenchman into an open battle. Every day the British lost several soldiers to American snipers. Lafayette's hit and run tactics were taking a toll on the British army. Not all of Lafayette's men escaped the British. Tarleton's troops chased, killed and captured Americans in skirmishes. Lafayette was forced to change his route and headed to the woods, where Tarleton's troopers were less effective.

Lafayette desperately needed Wayne's Pennsylvanians.

Cornwallis, while camped outside Hanover Court House, captured dispatches from Lafayette to Greene, Jefferson and von Steuben. The dispatches alerted Cornwallis to the Virginia's assembly being in Charlottesville and a store of munitions near the James River. Cornwallis dispatched Tarleton and Colonel John Graves Simcoe of the Queen's Rangers to capture the assembly and supplies.

Lafayette feared such a foray by the British. On June 3, Lafayette wrote Greene, "It is possible they mean to make a stroke towards Charlottesville."[131] On the same day, Tarleton, with 250 of his dragoons riding prime Virginia horses, set out to capture Jefferson and the Virginia elected officials and also release British prisoners of war. Those taken at the battle of Saratoga were being held in the vicinity of Charlottesville. Cornwallis hoped to double the size of his army when the captives were liberated.

Swiftly, Tarleton traveled the 70 miles to Charlottesville. The ride of the dragoons to Charlottesville didn't go unnoticed. Jack Jouett, a captain in the Virginia militia, discovered Tarleton's movements and rode swiftly to warn the Virginia legislature.[132]

On June 4, Tarleton rode into Charlottesville. Taken into custody were members of the Virginia legislature, including Daniel Boone, who didn't act quickly enough on Jouett's warning,[133] Boone was later paroled by Tarleton. Also, Charlottesville officials didn't heed Lafayette's instructions to move supplies out of the town. Tarleton was able to seize weapons, munitions, clothing and tobacco stored in the town. A second British raiding party, under the command of Simcoe, on June 5 also was successful in capturing supplies under von Steuben's protection. Cannons were part of the munitions seized in the Simcoe raid.

Jefferson was at his Monticello home with Benjamin Harrison and John Tyler at the time of Tarleton's raid. Jefferson, because of the advance warning, fled just ahead of Tarleton's arriving dragoons. Eventually, Cornwallis had Monticello looted and the grand home suffered severe damage.

Losing Jefferson caused Cornwallis great anguish. He was equally distressed when Tarleton reported that only 20 of the

---

[131] John R. Maass, *To Disturb the Assembly: Tarleton's Charlottesville Raid and the British Invasion of Virginia, 1781*. University of Virginia Library, 2000.

[132] Maass.

[133] Maass.

interned British soldiers were going to rejoin the army. Many of the prisoners of war started their own little conclave, bonded with Americans and some married American women. For most of the one-time British soldiers turned prisoners, no more war for them-as they were staying put in their new community.

Lafayette's small force couldn't oppose the stronger British troops at Charlottesville without General Wayne's troops. On June 10, the Pennsylvanians were seen camping along the shore of the Rappahannock River. Lafayette's little band rejoiced. Wayne and the Pennsylvanians brought much needed supplies for Lafayette's men. Wayne also had much needed information for Lafayette. Wayne informed Lafayette of Washington's grand plan to trap Cornwallis.

Cornwallis presently confronted the same difficulties that challenged Lafayette earlier in the campaign. Supplies were running low. Cornwallis was losing men to the constant sniping of Lafayette's forces. Also, the British soldiers were not holding up well in the heat of the Virginia summer. Cornwallis decided to march to Richmond. His army would then be nearer the sea where, if needed, the British navy could whisk his army to New York.

Lafayette reported to Washington that twice he offered the British a chance to fight and twice the British declined. "The enemy have been so kind as to retire before us," Lafayette wrote his commander as he followed Cornwallis towards Richmond.

The outskirts of Richmond turned into a field of dreams for Lafayette. From almost every direction, additional American troops added to Lafayette's growing band of men. Weeden arrived from his Fredericksburg recruiting trip with almost 1,000 new militiamen. Von Steuben brought his 650 members to Lafayette's Virginia army. Civilians, tired of the British rule and maltreatment by the British army, joined on their own accord. Suddenly, Lafayette's force numbered near 5,000 members. Of that number, 2,000 were veterans of the American army.

Even though the British army still was larger than Lafayette's forces by 2,000 men, Lafayette was emboldened. No longer would the young French general be the mouse in a cat-and-mouse game with Cornwallis. The time had come for Cornwallis to be the rodent.

IN CONGRESS, JULY 4, 1776.

The unanimous Declaration of the thirteen united States of America,

The Declaration of Independence

·16·

Yorktown

The momentum of the Virginia campaign was swiftly changing from Cornwallis to Lafayette.

Cornwallis could sense the growing strength of Lafayette's command. The veteran British general requested additional support from his commander, Clinton, in New York City. Clinton had exactly the opposite idea. Clinton wanted part of Cornwallis's command to help protect New York against a suspected attack by Washington.

Both Lafayette and Wayne strongly believed Cornwallis was vulnerable. The two American generals were set to test their conviction. Lafayette, cautious for once, overruled Wayne's call for an immediate attack on the British army. Lafayette decided to follow Cornwallis at a safe distance as Cornwallis made his way from Richmond to Williamsburg.

A skirmish did take place on June 26 at Water Plantation, near Williamsburg. A small force of Lafayette's command chased a contingent of British regulars, causing a number of casualties to the British. The minor victory uplifted the spirits of Lafayette's forces and area civilians supporting the cause of independence.

As his army needed some refitting of armaments, Lafayette took several days to prepare for the crucial upcoming battles.

Lafayette and his troops also grandly celebrated the fifth anniversary of the Declaration of Independence. Lafayette took time to praise his small army, a unit that confounded British General Cornwallis throughout Virginia. Cornwallis chased Lafayette and then retreated, leaving control of Virginia in Lafayette's hands. "For American Patriots, the Virginia campaign, according to Rochambeau's chaplain, make the word *marquis* 'a beloved symbol which rouses their admiration and gratitude.'"[134]

Under orders from Clinton, Cornwallis withdrew from the James River towards Yorktown. The maneuver gave Lafayette an opportunity to attack Cornwallis's vulnerable rear guard. On July 6, Wayne advanced to Green Spring Plantation, near the site of the Water Plantation engagement.

Wayne wasn't facing just the British rearguard. The majority of Cornwallis's forces were waiting for Wayne, who was outnumber by more than 5-to-1. Instead of sending the majority of his troops across the James, as Lafayette and Wayne believed, Cornwallis crossed only his wagons and baggage. Cornwallis had been told of Lafayette's plan to attack.

When Wayne encountered unexpected opposition, Lafayette moved along the James to obtain a better observation post. There, Lafayette recognized Wayne was about to fall into a trap. Lafayette ordered reinforcements. Lafayette led a charge through the British line to give Wayne an avenue of escape. After Lafayette's horse was mortally wounded, Lafayette continued on foot to Wayne. "Not a man was more exposed than Lafayette," Wayne reported.[135] Together, Wayne and Lafayette extricated their men.

Even though Wayne suffered about twice as many losses as the British, Wayne received praise for his actions in extracting his troops from danger. The American losses were reported to be about 140. The British casualties were approximately 75. Lafayette wrote, "The General is happy in acknowledging the spirit of

[134] Unger, p. 150.
[135] Unger, p. 150.

the detachment commanded by General Wayne, in their engagement with the total of the British army, of which I happened to be an eyewitness. I request General Wayne, the officers and men under his command, to receive my best thanks."[136] For his actions at Green Springs, Lafayette, in turn, received congratulations from Washington.

Wayne did receive a caution from General Greene; Cornwallis was not yet beaten. Lafayette was in agreement with Greene. On July 9, Lafayette was quoted as saying, "This devil Cornwallis is much wiser than the other generals with whom I have dealt. He inspires me with a sincere fear, and his name has greatly troubled my sleep. This campaign is a good school for me. God grant that the public does not pay for my lessons."[137]

Lafayette's lessons were put on hold for a time as Green Springs was the last major engagement before the siege of Yorktown.

Lafayette followed Cornwallis as the British army moved towards Portsmouth. The young French general believed the British army was about to be removed by the British navy to New York City. Lafayette informed Greene of his conviction.

Instead of boarding ships, Cornwallis began fortifying Yorktown and the opposite settlement, Gloucester Point, on the York River. Lafayette's surmise of a British departure to New York City was incorrect. In hindsight, the British would have been better off if they had followed Lafayette's instincts. Yorktown would soon become a deadly trap for Cornwallis and the British army.

An opportunity for destroying Cornwallis's forces was tantalizingly close to Lafayette's reach. Lafayette desired the British army to camp at Yorktown. Lafayette reasoned the enemy would have no avenue of retreat. Lafayette alerted his superiors and called for assistance. "If the French army could all of a sudden arrive in Virginia and be supported by a squadron, we would

[136] National Park Service website for Yorktown.

[137] National Park Service website for Yorktown.

do some very good things," Lafayette wrote to Chevalier de La Luzerne, French minister to the United States.[138]

Lafayette made the same plea to Washington in August. Victory would surely be obtained, Lafayette implored, if Washington could lead a combined American-French army against Cornwallis and the French navy controlled the bays and rivers off of the coast of Virginia.

This time, Washington was several steps ahead of Lafayette. Washington and the French forces under Rochambeau were already on the move to Yorktown and the French navy, under de Grasse, was sailing towards the Chesapeake Bay with an impressively large fleet. On August 19, 6,500 troops, including 4,000 French soldiers, departed for Virginia. Presently, Washington would command an overwhelming force of 17,000 French and American soldiers at Yorktown and outnumber the British by more than 2–1.

By the end of August, the American army was south of Philadelphia, and de Grasse's naval contingent of about 40 ships was approaching the mouth of the Chesapeake Bay. An anxious Washington desired updates on news from Virginia. On September 2, Washington wrote Lafayette, "You see, how critically important the present moment is. If you get anything new from any quarter, send it I pray you on the spur of speed, for I am all impatience and anxiety."[139]

Lafayette's immediate task was to make sure Cornwallis didn't escape by land before Washington, de Grasse and Rochambeau arrived. Lafayette strategically positioned artillery surrounding Yorktown and deployed his troops. The perpetual lack of supplies caused Lafayette to secure needed food, medicine and munitions. Lafayette quickly needed assistance.

To obtain information on the movements of British troops, Lafayette sent spies into Yorktown. Their reports gave Lafayette

---

[138] National Park Service website for Yorktown.

[139] Ellis, p. 134.

valuable information, assisting him in formulating his plan to keep Cornwallis within the confines of Yorktown. Lafayette was spurred to do his duty as Washington implored Lafayette to not allow Cornwallis to escape to the Carolinas.

Washington had another worry; he wasn't sure of the location of de Grasse's armada. Washington wrote Lafayette, "I am distressed beyond expression to know what is become of the Count de Grasse, and for fear the English fleet, by occupying the Chesapeake . . . should frustrate all of our flattering prospects in that quarter."[140]

All of the elements necessary for a grand American victory were present, but not all of the pieces were in place. No wonder Washington was anxious and concerned.

Dutifully, Lafayette kept a close watch on Cornwallis's daily troop movements. Lafayette made sure Cornwallis was aware any attempt to depart Yorktown by land would be met by stiff resistance from Lafayette's troops. The two armies spent days eyeing and testing each other while waiting for reinforcements; Lafayette from Washington and the French and Cornwallis from Clinton and New York.

The shortage of provisions for Lafayette's troops was solved when de Grasse's force landed. Besides arms, ammunition and other supplies, de Grasse brought 3,000 French soldiers commanded by Marquis de Saint-Simon. The arrival cheered the spirits of the American troops. Wayne reported the "universal joy" felt by his troops. The night of de Grasse's arrival, Wayne hurried to meet with Lafayette. Wayne failed to hear a challenge by an American guard and the guard fired his weapon, wounding Wayne in the thigh. The injury kept Wayne out of action until September 12, two days before Washington's arrival in camp.

The French fleet approached the Chesapeake on the evening of August 29 and anchored at sea, about nine miles southeast of Cape Henry. At Lynnhaven Bay, 40 boatloads of Saint-Simon's

---

[140] Leckie, p. 651.

men landed. One of the disembarking French divisions had a special meaning for Lafayette. Lafayette's father was a member of the unit when he was killed at Minden.[141]

De Grasse's force controlled the headwaters of the James River, blocking any rescue attempt by the British navy of Cornwallis's troops. In the meantime, too late to save Cornwallis, Clinton realized Washington had outfoxed him in New York and dispatched a rescue team of soldiers and ships.

Before Washington arrived, de Grasse advocated for an immediate attack on Cornwallis. Lafayette faithfully followed Washington's instructions to prevent the British from escaping, not attacking. While a victory under Lafayette's leadership would secure him great accolades, Lafayette knew such an assault would lead to the deaths of many of his men. Lafayette waited for Washington.

When a British fleet under the leadership of Sir Thomas Graves did attempt a rescue of Cornwallis's troops, the strong French navy foiled the effort in an engagement known as the Battle of the Virginia Capes on September 5. Graves eventually returned to New York to form a more formidable British fleet. By the time Graves was able to return to Yorktown, Cornwallis had surrendered.

In Williamsburg on September 14, Rochambeau and Washington were reunited with Lafayette. All seemed to be going as planned until Washington met with de Grasse on his flagship, *Ville de Paris*. De Grasse informed Washington he was going to depart Virginia for the French West Indies because of the expected return of a large British flotilla. Washington issued an angry response to de Grasse, saying such a withdrawal would be a disgrace for the French and a disaster for the United States.

With a major victory slipping from his grasp, Washington once again turned to Lafayette to save America's independence.

---

[141] Jerome A. Greene, *The Guns of Independence: The Siege of Yorktown, 1781*, Savas Beatie, 2013, p. 70.

Lafayette met with de Grasse and urged the French admiral to stay the course and not to retreat to the French West Indies. De Grasse left five ships to block Cornwallis's escape from the York River and turned the rest of his fleet, 35 ships, to the Chesapeake Bay to face the British.

In his memoirs, Lafayette wrote, "The whole expedition was on the verge of failing. Washington begged me to go and see de Grasse and get him to change his mind. I succeeded and the siege of Yorktown began."

Once again, Lafayette's diplomatic abilities saved the United States.

Lafayette did suffer one negotiating setback. Lafayette made several requests to Washington to be placed second in command, under Washington, of all American forces at Yorktown. Since General Benjamin Lincoln was the senior officer, Washington insisted Lincoln remain second in command.

The siege of Yorktown was under way on September 28 as the combined French and American armies moved from Williamsburg to Yorktown. The allied forces tightened the circle around Yorktown and the British abandoned its outer defenses. From a journal of the Yorktown siege, "We would have been obliged to attack them by storm, which would only have been done with many losses. But the enemy abandoned the redoubts and batteries on the night of 29 to 30 Sept. We became aware of that on the morning of the 30th; our troops took possession of the area immediately; 100 men went into the redoubt of Pigeon Quarter and 50 into the one on Penny Hill. One of the neighboring batteries was changed into a redoubt, and we constructed an intermediate one at the head of the big ravine — this work was very much harassed by enemy fire."[142]

Cornwallis was not about to abandon hope, despite the setback. On September 29, a ship dispatched by Clinton made it

[142] American Friends of Lafayette: Journal of the siege of York in Virginia in the month of October 1781.

through the French blockade with a message for Cornwallis. Reinforcements were on the way, 23 ships and 5,000 men. The rescue team's expected departure date from New York City was October 5.

The defensive shell Cornwallis devised to protect the British army at Yorktown was frail. Washington ordered an artillery bombardment of the British defenses on October 6. "On the afternoon of the 9th, some batteries, both French and American, were ready to operate, and they opened fire. General Washington had proposed to M. le Marquis de Saint-Simon to take command on the left, which he did. Immediately the frigate and other warships withdrew precipitously. All the batteries opened fire and silenced the cannon of the enemy. On the same day, the shells on the left set fire to the moored vessel; it was sunk along with two other enemy ships. Most of the others stationed themselves on the opposite shore, next to Gloucester, to avoid the same fate."[143]

The capitulation of the British army was nearing.

Despite the shelling, Cornwallis's defense held firm at several sections of its inner defensive perimeter. Lafayette's light infantry opposed one of the stubborn British units. Washington reinforced Lafayette with two units, one under Hamilton and the other under John Laurens, the son of the former President of Congress. Washington's three young champions, Lafayette, Hamilton and Laurens, were ready to strike a crippling blow to the British defenses. To aid Laurens, Washington sent Colonel Gimat, Lafayette's former aide who helped rescue Lafayette at Brandywine. Lafayette wanted Gimat to lead one contingent, but Hamilton objected and Washington ordered Hamilton to lead the group of American soldiers.

After another shelling greatly weakened the British positions, Washington ordered an assault. Two columns, one French and one American participated. Lafayette was in command of his

---

[143] American Friends of Lafayette: Journal of the siege of York in Virginia in the month of October 1781.

wing as his troops stormed the Rock Redoubt fortification near the river during the early evening of October 14. The ferocious Americans quickly overwhelmed and drove the British from their fortifications.

In Lafayette's report to Washington on October 16, Lafayette heaped praise on Gimat, who was wounded in the foot, Laurens and all the men under his command. "Colonel Gimat led the van, and was followed by that of Colonel Hamilton, who commanded the whole advanced corps. At the same time, a party of 80 men under Colonel Laurens turned the redoubt. Hamilton's bravery and talents were on display. Not one gun was fired as the redoubt was quickly stormed. The Colonel was slightly wounded. The rest of the column under General Muhlenberg and Hazen advanced with admirable firmness and discipline. Major Barber distinguished himself and was wounded by a cannon ball. Wayne's Pennsylvanians were ready to give any assistance needed."[144]

As the allies bombarded Yorktown, Cornwallis made a desperate counterattack on October 15 but had no luck breaching Washington's strong position. The British retreated to the York River in a driving rain storm.

On October 17, the pounding by the allies was too much for the British troops to endure. Cornwallis sent a message to Washington. "Sir, I propose a cessation of hostilities for twenty-four hours, and that two officers may be appointed by each side . . . to settle terms for the surrender of the posts of York (Yorktown) and Gloucester."

Washington refused to halt hostilities for a day, as Cornwallis requested. Later on October 17, Cornwallis conceded and an offer to surrender was proffered. Washington entered into negotiations with Cornwallis for the British army's surrender. Washington wouldn't agree—at Lafayette's insistence—to Cornwallis's request to be allowed to surrender with "customary honours." Cornwallis had denied the "customary honours" request when

---

[144] Lafayette memoirs, pp. 443–444.

American General Lincoln surrendered at Charleston. Under "customary honours" a surrendering garrison was permitted to march out with drums beating and flags flying, after which they would become prisoners of war or granted free passage.

The formal orders of capitulation were signed on October 19. Cornwallis claimed he was ill and wasn't able to attend the surrender ceremony at a field just outside Yorktown. Cornwallis sent General Charles O'Hara in his place. When O'Hara attempted to surrender Cornwallis's sword to Frenchman Rochambeau, Rochambeau declined. Washington was the American commander-in-chief and should receive the honor. Lafayette stood by Washington as Washington ordered O'Hara to present the sword to General Lincoln.

Lafayette watched as the British silently marched between lines of American and French soldiers and laid down their arms.

> It was evident to us that the English, in their misfortune, were particularly driven to despair by being obligated to lay down their arms before the Americans; for their officers and soldiers put on a show of turning their heads toward the French line. Lafayette noticed this and avenged it in a very pleasant manner; he ordered the band of his light infantry to play the melody of *Yankee Doodle*, a melody which the English had applied to a song they had composed to ridicule us at the beginning of the war, and which they had never failed to sing in front of the prisoners that they had made of us. They were so thin-skinned at this pleasantry that many of them smashed their arms in anger while laying them down on the slopes.[145]

---

[145] Lafayette in America in 1824 and 1825, pp 210–211.

The surrender by Cornwallis marked the beginning of the end of England's oppressive rule of Americans. Independence was in the not too far distant future.

Lafayette wrote to French Prime Minister Maurepas on the day after the surrender,

"The play is over, Monsieur le Comte, the fifth act has just come to an end."[146]

The headline star player in the Virginia play was none other than Lafayette. In just a few months, The Marquis dueled Cornwallis's superior army across the state, boxed in Cornwallis forces at Yorktown, alerted Washington to a golden opportunity to cripple the British army, stormed a British stronghold at Yorktown and mended a potentially disastrous disagreement with the allied French navy.

The young French General who first shed blood on the field of the Battle of Brandywine, earned the right to be called an American hero.

---

[146] Unger, 159.

17

Return to Adrienne

With Lafayette's stature as an American hero fully earned, recognized and documented by the leaders of the American Revolution, the young Frenchman's next goal was a return to France and a reunion with Adrienne and his young family.

Lafayette wrote his wife on October 22: "The end of this campaign is truly brilliant for the allied troops. There was a rare coordination in our movements, and I would be finicky indeed if I were not pleased with the end of my campaign in Virginia. You must have been informed of all the toil the superiority and talents of Lord Cornwallis gave me and of the advantage that we then gained in recovering lost ground, until at length we had Lord Cornwallis in the position we needed in order to capture him. It was then everyone pounced on him. I count this amongst the happiest epochs of my life."[147]

In the letter, Lafayette had some kind words for his Virginia opponent. "I pity Lord Cornwallis, for whom I have the highest respect; he is kind enough to express some esteem for me." The slight of General Lincoln at Charleston had been repaid, according to Lafayette, and he promised not to pursue his vow of vengeance.

---

[147] Lafayette memoirs, p. 446.

According to Lafayette's memoirs, he wrote to French Foreign Minister Vergennes on October 20 and told him of the Yorktown victory. No English general will again attempt to conquer America, Lafayette vowed. Vergennes, who vehemently opposed Lafayette's first voyage to the United States in 1777, praised Lafayette and gave Lafayette primary credit for subduing Cornwallis.

Lafayette approached Washington for his blessing to return to France, and Washington whole-heartedly agreed. Since the war was not over and America still needed France's involvement, Washington asked Lafayette to once again be an advocate in France and Europe for the United States. Washington was especially concerned about France continuing to offer naval support. Lafayette's memoirs stated a "constant naval superiority would terminate the war speedily. Without it, I do not know that it will ever be terminated honorably."

The month after Cornwallis's surrender at Yorktown, Lafayette traveled to Philadelphia to petition Congress for permission to take a leave of absence from the American army. Lafayette noted he saw no prospect of active operations in the near future. In fact, Lafayette had held his sword in defense of America for the last time. Congress granted his request to return to Adrienne and praised Lafayette's conduct in America. Congress also wanted Lafayette to help secure a loan from France and continue to be a liaison between the United States and France.

Lafayette was promised a royal welcome in France. A letter dated December 5 from the Minister of Defense Marquis de Segur to Lafayette indicated King Louis XVI was pleased with Lafayette's accomplishments in America. Lafayette could count upon the King's future kindness, according to de Segur. Also, Lafayette was informed the King had renewed his rank of brigadier general in France's army. De Segur wrote France's old warriors admired Lafayette and young ones made Lafayette their model.

In France, all of the royalists who opposed Lafayette in 1777 now universally praised him. King Louis XVI awarded Lafayette the highest military honor available, the Cross of St. Louis.

The Château de Chavaniac was constructed in the 14th century. The General Lafayette was born here in 1757. He was married in 1774 to Adrienne de Noailles. They had four children together. Henriette, who died at a young age, Anastasie, Georges and Virginie who lived in the castle. The French and American flags fly permanently over the château in honor of the key role Lafayette played in the French and American revolutions.

Wife of Lafayette,
Marie Adrienne
Francoise de Noailles.
French School
18th Century Art

The Marquis de Lafayette

The Marquis de Lafayette first meets
George Washington on August 5, 1777.
Postcard By Currier & Ives

Lafayette (center) being introduced by Baron Johann de Kalb (left) to Silas Deane. 1879 Alonzo Chappel print.

Ceremonial Sword of Gilbert du Motier, Marquis de Lafayette

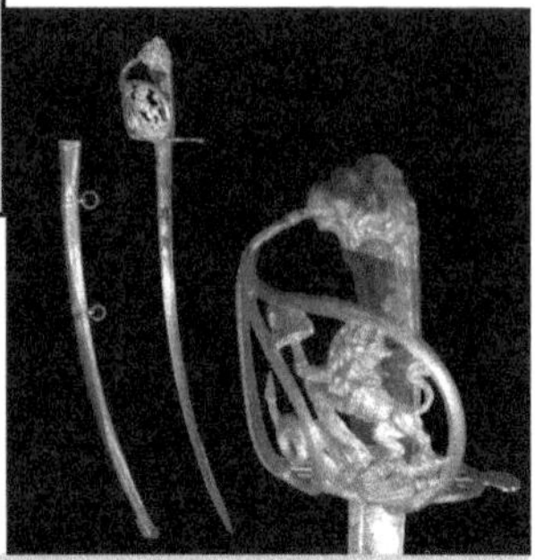

Statue of Lafayette in front of the Governor Palace in Metz, where he decided to join the American cause.

Anonymous miniature of
Patrick Ferguson,
c. 1774-77
from a private collection

During the American War for Independence, a young Scottish officer by the name of **Patrick Ferguson** introduced his version of a military breech loading rifle. It was an adaptation of an earlier breech loading sporting arm first developed by Isaac de la Chaumette. After receiving a patent in 1776, the design caught the eye of the British War Office. Compared to the standard British firearm of the time, the "Brown Bess," the Ferguson Rifle outperformed it in accuracy and speed of loading and firing. Ferguson's demonstrations for King George III and the British War Office won its approval. The rifle became the first breech loading rifle to be placed into official service by any army in the world.

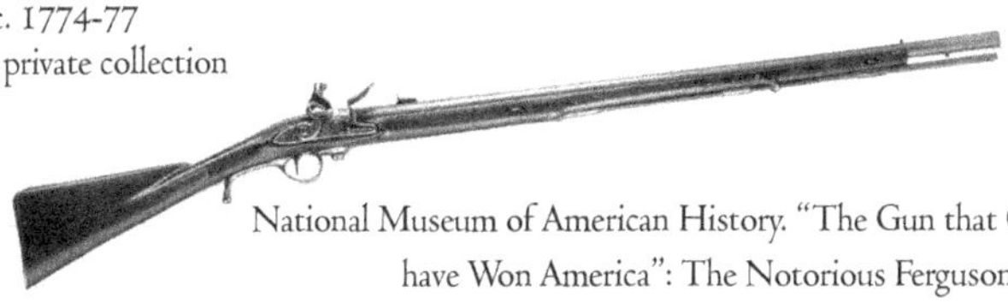

National Museum of American History. "The Gun that Could have Won America": The Notorious Ferguson Rifle

Lafayette wounded at the Battle of Brandywine. Lafayette recovered to finish the war and enjoy victory. Jean-Joseph Sourbader de Gimat noticed Lafayette's loss of blood after Lafayette received his leg wound. Gimat helped Lafayette to his horse and away from the advancing British army.

The John Chad House. Lafayette and General George Washington spent part of the morning of September 11, 1777 at the John Chad house observing the British army on the western side of the Brandywine River. The house, built in 1712, is owned by the Chadds Ford Historical Society.

— Lafayette's Headquarters —

The Barn

Lafayette visited Gideon Gilpin, a Quaker farmer, when he returned to Brandywine in 1825. Lafayette's secretary stated Lafayette stayed with Gilpin the night before the Battle of Brandywine. Gilpin's farm and home is known as Lafayette's Headquarters, even though no direct evidence exists that Lafayette did or did not spend September 10, 1777 with Gilpin.

Paintings by Heather Davis, Everett, PA

Portrait of Louis XVI
King of France and Navarre
(1754-1793)
Artist: Joseph Duplessis

James Armistead Lafayette

James Armistead volunteered to be a spy for Lafayette with the permission of William Armistead, his master. James Armistead, acted as an escaped slave within Cornwallis's camp. Later, James Armistead changed his name to James Armistead Lafayette.

The Battle of Cowpens, painted by William Ranney in 1845.
The scene depicts an unnamed black U.S. soldier (left) firing his pistol and saving the life of Colonel William Washington (on white horse in center).

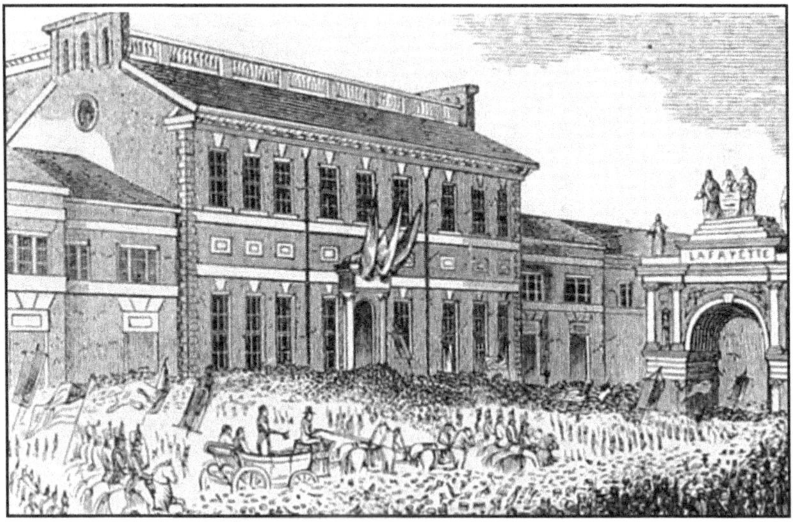

Lithograph of The Lafayette Welcoming Parade of 1824 was a parade held in Philadelphia to welcome the arrival of the Marquis de Lafayette on the occasion of his visit to the United States for a sixteen-month tour. Date: September 28, 1824
Organized by City of Philadelphia

King George III of England

Henry Laurens served as a President of the Continental Congress. On a mission to France, the British took him prisoner and incarcerated him in the Tower of London. After a brutal captivity he gained his freedom through a prisoner exchange.

James Monroe was the fifth President of the United States (1817–1825) and the last President from the Founding Fathers.

Portrait of James Monroe, The White House Historical Association. Created circa 1819

Bronze Mourning medal for Lafayette marking his death. Used by Adam Wert as a paper weight on his desk.

J. Howard Wert Gettysburg Collection ™

1. Silk ribbon honoring Lafayette's return to Philadelphia for the 50th Anniversary of the United States in 1826. The ribbon was worn Adam Wert of Gettysburg. Several Wert family members were commissioned officers during the Revolution. **2.** Patriotic silk ribbon commemorating Lafayette's Grand Visitation in 1824 and 1825 and marking the 50th Anniversary of the United States in 1826. Given to J. Howard Wert by Col. Aylette, grandson of Patrick Henry of Virginia. **3.** Mourning ribbon marking the death of Lafayette. The ribbon honored Lafayette and was worn by Adam Wert, soldier of the War of 1812.

1

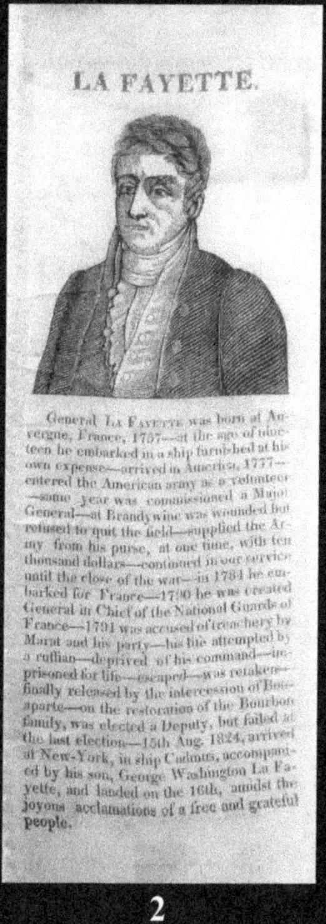

2

3

Plaza Lafayette in Pauillac, France where Lafayette set sail to America on March 25, 1777

The Nathanael Greene Monument in Savannah, Georgia. Located in Johnson Square, the monument honors Nathanael Greene, a general in the Continental Army during the American Revolutionary War.

American General John Pershing sent his aide Colonel Charles E. Stanton to Lafayette's grave to plant an American flag.

Lafayette's grave in Picpus cemetary in Paris, France

The Cross of Saint Louis, the highest military honor available, was awarded Lafayette

Reports of Lafayette's triumphs throughout America were recounted throughout his home country. A newspaper article relating to Yorktown stated: "The general who contributed most to the success of this great enterprise is without contradiction the Marquis de Lafayette. It is he who followed Cornwallis step by step, who harassed him unceasingly, who drove him back into Yorktown, and who prepared his downfall. Americans as well as Frenchmen, and even the enemy, pronounce the warmest praise of this young nobleman."[148]

Americans joined in praising Lafayette. An American officer wrote, "It is no trifling compliment to say that next to the Commander in Chief and the intrepid Greene, no general stood higher in the public favor or more constantly commanded the admiration of the army than Lafayette."[149]

---

[148] Lane, p. 68.

[149] Lane, p. 69.

Lafayette was the guest of honor at many celebrations as he made his way to his departure point, Boston. Lafayette's fellow French officers returning home with Lafayette joined in the festivities. One Frenchman was quoted as saying fighting through the British army was easier than navigating the celebrations thrown in Lafayette's honor.

After writing a farewell note to Washington, Lafayette departed from Boston on Christmas Day, 1781, on the frigate *Alliance*. He touched French soil on January 17, 1782. Immediately, Lafayette took a coach to the Hôtel de Noailles and reached home on the afternoon of January 21. Adrienne was away, attending a royal function. When news of Lafayette's return reached Queen Marie-Antoinette, the Queen escorted Adrienne in one of her carriages to greet Lafayette. The Queen personally congratulated Lafayette on his successes.

Lafayette's daughter wrote that her mother was overjoyed to see Lafayette and for days Adrienne would feel faint every time Lafayette left her side. One of Lafayette's first tasks was to find a home for his family. That task was accomplished in the summer.

Visitors were aplenty, especially Americans as Lafayette was a magnet for those wishing to discuss America's freedom and independence. Lafayette did more than discuss America's situation. As he promised Washington and Congress, Lafayette acted on behalf of the United States in Versailles and attempted to secure more loans and other assistance from France. Lafayette kept in close contact with his friend Benjamin Franklin, even though gout slowed Franklin's movements. Franklin assured Washington that Lafayette continued to be dedicated to assisting the United States.

After Yorktown, peace was tantalizing close. As England indicated a willingness to talk with both the United States and France, Lafayette couldn't resist becoming deeply involved in the negotiations. Lafayette insisted the British release an important American prisoner before any talk of peace could commence.

Since his capture in 1780, former Congressional President Henry Laurens had been held in the Tower of London, the only American prisoner in history to be so confined. After months of captivity, Laurens was released from the London fortress and paroled on December 31, 1781. Laurens' kindness to Lafayette after the Battle of Brandywine was repaid in full. As Laurens was without income or assets in England, Lafayette financially supported Laurens until Laurens was able to depart London. Laurens was exchanged for Cornwallis, who was paroled by Washington after Yorktown.

In February 1782, the English Parliament voted to discontinue the war against the United States, expressing total dissatisfaction with the way the war was handled. By the end of March, England began peace talks with French representatives and Franklin.

England at first seemed willing to agree to a peace pact with the allies. The English attitude changed somewhat after English naval victories over a French and then a Spanish fleet. In one of the engagements, the Battle of the Saintes, French Admiral de Grasse was captured.

England was having second thoughts about giving the United States its freedom.

The negotiations among the representatives of France, England, Spain and the United States were tense. An agreement was not assured. The War of Rebellion was on the verge of reigniting. At one point, Lafayette accused the English representative, Richard Oswald, of not negotiating in good faith.

Lafayette had more on his agenda than the peace talks with the British. He was attempting to secure a loan from Holland for the United States. He also tended to other diplomatic matters for the United States and attended court functions at Versailles. Adrienne was included in royal assignments. She was an official royal escort when Russian royalty visited Versailles. In the coming troubling years for her family, Adrienne would use her royal contacts to help her family survive.

In the summer of 1782, Adrienne's duties at court dwindled as she and Lafayette oversaw the renovations of their new home in Paris. Also, Adrienne was pregnant. She delivered a daughter, two months premature, in September. Adrienne and Lafayette called her Marie Antoinette-Virginie. The name, obviously, honored the French queen and Lafayette's association with the United States.

With England balking at signing a peace accord, Lafayette advocated for additional French military aid for the United States. France did not have the financial ability to solely pay for a renewed war against England. France made arrangements to team with Spain to oppose their mutual enemy, England. A huge joint operation against England in the West Indies, Canada and the United States was being planned by France and Spain. Of course, Lafayette was prepared to lead troops against England. Lafayette sailed to Cádiz, Spain, to join the newly formed French-Spanish taskforce.

Learning of the joint operation against the forces of King George III, England agreed to a preliminary peace treaty. More intrigue was taking place behind the scenes as England maneuvered to prevent France from controlling the United States after the war concluded. At the same time, the United States was wary of France's ultimate goals for the new country. After all, early in the war French officials wanted its own general to lead the American forces and desired to recapture land lost to the British in the Seven Years War.

Lafayette intended to take news of the peace agreement to the United States but abruptly cancelled his travel plans. His diplomatic skills and stature as a nobleman and world leader were desperately needed by the United States. Spain was balking at recognizing the United States as a nation and refused to officially receive any American official at court. The implication was frightening to the United States. If Spain failed to recognize the United States, a war with Spain was almost assured.

Spain's desires were questioned by Congress. Did Spain want to become the third country, along with France and England, to dominate America?

Spanish King Charles III refused to see American representatives but couldn't turn down a request by Lafayette for an audience. Dressed in his American uniform, Lafayette was granted a session with the King. After answering questions about his exploits in the American War of Independence, Lafayette assured King Charles III that America sought peaceful relations with Spain and didn't intend on liberating Spanish possessions in America. After two weeks of negotiations, Spain recognized the designated American envoy, William Carmichael, former aide to Franklin. Lafayette was credited with paving the way for Spanish recognition of American independence.

While not being about to personally deliver the good news, Lafayette did send letters to Washington and other American officials concerning the peace agreement with England. As news spread in America, Lafayette was once again hailed as a key player in attaining America's independence.

With his service to America concluded, Lafayette turned to personal matters. He visited his boyhood home, tended to his family and even took a vacation with his wife. He wrote a farewell letter to Washington, asking Washington to remember his adopted son.

On September 3, 1783, the United States and England agreed to the Peace Treaty of Paris. The signing took place near Lafayette's new French home. The United States officially won the war and its freedom. At the same time, French and Spanish diplomats entered into a similar agreement with England at the Palace of Versailles.

England was a defeated world power. The United States was a fledging nation.

Peace did not uncouple Lafayette from the United States or Washington. Correspondence continued and Washington invited Lafayette for a visit. In return, Lafayette and Adrienne invited George and Martha Washington to visit France. The Washingtons declined the invitations, citing family obligations and age considerations.

Despite admitting leaving Adrienne and his children would be difficult, Lafayette pursued his visit to see Washington. Lafayette and his aide, Chevalier de Caraman, departed on the ship *Le Courrier de l'Europe* for New York City. During the journey, Lafayette rediscovered seasickness.

In August 1784, Lafayette was back in his adoptive land, America. The returning hero received lavish welcomes as he journeyed across the country. The celebrations were just a prelude to the wild welcoming festivities he would receive during his 1824–1825 grand visit.

During his years of fighting with Washington, Lafayette never had the opportunity to visit New York City. The British controlled the town all during the revolution. On August 5, 1784, Lafayette entered the vibrant American city for the first time. Adoring Americans turned out to see the great Marquis. Lafayette was feted that night by former comrades in arms. The next day Lafayette was given a tour of the city by General Gates, the same general who was a member of the Conway Cabal. Lafayette's clash with Gates about Washington's leadership was not an issue.

After another day full of honors, Lafayette departed New York City for Philadelphia. The elite City Troop of Horse of Philadelphia and civilians joined Lafayette for the final miles of the journey into the city. Not to be outdone by New York citizens, Philadelphia inhabitants celebrated his arrival in style. During his stay, an honor was bestowed upon Lafayette by the Pennsylvania legislature; the county of Fayette was named in his honor. Counties and towns throughout the country would eventually be named for Lafayette.

The celebrations continued as General Wayne and officers of the Pennsylvania Line that served with Lafayette, hosted a dinner for the visiting French hero. Lafayette called the Pennsylvania officers his "brothers."

Lafayette had another "adopted" family member, Washington, to visit during his return to America. After a stop at Baltimore,

Lafayette traveled to Mount Vernon. Lafayette wrote to Adrienne that the meeting was joyful and deeply moving. Lafayette proudly informed Adrienne that portraits of them and their family were hung in honor in Washington's home.

Lafayette had a surprise for Washington. Lafayette presented a treasured gift to Washington from Adrienne, a Masonic apron she made for her husband's surrogate father. Washington reportedly proudly wore the apron to Masonic events for years.

For 10 days, Lafayette lived with Washington and Washington's family. Many visitors called upon Lafayette at Mount Vernon, including George Augustine Washington. He was Lafayette's aide in the Virginia campaign. Lafayette's days were filled with chats with Washington concerning past experiences and current events. Lafayette spent hours touring Mount Vernon with its proud owner, Washington.

Lafayette took his leave of Washington on August 28 and then traveled to Annapolis and Baltimore, where the celebrations continued. New York, Maryland and other states all joined in declaring Lafayette an honorary citizen. Years later, Congress officially approved Lafayette as the sixth foreign national to be given honorary American citizenship.

While in New York City, Congress asked Lafayette to join a delegation tasked with making peace with Six Nations, the Indian consortium, at Lake Oneida in the northern section of New York State. Lafayette journeyed 200 miles through cold weather to participate in the vital meeting. At the conference, Lafayette was a central character in the negotiations. Lafayette was introduced to the attendees by his Iroquois name, Kayewla. Lafayette urged the Six Nations to make a peace settlement. Such an agreement was reached after Lafayette departed.

Lafayette continued his tour with stops in Hartford, Connecticut, and in Boston. General Knox was waiting for his old friend with a fife and drum corps as Lafayette approached the Massachusetts town. Lafayette took time to visit another dear military friend, General Greene, in Providence, Rhode Island.

After two weeks, Lafayette set sail for an American Revolution sacred location, Yorktown. More celebrations were held in Virginia at Williamsburg and Richmond.

A return visit to Mount Vernon was next on Lafayette's schedule. For four days Lafayette and Washington continued their intimate discussions. Washington decided to accompany Lafayette to New York City, where the Marquis would embark for his trip back home to France. After a number of lengthy celebrations along the way, Washington decided to cut short his escort of Lafayette. On December 1, 1784, the two close friends and comrades parted company for the last time. Washington returned to Mount Vernon. Lafayette continued to Philadelphia and then to Trenton to bid Congress farewell before continuing to New York City. At Philadelphia, James Monroe wrote he was thrilled to see his old comrade, Lafayette.

While waiting for his ship to be repaired in New York, Lafayette spent time with his friends, Greene, Hamilton and Knox. The frigate *Nymphe* was ready to sail on December 22, 1784. Lafayette would return to French soil on January 20, 1785.

·18·

Slavery

As Lafayette and Washington enjoyed the pleasures of Mount Vernon, some of their intimate conversations undoubtedly included the subject of slavery. At least, reminders of slavery surrounded them as the more than 100 slaves Washington owned worked the vast Virginia estate. Additional slaves belonging to Washington's wife also tended to Mount Vernon.

For some time, Lafayette advocated ending slavery. In a February 5, 1783, letter, according to Diane Windham Shaw, was the "first inkling that Lafayette wished to take action in the cause of emancipation." Shaw is director Emerita of Special Collections and College Archives at Lafayette College, a Lafayette expert and a member of the American Friends of Lafayette.

The lengthy letter, Shaw noted, "contained a startling paragraph requesting Washington's collaboration in an experiment to emancipate slaves and use them instead as tenant farmers."

Slavery was an issue that bothered Washington all during his life. Washington frequently spoke about the subject and many times expressed his desire to end the inhuman practice. On April 12, 1786, Washington wrote to his friend and the financier of the American Revolution Robert Morris, "I can only say that there is not a man living who wishes more sincerely than I do to see a plan adopted for the abolition of (slavery)."[150]

In a lecture Shaw gave for The American Friends of Lafayette titled *A Sanctuary for the Rights of Mankind: Lafayette and Human Rights,* she said, "As radical as the suggestion may have been, it is not surprising that it was Washington's aid that Lafayette hoped to enlist. The relationship between the two men was like that of father and son, and Lafayette knew how influential such an action by Washington could prove. Promising to lend his own support to make such a plan work in the West Indies, Lafayette told Washington: 'If it be a wild scheme, I had rather be mad that way, than to be thought wise on the other track.'"

Lafayette's letter to Washington, referenced by Shaw, stated, "Now, my dear General, that you are going to enjoy some peace and quiet, permit me to propose a plan to you which might become greatly beneficial to the black part of mankind. Let us unite in purchasing a small estate where we might try the experiment to free the Negroes and use them only as tenants. Such an example as yours might render it a general practice, and if we succeed in America, I will cheerfully devote a part of my time to render the method fashionable in the West Indies. If it be a wild scheme, I would rather be made this way than to be thought wise in the other tack."[151]

"Washington," Shaw said, "responded warmly to Lafayette on this occasion." Washington's reply to Lafayette on April 5, 1783, stated, "Your scheme . . . to encourage the emancipation of the black people of this country from that state of bondage in which they are held is a striking evidence of the benevolence of your heart. I shall be happy to join you in so laudable a work."[152] Washington never did so.

[150] Bruce Chadwick, *George Washington's War: The Forging of a Revolutionary Leader and the American Presidency*, Sourcebooks, Inc., Naperville, Illinois, 2004, p. 403.

[151] Lane, pages, 79–80.

[152] Chadwick, p. 403.

Washington, who inherited a slave at age 11 when his father died, did not free his slaves during his lifetime. Washington's will directed that his slaves be set free upon his death.

While John Adams was minister to England in 1786, Lafayette wrote a pointed letter about slavery and the United States. "Whatever be the complexion of the enslaved, it does not, in my opinion, alter the complexion of the crime which the enslaver commits. . . . It is to me a matter of great anxiety and concern, to find that this trade is sometimes perpetuated under the flag of liberty, our dear and noble stripes, to which virtue and glory have been constant standard bearers."[153]

In 1785, Lafayette began negotiations to purchase two plantations with slaves in the French colony of Guyane, known today as French Guiana. The number of slaves involved was 48. Another 22 slaves were included when a third location, called La Gabrielle, was included in Lafayette's design. The plantations were located on the coast near the city of Cayenne.

Shaw explained Lafayette's idea, "According to the plan, which was administered by Lafayette's agents in Cayenne, the slaves were paid for their labor, schooling was provided, and the sale of any slave was expressly forbidden. Lafayette hoped to show that the birth rate would rise and infant mortality would decrease under these more favorable conditions, thus undercutting the need for the slave trade."

Also, Lafayette changed the disciplinary system and mandated blacks and whites were punished the same for like offenses. The hoped end result for Lafayette was to eventually divide the land among the former slaves.

Adrienne was an enthusiastic partner in the Guyane project. Her daughter Virginie wrote, "My mother had a deep need to propagate good and was horrified by all injustice. She was thrilled by my father's decision to work for abolition of the slave trade. When he bought La Belle Gabrielle, her zealous belief in just and

153 Lane, p. 93.

liberal ideas made her search ardently for means to put those ideas into immediate practice."[154]

Alas, Lafayette's grand idea failed. Shaw explained, "As Lafayette's attentions were increasingly drawn to the unfolding revolutionary drama in France of 1789, the running of the Cayenne estates fell to his wife Adrienne. She relished the role and corresponded frequently with the estate managers as well as with the priests at a nearby seminary whom she asked to look after the religious welfare of the slaves. When Lafayette became a prisoner-of-war of the Austrians in 1792, his properties were confiscated and the Cayenne blacks were resold as slaves."

Before the French Revolution subjugated his life, Lafayette became active in several anti-slavery societies in Europe and America. "Lafayette took an active role in the French Society of the Friends of Blacks formed in 1788 to promote the abolition of the slave trade and he was influential in the passage of the 1791 decree which gave rights of citizenship to free men of color in the French colonies," Shaw wrote in her presentation.

Speaking in the National Assembly Lafayette "argued eloquently that free men are citizens, that free men of color are also men and therefore deserving of the same rights. 'Now I ask,' he said, 'Are they human beings? I do think so!' Even though this decree affected only a small proportion of blacks in the French colonies, the white colonists refused to honor it, setting off a slave revolt that would eventually become the Haitian Revolution," Shaw stated.

Washington was not the only one closely connected with Lafayette's service in America who was conflicted about slavery. Members of the Laurens family held divergent views.

Henry Laurens, President of the Continental Congress, assisted Lafayette after his wounding at Brandywine, and later Lafayette helped to secure Laurens's release from the Tower of London. Laurens himself was a rice planter and slave trader from

---

[154] Unger, p 210.

South Carolina. He was a partner in the Austin and Laurens slave-trading firm, reputed to be one of the largest in the South. Laurens' son, John, was an aide to Washington and a Revolutionary War friend of Lafayette. John Laurens opposed the family business of slavery.

Shaw wrote, "At some point during his service in the American Revolution, Lafayette began to be interested in the welfare of the enslaved people that he had encountered when he first arrived on American shores. Lafayette was undoubtedly influenced by the ideas of his friend, John Laurens, a fellow aide-de-camp to George Washington and the proponent of a plan to offer slaves their freedom in exchange for their service in the Continental Army."

In 1779, John Laurens gained approval from Congress for his plan to recruit a brigade of 3,000 slaves by promising them freedom in return for fighting. The plan was defeated by political opposition in South Carolina. Laurens was killed in the battle of the Combahee River, near Beaufort, South Carolina, in August 1782.

Lafayette's 1784 visit to America provided an opportunity for the Frenchman to help a slave gain his freedom. The slave acted as a spy for Lafayette during the Virginia campaign.

James Armistead volunteered to be a spy for Lafayette with the permission of William Armistead, his master. James Armistead, acted as an escaped slave within Cornwallis's camp. The British recruited James to be a counter spy, but James remained loyal to Lafayette and gave Lafayette valuable information during the siege of Yorktown. According to reports, Cornwallis visited Lafayette after the surrender and saw his spy James "looking at home in Lafayette's quarters."[155]

Lafayette wrote a testimonial in 1784 that was offered to the Virginia General Assembly. In 1787, James was granted freedom and changed his surname to Lafayette. Lafayette wrote, "This is to certify that the bearer by the name of James has done essential services to me while I had the honor to command in this state.

[155] Diane Shaw, *Rights of Mankind: Lafayette and Human Rights.*

His intelligences from the enemy's camp were industriously collected and faithfully delivered. He perfectly acquitted himself with some important commissions I gave him and appears to me entitled to every reward his situation can admit of. Done under my hand, Richmond, November 21st, 1784."

Lafayette clashed openly with one American leader, Thomas Jefferson, on the slavery issue. In 1807, Lafayette wrote to Jefferson that he was pleased that the slave trade in England had been abolished. Jefferson stated slavery was wrong but kept his own slaves.

"Lafayette and Jefferson had argued vigorously about allowing slavery into the western territories of the United States. Jefferson defended it saying that it would not increase the total number of slaves in America. Lafayette was aghast, asking how he could possibly condone the spread of so abhorrent a system. Thomas Clarkson, the great British abolitionist always claimed that Lafayette had told him: "I never would have drawn my sword in the service of America, if I could have conceived thereby that I was founding a land of slavery," Shaw reported in her lecture.

Shaw also reported on an exchange between Jefferson and Lafayette during a carriage ride reported by the driver, Israel Jefferson. "The conversation turned upon the condition of the colored people—the slaves. . . . On this occasion my ears were eagerly taking in every sound that proceeded from the venerable patriot's mouth. Lafayette remarked that he thought that the slaves ought to be free; that no man could rightly hold ownership in his brother man; that he gave his best services to and spent his money in behalf of the Americans freely because he felt that they were fighting for a great and noble principle—the freedom of mankind; that instead of all being free a portion were held in bondage (which seemed to grieve his noble heart)."

After surviving the horrors of the French Revolution and imprisonment, Lafayette again addressed the issue of slavery during his tour of the United States in 1824–1825. Shaw quoted one talk by Lafayette:

> I have been so long the friend of emancipation, particularly as regards these otherwise most happy states, that I behold with the sincerest pleasure the commencement of an institution, whose progress and termination will, I trust, be attended by the most successful results. I shall probably not live to witness the vast changes in the condition of man, which are about to take place in the world; but the era is already commenced, its progress is apparent, its end is certain. France will, ere long, give freedom to her few colonies. In England, the Parliament leaders, urged by the people, will urge the government to some acts preparatory to the emancipation of her slave holding colonies. . . . South America is crushing the evil. . . . Where then, my dear sir, will be the last foothold of slavery, in the world? Is it destined to be the opprobrium of this fine country?

During the southern part of Lafayette's tour, he took time to greet a delegation of black War of 1812 veterans in New Orleans, shaking hands with each. He also visited homes of slaves and free blacks.

Lafayette's promotion of emancipation was not looked upon kindly by southern leaders. At least three newspapers, Shaw reported, printed notices that owners should keep their slaves away when Lafayette spoke.

As Shaw's lecture reported, "The *Savannah Georgian* printed a letter from the mayor that read: 'The citizens of Savannah are respectfully requested as much as possible to confine to their own yards and houses, their servants and especially the children, whilst military honors are paying to General Lafayette. The City Marshals and City Constables are required to take into custody all such negroes and persons of color as may be found at all trespassing upon or attending the procession, parades, etc., during the stay of General Lafayette in this city.'"

Among the former slaves visited by Lafayette were James Armistead Lafayette and Hannah Till, a 104-year-old black woman who had been a servant for both Lafayette and Washington during the revolution. When Lafayette discovered Till was to be evicted from her home, he paid her rent, according to Shaw.

During the tour, Lafayette greatly impressed a future Boston abolitionist, Lewis Hayden. Hayden was 10 years old when he saw Lafayette. Shaw reported Hayden's reaction:

> Lafayette . . . was in full march under the town militia escort, with Henry Clay as its immediate conductor. I went a mile to meet them and found the fences lined with people. Lafayette was in a barouche drawn by four horses and as he passed the people he bowed to them on both sides. When he passed me he bowed to the fence I was on. I looked around and saw no one else on the fence and what did I do but roll right down on the ground, frightened almost to death . . . Lafayette was the most famous man I had ever heard of, and you can imagine how I felt, a slave-boy to be favored with his recognition. That act burnt his image upon my heart so that I never shall need a permit to recall it. I date my hatred of slavery from that day, and I tell you that after I allowed no moving thing on the face of the earth to stand between me and my freedom.

The American Revolution spurred Lafayette to devote his life to freedom and independence. For many African Americans, those goals wouldn't be achieved until the next major American conflict, the Civil War.

·19·

French Revolution

Life was grand for Lafayette when he returned to France from his 1784 visit to America. Lafayette was hailed as a hero in two worlds; he had a loving family; he was financially secure despite his lavish spending on the American Revolution; he was respected by his fellow French citizens; and he was a favored member of the royal court.

Lafayette and Adrienne hosted parties where visiting American dignitaries mingled with French leaders. Working hard, Lafayette attempted to strengthen commercial ties between France and America. The Lafayette home was considered a home away from home for those from the United States.

In the royal court, Lafayette and Adrienne became favored members. The King welcomed Lafayette, partly because of his hero status and partly because Lafayette was a favorite of his subjects. Lafayette brought favorable attention to the King and his country. Adrienne retained her connections in the royal court as the Queen considered Adrienne a confidant.

All would change for Lafayette, Adrienne, their family and all of France in the coming French Revolution. Lafayette and Adrienne were imprisoned and their lives threatened. Family members and friends were executed. To keep their son safe, Adrienne sent their son George Washington Lafayette to the United States to stay with General George Washington. Lafayette and Adrienne became destitute.

A decade of misery was ahead for Lafayette and Adrienne.

Major causes of Lafayette's decline included his dedication to personal liberty for all; his endorsement of an Americanized governing system in France, or at least one modeled after England; his refusal to bend on his principles; and his powerful political enemies.

Despite what Lafayette meant to America, a lifeline would not come his way from his adopted country, the United States. The newly established country desperately needed the commerce trade with France to grow and thrive. Also, the United States couldn't survive a disastrous war between France and the United States. By intervening on Lafayette's behalf, a conflict was possible.

For a myriad of reasons, the citizens of France were becoming increasingly angered by the rule of King Louis XVI. The monarchy was in financial difficulty and taxes became burdensome for the citizens. A food shortage existed along with a sense of lawlessness, as bands of robbers prayed on countryside travelers. The French citizenry was broke, hungry, threatened, and without a voice in their government.

Besides the pockets of Frenchmen being empty, French government coffers were bare. The country was heavily in debt because of the costs of fighting the losing Seven Years War, the building of a first-rate navy and support for America's War for Independence. Also, citizens were questioning the exemption from taxation of land owned by the Catholic Church and the nobility. A religious conflict was ongoing in France. Queen Marie Antoinette didn't escape criticism as she was chastised for her outlandish spending on her lavish lifestyle.

In 1787, An Assembly of Notables was called by King Louis XVI to approve new taxes. Lafayette was appointed to take part in the assembly but didn't agree with the royal proposal. The

King continued to push implementation of his taxes, and the King continued to receive resistance.

During the French Revolution, in true Lafayette fashion, he tried to mediate between the King and his nobles, and the people. He spent time composing a bill of rights and a constitutional monarch with the people being empowered in a legislative assembly. As time passed, despite Lafayette's heroic efforts, he ultimately failed. By 1792, Lafayette was reviled by both the royalists and the radicals who had then control of France.

From the shores of the United States, Washington saw the dangers swirling around his trusted comrade Lafayette, and warned the Frenchman, in letters, to be careful. "I do not like the situation of affairs in France," Washington wrote. "Little more irritation would be necessary to blow up the spark of discontent into a flame that might not easily be quenched."[156]

Washington was a soothsayer in this instance. A spark ignited a bloody revolution unlike the one just won in America.

Lafayette and some other like-minded nobles met with clergymen and representatives of the citizens of France to discuss the financial issues facing France. The Estates General of 1789 was a general assembly representing the clergy, the nobility and the commoners. The exercise was doomed from the beginning. King Louis XVI wasn't about to allow the common people be involved in the decisions of his country, especially when they opposed his desires. As the negotiations failed, the French Revolution began. By 1789, the populace was in open rebellion.

The storming of the Bastille—the government's castle prison—took place on July 14, 1789. Almost immediately, Lafayette was appointed to lead the Parisian National Guard, an organization of citizen-soldiers formed to restore order and advance the goals of the French Revolution. Lafayette told them no true liberty was possible without order. At first, Lafayette's leadership was praised and the French Declaration of the Rights

---

[156] Unger, p 227.

of Man and the Citizen, which he helped to draft, was adopted. The document was patterned after the American Declaration of Independence.

Lafayette was walking a tightrope, one where the rope was thinning by the second. As both Lafayette and Adrienne tried to help the impoverished working families of Paris, the revolution careened forward. Not all of Lafayette's decisions favored the working man. Presently, Lafayette fell out of favor and mobs grew unruly and violent against those supporting the royal system of government and the royals themselves. One mob threatened Queen Marie-Antoinette on October 5, 1789, at Versailles, but the angry populace was thwarted by Lafayette and the National Guard. While Lafayette didn't believe in the infallibility of the monarchy, he also didn't believe in harming members of the royal family.

Support for a parliamentary monarchy, like the one in England, caused Lafayette to lose additional popular support. Acting as the voice of reason didn't endear him to the fervent segments fueling the passion of the French Revolution. The radicals wanted a republic and the removal of the royal family from power. After the King and Queen attempted to flee France, their demands escalated to include the guillotine.

The King and Queen were well aware they were in danger. Lafayette was wrongly accused of aiding in the escape. In a show of support for the revolutionaries, and in an ironic twist, Lafayette issued orders to stop and detain the royal couple. Not too many years before, the King issued orders to stop Lafayette from departing France. Louis XVI and Marie-Antoinette were apprehended and taken into custody. The arrest didn't quell the mob's desire for vengeance and chaos filled the streets. Some called for the King and Lafayette to be executed.

The escalating violence disturbed Lafayette. After a new constitution, destined to be stillborn, was enacted by the National Assembly, Lafayette resigned his command of the National Guard and returned to his ancestral home, Chavaniac. Lafayette's respite from national service didn't last long. The next year, Lafayette was appointed to lead a French army against Austria and Prussia. France declared war on Austria on April 20, 1792. Later, Prussia joined Austria against the French. The Austrian-Prussian forces supported monarchies, including deposed King Louis XVI and Queen Marie Antoinette, and opposed the French Revolution.

The beginning of the war was a disaster for the French.

In June, Lafayette protested against the latest attack on the French royal family. He discovered he had little support. In August, government leaders, the Jacobins, proclaimed Lafayette a traitor. The Jacobins falsely claimed Lafayette planned to lead an army to Paris and take over the government. The false charges against Lafayette were believed by many. On August 13, an arrest warrant was issued for Lafayette. Instead of returning to Paris to face the guillotine, Lafayette decided to flee to America.

Lafayette and other French officers, including La Columbe who was with Lafayette throughout the American Revolution, made it to Austrian-held property in Belgium. The Jacobians threatened to hold Lafayette's family as hostages until Austria returned Lafayette. Lafayette requested the Austrians to allow him to continue to England and then America. His request was refused. The Austrians arrested and made Lafayette a prisoner of war.

In October, Adrienne was informed of her husband's imprisonment. There, Lafayette received harsh punishment as he was considered a traitor to the monarchy. Prussia and Austria, because of family ties and political considerations, wanted King Louis XVI reinstated to the French throne.

When Adrienne discovered plans to attack and burn their chateau at Chavaniac, she took steps to protect her family.

Adrienne sent her 13-year-old son George and his tutor, Felix Frestel, to a mountain village, Conangles. Her two daughters, Anastasie and Marie Antoinette Virginie, and an aging governess were dispatched to a chateau in Langeac. When the attack on

Chavaniac didn't materialize, her daughters returned to Adrienne. Still, Lafayette's family was not safe. An order for Adrienne's arrest and confinement, along with her children, was issued in September 1792. Adrienne, Anastasie and Aunt Charlotte, Lafayette's only remaining relative, were taken into custody and held in prison as the governess and Marie Antoinette Virginie hid and escaped immediate capture.

At the time of Adrienne's detention, many victims, estimated to be 1,500, who were being held for crimes or for just being born of noble birth, were summarily executed in Paris. Adrienne appeared before government representatives and after some negotiations was allowed to return to Chavaniac on parole.

Lafayette spent time in several damp and desolate prisons, including ones in Wesel, Magdeburg and Neisse. Lafayette later became known as the prisoner of Olmutz. The heralded military hero was at a low point in his life. The French Revolution was in the hands of radicals. One faction wanted to execute him and another faction despised him. He had lost his power and his wealth. His family was suffering.

During his time in prison, Lafayette had one thought that consoled him. "The tree of liberty which he had helped to plant was bearing fruits as sweet as they were plentiful, and that there existed a people both happy and worthy of it, who maintained toward him a lively sense of gratitude; but restrained by reasons of more than one kind, he could only harbor the desire of seeing America again without foreseeing, however, whether he would be able to return there one day."[157]

On October 8, 1792, Adrienne wrote to President George Washington. Adrienne implored her husband's surrogate father to take steps to obtain Lafayette's release. She informed Washington that her husband was caged in a small, filthy vermin-infested cell. Lafayette wanted to join him in America to enjoy liberty. Adrienne reminded Washington that Lafayette had stood

---

[157] Auguste Levasseur, *Lafayette in America in 1824 and 1825*, p 1

by Washington in times of trouble. After not receiving a reply, in March 1793, Adrienne wrote a stronger letter to Washington, despairing over Washington's lack of action.

Washington had taken some steps to assist Lafayette and Adrienne before Adrienne's first letter was received. Washington forwarded funds to Amsterdam, where Washington believed Adrienne was residing. Washington and his Secretary of State Thomas Jefferson were not inclined to vigorously petition for Lafayette's release, as it might lead to tensions with France, one of the United States' top economic and political partners.

Washington explained the country's inaction to Adrienne and offered his personal wish that Lafayette be released and reunited with his family. "I do it in all sincerity of my friendship for him, and with the ardent desires for his relief; in which sentiment I know that my fellow citizens participate."[158] Lafayette's status was discussed at a cabinet meeting in January 1794. Washington proposed writing a personal and unofficial letter to the King of Prussia, requesting Lafayette's release. The letter, according to government documents, was finally written in May 1796.

While the United States government stood firm in not interfering with Lafayette's imprisonment, some of Lafayette's American friends did what they could for him and his family. Gouverneur Morris, America's minister in Paris, loaned Adrienne money to pay debts and make Lafayette's time in prison more bearable. Prison conditions were wrecking Lafayette's health. Adrienne continued to seek help, without success, from her personal contacts. Members of the nobility were no longer friends with Adrienne, as some of the changes Lafayette championed led to the execution of King Louis XVI on January 21, 1793. Queen Marie Antoinette was executed on October 16, 1793.

Adrienne's life was placed in jeopardy on November 13, 1793; she was arrested and imprisoned. A new law that all relatives of those believed traitors were themselves suspected of being

---

[158] Lane, p 194.

traitors. Lafayette was deemed to be a traitor. In May 1794, Adrienne was transported to a prison in Paris where she expected to be executed. Adrienne's life was spared because of the intervention of Morris. The United States representative reminded the French of their love for Lafayette and that at that moment the United States was one of the few nations still friendly with France. Adrienne's life was spared but she remained imprisoned.

American representative James Monroe vowed to help gain Adrienne's release from prison. Monroe, the future President of the United States, assisted Lafayette after he was wounded at Brandywine. Monroe was not sure if proper diplomacy would work in the case of Adrienne, who was not an American citizen. Also, the French considered Lafayette a traitor and did not look kindly upon Adrienne. Monroe's wife, Elizabeth, found a solution. Elizabeth Monroe visited Adrienne in Plessis prison, taking her food and arriving in a fine coach. Elizabeth's mercy mission became public knowledge. and Monroe began informal negotiations to have Adrienne released. James and Elizabeth Monroe visited Adrienne on a regular basis. Finally, Adrienne was told she could depart prison.

Upon securing her release in early 1795, Adrienne worked tirelessly to rejoin Lafayette, even though he was in prison in Austria. Also, Adrienne wanted to make sure her son was safe. Adrienne believed George Washington Lafayette would be out of harm's way if he was under the care of General George Washington in America. Without prior approval from Washington and still stinging from the inaction of the United States to free Lafayette, Adrienne sent her son and his tutor to live with Washington.

When young Lafayette arrived in the United States, Washington made sure Lafayette was safe and housed, but not initially at Mount Vernon. Washington didn't want to anger France. Finally, in April 1796, young Lafayette and his tutor were sheltered with Washington, first in Philadelphia and then at Mount Vernon.

Finally, Adrienne and her two daughters were reunited with Lafayette on October 15, 1795, at Olmutz prison. They hadn't seen Lafayette in almost four years. The Austrians confiscated all of Adrienne's possessions and then allowed her and her daughters to share prison life with Lafayette. During her time in prison with her husband, Adrienne's health deteriorated as did the health of her daughters. Supporters in the United States and England continued efforts to gain the Lafayette family's release but failed to do so.

Imprisonment continued until Napoleon became the military leader of France. His armies were strong enough to force Austria into a peace agreement. A condition of peace was the release of Lafayette. Another condition, imposed by Napoleon, was that Lafayette not return to France. Lafayette was viewed as a possible rival to Napoleon's control of France.

On September 16, 1797, Lafayette, Adrienne, Anastasia and Virginie all departed the prison at Olmutz. Lafayette had been in custody for more than five years and Adrienne and his daughters spent 23 months with him. For more than two years, Lafayette remained officially in exile as the family stayed in northern Europe, living in Hamburg, Holstein and Holland. Son George Washington Lafayette returned from America during this period and rejoined his family.

Lafayette thought about traveling to the United States to retire but was warned the relationship between France and the United States had become so strained while he was in prison that Lafayette should not think about making the trip.

During his exile, Lafayette received news of the death of George Washington, who died December 14, 1799, at Mount Vernon. Lafayette and his son George Washington Lafayette expressed their sadness in letters to Martha Washington. She wrote back, thanking them for their thoughts and acknowledging Lafayette's closeness to her husband. If he returned to America, Lafayette would be welcomed at Mount Vernon, Martha Washington assured him.

Napoleon signed a decree on March 1, 1800, restoring the political and civil rights of Lafayette, and others. Napoleon embraced Lafayette and offered him a number of official positions, including becoming France's minister to the United States. Lafayette declined all proposals, as he didn't approve of Napoleon's rule.

Napoleon did not want Lafayette in Paris. A compromise was reached. The Lafayettes would live in Adrienne's inherited chateau and estate of La Grange, about 40 miles from Paris. For the next 35 years, La Grange would be Lafayette's home. Lafayette and Adrienne spent the following years rebuilding their wealth and attending to family matters. They became grandparents.

In 1805, Lafayette rejected an offer by President Thomas Jefferson to become Governor of Louisiana in the United States. The couple were content at La Grange where Lafayette copied and installed some of the luxurious innovations he had seen at Mount Vernon when visiting Washington.

During a visit to a Paris relative in 1803, Lafayette asked to see an old friend, Monroe. The two former soldiers of Washington's army had not been together in more than 20 years. The reunion was nine years after Monroe assisted Adrienne to escape a French prison. The meeting was not under the best of circumstances as Lafayette was bedridden. Lafayette had fallen and seriously injured his hip. Monroe had some good news for Lafayette, Congress had granted him 2,500 acres of land along the Ohio River for his service during the Revolution. Later, the land was transferred to an additional grant from of property acquired during the Louisiana Purchase. The timing of the grant was perfect as the family fortune had evaporated. Adrienne asked Monroe if a loan could be obtained on the Ohio property. Monroe arranged the transaction.[159]

Lafayette's plight troubled Monroe, who aided the Lafayette family as much as possible. Monroe wrote to Madison, "Can nothing further be done for the unfortunate & most estimable Genl. Lafayette?"[160]

---

[159] Tim McGrath, *Monroe, A Life*, Dutton, New York, N.Y., 2020, p 243.

[160] McGrath, p. 243

Adrienne's physical conditioned deteriorated from her suffering in the French Revolution and her time with Lafayette in a prison cell. Adrienne died on Christmas Eve 1807. She was 48 years old.

Adrienne's death greatly affected Lafayette. Lafayette wrote a friend, "During the thirty-four years of a union in which her tenderness, her goodness, the elevation, the delicacy, the generosity of her soul charmed, embellished, honored my life. I felt so accustomed to all that she meant to me that I did not distinguish her existence from mine."[161]

[161] Lane, p 263.

·20·

A Hero's Celebration

Adrienne's death left a huge void in Lafayette's life. In the following years, Lafayette mended his own health, tended to his estate and enjoyed his family. Lafayette's financial condition improved somewhat as the estate prospered. Life was somewhat more tranquil for Lafayette, at least compared to Lafayette's earlier life, after his release from prison. Of course, Lafayette kept an eye on the ever-changing structure of the French government and the various intrigues surrounding the country's leadership. Liberal causes, always close to Lafayette's heart, continued to receive his support.

Louis XVIII was made King and a constitutional monarchy was put in place in 1814 after the defeat of Napoleon's forces in Europe. Lafayette had an uneasy relationship with the new King as he wasn't in favor of the new Chamber of Deputies because it represented only a small portion of France's inhabitants. The King didn't embrace Lafayette's dream of individual personal freedom for all. Napoleon rallied troops and regained control of Paris as Louis XVIII fled.

Again, Lafayette landed in a deadly controversy. After Napoleon's defeat at Waterloo in June 1815 by British and Prussian troops, Napoleon wanted the Chamber to dissolve itself and hand over all governance, and emergency dictatorial powers, to him.

Not a good idea, according to Lafayette. Lafayette's refusal to abandon his personal integrity in face of Napoleon's wrath, led to another charge of disloyalty to the government. Lafayette then led a group calling for Napoleon's abdication. When Napoleon refused, Lafayette urged the Chamber to dethrone Napoleon.[162] Four days after Waterloo, Napoleon did abdicate. Once again under the rule of Louis XVIII, France was again in turmoil and a second French Revolution was more than possible.

Lafayette was called back to national service in 1818 by the French people, having been elected to the Chamber of Deputies, the French national legislature. His son, George Washington Lafayette, also won a seat in the legislature.

The idea of liberty, Lafayette wrote to American President James Monroe, was seeping into many lands throughout Europe. Lafayette had not given up on the idea of "pure liberty" taking hold in the world. The liberty Lafayette sought all of his life was not welcomed in France. At age 66, Lafayette lost his re-election bid in 1823. George Lafayette was also defeated by those supporting a royalist government.

Lafayette's political life appeared to have ended with his election loss. His quest to bring American-style independence and freedom had failed. Lafayette wrote to President Monroe, "I often dream of the day when I will be able, without remorse, to enjoy the happiness of finding myself once again on American ground."[163]

A dejected Lafayette was rescued from his disappointment by his adopted country of the United States.Monroe sent a letter saying Lafayette would be welcomed in the United States as the "nation's guest." What better way to celebrate the upcoming 50th anniversary of the nation and remind American citizens of the

[162] Unger, p. 345.

[163] McGrath, p. 542.

sacrifices made for their freedom than to have the heroic Lafayette alight upon its shores.

By letter dated February 7, 1824, from "Washington City," Monroe wrote in part, "Congress has passed a resolution on this subject in which it expresses to you the sincere attachment of the entire nation, which ardently desires to see you again in its midst . . . bring you to this adopted country of your youth, which has always retained the memory of your important services . . . I add to it the assurance of my high esteem and affectionate feelings."[164]

While Monroe and Congress were happy to have Lafayette visit, French King Louis XVIII was not. The King took the offer from Monroe as an indication the United States had belligerent designs on French foreign holdings. Lafayette would betray France and aid Monroe, according to the royal thinking. King Louis XVII called Lafayette "that animal."[165] Lafayette could make the trip, but the government deterred any farewell celebrations for Lafayette.

Aware that the relationship between France and the United States was strained, Monroe had the invitation be issued by Congress as an unofficial visit. Lafayette was in complete agreement and declined passage to America on an American government frigate.

Without fanfare, Lafayette, son George, private secretary Auguste Levasseur and valet Bastien sailed on the private American packet ship *Cadmus* from the port of Le Havre on July 13, 1824. Levasseur recorded in detail Lafayette's voyage and trip throughout the United States and wrote a book, *Lafayette in America in 1824 and 1825*, which was translated by Alan R. Hoffman, President of the American Friends of Lafayette. The book contains more than 500 pages of detailed descriptions of thousands

---

[164] Levasseur, p. 2. Most of the details of Lafayette's trip in this book come from Lavasseur's reports.

[165] McGrath, p. 542.

of speeches and events and vignettes. The following conveys some of the highlights.

Upon arrival in New York harbor, Lafayette's American greeting was the exact opposite of his French farewell. The harbor was jammed with ships with welcoming messages for Lafayette. Since the ship arrived on a Sunday, August 15, Lafayette's grand entrance to the city was delayed until Monday.

Bands were playing and a vast, cheering crowd greeted Lafayette. Levasseur wrote, "Finally, at two o'clock, the General disembarked in the Battery, in the midst of acclamations of 200,000 voices, which hailed and blessed his welcome." Within the crowd were soldiers that served with Lafayette during the American Revolution. A "Lafayette Guard" was formed, each wearing a likeness of Lafayette on their blouses, to lead Lafayette through the city's streets.

For the next four days, Lafayette met with delegations and dignitaries from New York and beyond. Every moment was filled and still Lafayette did not have enough time to meet with all who wished an audience.

Lafayette's greeting was just the forerunner of the adulation he would be shown in the next 13 months as he visited all of the then 24 states and was the featured star at a multitude of celebrations, dinners and fireworks displays in big cities and small hamlets.

The second major destination was Boston. Lafayette's party departed New York City on August 20 and the journey took five days to complete. During the trip, Lafayette was escorted by the military and by civilians. "Each village had raised a triumphal arch, on which we almost always saw the names of Washington and Lafayette joined, or the date of the Battles of Brandywine and Yorktown," Levasseur wrote.

Levasseur indicated Lafayette would have lingered in Rhode Island to visit some of the sites of his Revolutionary War experiences but didn't do so as festivities were planned in Boston. Lafayette didn't need an alarm clock in the city as at daybreak he was awakened by the sound of martial music. The evening festivities included a toast to King Louis XVI, who financially supported American independence and later was executed in the French Revolution. "Those who had favored liberty ought not to be forgotten, even when they had worn the crown."

At Harvard University, Levasseur recorded a grand celebration for Lafayette. "When the General appeared in the hall, the cheering and the rapture of the entire crowd was such that it was not possible to begin the exercises for a long time; it was a truly fascinating picture, namely, that of the immense benches full of young girls crowned with flowers waving their handkerchiefs above their heads in order to salute the one whom they called father, their friend, their defender, the companion of their great Washington."

A ceremony at Bunker Hill greatly affected Lafayette, according to Levasseur, who recorded the Frenchman's comments, "That I tread upon this hallowed ground, where the blood of American patriots, the blood of Warren and his companions, gloriously spilled, revived the force of three million men and secured the happiness of ten million who live now, and of so many others to be born. This blood has summoned the American continents to republican independence, and has awakened in the nations of Europe the necessity of, and assured for the future, I hope, the exercise of their rights."

As President Monroe envisioned, Lafayette's tour not only celebrated the American French hero but also those patriots who fought with Lafayette to gain independence.

Lafayette sought out a private meeting with 89-year-old John Adams, his Revolutionary War friend and second President of the United States. Levasseur believed Lafayette's time with Adams revived the aging former President. "(Adams) could not tire of repeating how great was the joy that the recognition of his fellow citizens for Lafayette caused him."

After additional celebrations, Lafayette began making his way to New Hampshire and on to New York City but not before stopping at Lexington and Concord, two of the early historic sites of the American Revolution. Another stop was at Salem, Massachusetts, where Levasseur recorded wording of several banners saluting Lafayette. They read:

> *Honor to Lafayette! Honor to the one who fought and spilled his blood for the peace and happiness which we enjoy.*" And, "*Lafayette, friend and defender of liberty, welcome to your favorite land!*" And, "*At the time of our adversity, you helped us: in our prosperity, we recall your services with gratitude.*

The time in Portsmouth, New Hampshire, was grand but tiring for Lafayette. The days were filled with well-wishers, official meetings and speeches. On his way back to New York, Lafayette stopped in Connecticut where he was presented with a medal saying, "The children of Hartford, to Lafayette, September 4, 1824."

Lafayette had hoped his return to New York City on September 5 would be low key, but the reception was again lively. A naval ship saluted his return with 13 blasts from its cannons, and the pier was full of cheering citizens.

For his 67th birthday celebration, the Society of Cincinnati, an organization dedicated to remembering the American Revolution, hosted a dinner. At the time members were mostly veterans of the War of Rebellion. Levasseur wrote, "A truly moving tableau was offered by these old warriors, the vestiges of the glorious War of Independence, conducting in their midst the companion of Washington, the adopted son of America." Levasseur described a wonderful evening of camaraderie.

The rest of the time in New York City was filled with visits to cultural institutions, schools, hospitals, churches and the forts protecting the city, including Fort Lafayette. Lafayette and his son also attended a Masonic festival of the Knights Templar where they were presented with medals to celebrate the 47th anniversary of the Battle of Brandywine.

Before departing the city, officials organized one of the grandest events for Lafayette at Castle Garden on the Hudson on September 13. Levasseur described the event beginning with a 300-foot bridge with a luxurious carpet from one end to the other. "In the middle stood a pyramid 75 feet high, illuminated by colored pieces of glass and topped by a brilliant star in the middle of which one read the name of Lafayette." The hall for the dinner contained 6,000 people. "At the principal entrance was a triumphal arch of flowers and greenery, topped by a colossal statue of Washington resting on some cannon pieces . . . a shield with these words: 'To the Nation's Guest.' . . . In the front were two cannon pieces taken from Yorktown. . . . This circumference was lit up by more than 1,000 torches whose glare was reflected by a large number of stacked arms."

The next segment of Lafayette's tour was through the towns of the Hudson River Valley, including West Point, the scene of Arnold's betrayal of America. A stop in Albany, New York, included another welcoming ceremony. Levasseur recorded several spirited horses had to be restrained every time a cannon boomed. The crowds were so large on the street that a fear existed that someone would be crushed under the wheels of the carriages carrying Lafayette's party.

Towns across the upper region of New York state continued welcoming Lafayette in grand style. Upon returning to New York City, Lafayette requested a respite from the public ceremonies so he could meet with friends and take in the sights of the city as a tourist. When the tour resumed, Levasseur noted New Jersey towns, including Princeton and Trenton, treated Lafayette with "the same spirit of enthusiasm and gratitude" as New York and New England.

A special visit took place on September 16 in Bordentown, New Jersey. Lafayette met with Joseph Bonaparte, the ex-King of Spain and older brother of Napoleon. Bonaparte welcomed his guests and spent an hour with Lafayette in private conversation.

On September 28, Lafayette's welcoming committee in Philadelphia was impressive. "The horsemen and the carriages augmented the procession to such an extent that we advanced further only with the greatest difficulty. In a plain, a short distance from the city, were about 6,000 men of the voluntary militia in handsome uniforms and under arms, forming a square in the middle of which General Lafayette was received to the sound of cannon by the civil and military authorities," Levasseur recorded. "Never was it more truthful to say that the entire population had come to meet General Lafayette." The crowd estimates were 120,000 city residents and 40,000 visitors.

A reflective Lafayette was captured by Levasseur at Independence Hall. "In recognizing this hall in which the Declaration of Independence was signed, the hall at the door of which he waited in 1777 with so much anxiety for permission to dedicate his good right arm and his fortune to a cause then nearly desperate, General Lafayette felt an emotion that he had difficulty containing."

Another emotional encounter took place at Chester, Pennsylvania. Lafayette visited the same room where he had his leg wound treated after the September 11, 1777, Battle of Brandywine. One of the speakers recalled Lafayette's courage in rallying troops while suffering from his wound.

Not all of the festivities on the trip centered on Lafayette. During his excursion through Delaware, Lafayette found time to attend the wedding of a fellow Frenchman, Alfred Victor du Pont, in New Castle. Du Pont's father and family fled the French Revolution to save their lives and settled in the United States in 1800. Two years later, the family founded the famous E. I. du Pont de Nemours and Company, then a producer of a high-quality gunpowder.

All during the trip, native Frenchmen sought out Lafayette.

Two such compatriots made contact with Lafayette as he was making his way to Fort McHenry in Baltimore Harbor. One served with Pulaski during the war and the other helped prepare the ship Lafayette used to flee the wrath of the King of France in 1777.

At Fort McHenry an old friend, John Quincy Adams, the Secretary of State and future President of the United States, joined the group. Also, a relative of General Washington brought the Revolutionary War campaign tent of Washington to the public celebration. For Lafayette, the tent brought back fond recollections of Washington. "The memory of their old brotherhood, and of the cruel loss of the one who had served as their father, made them feel a mixture of pleasure and grief that they only express by the silence of theirs and of their embraces," Levasseur wrote.

After almost a week in Baltimore and another full round of public events and dinners, Lafayette journeyed to Washington city to see President Monroe, the man who aided Lafayette at Brandywine and was responsible for Lafayette's grand tour. "At the moment General Lafayette entered, all those assembled rose; the President went hurriedly to meet him, embraced him with all the affection of a brother."

The next scheduled stop on Lafayette's tour was the 43rd anniversary celebration of the surrender of Yorktown. First, Lafayette made an emotional pilgrimage to Washington's tomb. "General Lafayette descended alone at first into the burial vault, and some minutes later reappeared on the threshold, his face inundated with tears; he took his son and me by the hand, made us enter with him, and with the motion of his hand pointed out to us the coffin of his fatherly friend," Levasseur wrote.

A number of dignitaries jointed Lafayette at Yorktown, including the Chief Justice of the United States John Marshall, who fought at Brandywine in Maxwell's light infantry. Marshall said of Lafayette: "Some of us served under you in that memorable campaign; many in the course of the war. While duty required obedience, your conduct inspired confidence and love. Time which has thinned our ranks, and enfeebled our bodies, has not impaired these feelings, they retain their original rigour."[166]

The house used by British General Cornwallis during the siege was made available to Lafayette during his stay. At dawn on October 19, booming cannons interrupted Lafayette's sleep, according to Levasseur, and a full day of events began. After many speeches, presentations and a review of military units, a ball was held for Lafayette. During the day a box of candles was discovered that belonged to Cornwallis. Levasseur said despite the long day, the Revolutionary War veterans lingered at the ball until all of Cornwallis's candles were used.

As the journey continued, recording all of the events must have taken a toll on Levasseur. He wrote: "I will not undertake to describe the festivities prepared by the inhabitants of Norfolk to receive the Nation's Guest; they were, as everywhere stamped strongly with a patriotic character and the gratitude of the people."

A private reception was reserved for Lafayette and Thomas Jefferson, as the two seekers of freedom met at Monticello. Thereafter, Lafayette visited another former President, James Madison. For four days, Lafayette and Madison walked the grounds and spent the nights talking of America's history.

Lafayette's wanderings eventually took him back to Washington. Upon his arrival, Lafayette discovered invitations from parts of the United States that weren't on his original itinerary. After being informed of the lavish plans being made to welcome him, Lafayette couldn't resist accepting all of the requests. The tour would resume after the end of winter. Lafayette would use the time resting, visiting Congress and seeing friends.

In December, President Monroe addressed Congress about

---

[166] David Felsen, *The Gazette of the American Friends of Lafayette*, No. 93. Part II, p. 88.

Lafayette. He reminded Congress of the adulation Lafayette was receiving during his travels and the sacrifices Lafayette made for American freedom. Monroe then asked Congress to compensate Lafayette.

> The presence of the one who, guided by such noble ideas, took so active a part in our cause, could not fail to produce a profound impression on individuals of all ages. It was natural that we would take the most-lively interest in his future well-being, as we do. His rights to our gratitude all well known. For these reasons, I invite the Congress to take into consideration the services which he has rendered, the sacrifices that he has made, the losses that he has experienced, and to vote a grant in his favor which responds in a manner worthy of the character and the grandeur of the American people.

Congress heeded Monroe's call for compensation. Lafayette was warmly welcomed by Congress, and Lafayette gave a patriotic address in return. Congress granted Lafayette a sum of $200,000 and 24,000 acres of land in the most fertile part of the United States.

The scheduling of the 1825 leg of Lafayette's trip seemed almost impossible. To honor all of the invitations, Levasseur estimated more than 3,000 miles would have to be traveled in less than four months to make the June 17 appointment in Boston to attend the celebration of the anniversary of the Battle of Bunker Hill. On February 23, 1825, at 9:00 p.m. Lafayette and his troupe boarded a boat on the Potomac and sailed to the mouth of the Chesapeake Bay.

Soon after departure, Levasseur described what he believed to be "one of the sweetest moments" of Lafayette's life. The incident took place not at a lavish party, but at a small inn outside of Norfolk. While horses were being refreshed, the innkeeper beseeched Lafayette to take a few minutes to meet his family. A *Welcome Lafayette* sign was scrawled with charcoal on a white wall. "Modest refreshments were offered to us with a kindness and a cordiality that increased their value very much," Levasseur wrote.

The innkeeper then presented his wife and son, a young boy about three or four years old. The father placed his son's small hand on Lafayette's hand. The boy said, "General Lafayette, I thank you for the freedom that you have won for my father, my mother, for me and my country." Lafayette couldn't conceal his emotion and embraced the "child tenderly." Lafayette then "escaped into his carriage, where the blessings of this family, which was free and so worthy of being free, accompanied him."

Lafayette's travels brought him into contact with all strata of American life. Slaves, freed African Americans, American Indians, the poor, the rich, patriotic citizens and the well-connected all sought time with Lafayette. America's honored guest spent time with each group.

Through rainstorms, mud and small traveling mishaps, Lafayette continued visiting Southern towns. A fierce rainstorm greeted Lafayette as he stopped at Fayetteville, North Carolina, near the Cape Fear River, on March 4. The rain didn't deter the inhabitants, including the ladies dressed in all their finery, to catch a glimpse of Lafayette, Levasseur wrote. "This enthusiasm is more easily understood when one considers that it was manifested by the inhabitants of a city founded 40 years ago to perpetuate the memory of the services rendered by the very person whom they were honoring on this day."

Lafayette couldn't help but participate in an event to honor the memory of another Revolutionary War hero and friend, Baron de Kalb, at Camden, South Carolina. De Kalb, who traveled to America with Lafayette and fought beside Lafayette, was killed at the Battle of Camden in August 1780. Lafayette placed the first stone for a monument to de Kalb. "An inscription in a noble but unpretentious style recalls the patriotism, the services and the glorious death of de Kalb," according to Levasseur.

De Kalb and Lafayette landed near Charleston, South Carolina, in 1777. The city's inhabitants of 1825 greeted Lafayette in grand style. Included in the celebration was the son of Benjamin Huger who gave Lafayette shelter during his first days in America. The son, Francis, aided Lafayette during his imprisonment at Olmutz and joined in a failed attempt to break Lafayette out of prison.

Lafayette joined in honoring two other Revolutionary War heroes— Count Pulaski and General Greene—at Savannah. In a regal ceremony, Lafayette laid the cornerstone for a monument to Greene, his close Revolutionary War friend.

After departing Savannah, the sea voyage to New Orleans was somewhat rough for Lafayette and his compatriots. Seasickness overtook many before the batteries of the city fired 100 cannon blasts to announce the arrival of Lafayette. The governor of Louisiana further welcomed Lafayette as he noted the French history of the city. City officials found the perfect accommodations for Lafayette as he was quartered in the Lafayette House hotel. The sendoff was extra special as Levasseur noted hearing cries of "Vive Lafayette!"

For the next several days, Lafayette had a different type of tour as he traveled from Natchez to St. Louis by boat. Lafayette saw a portion of the country devoid of big cities, and observed wildlife and nature along the Mississippi. After a visit to see General Andrew Jackson, a hero of the War of 1812 and future President of the United States, this portion of the trip produced a frightening encounter for Lafayette and his traveling companions.

While sailing on the Ohio River on May 8, Lafayette spent the day answering letters and dictating notes to be given the caretakers of his French estate. George Lafayette remarked before going to bed that he was astonished that the captain didn't stop the ship for the night or at least slow down. The captain should have had George's intuition.

"At eleven o'clock, the utter silence that reigned on board was disturbed only by the muffled wailing of the steam engine and the rustling of the waves against the sides of our ship," Levasseur wrote. "Midnight had sounded, and sleep began to invite us to repose when suddenly our ship experienced a horrible jolt and stopped short. At this extraordinary impact, the General awakened with a start, his son leapt from his bed half-dressed, and I ran to inquire on deck."

What Levasseur was told was the ship had hit a sand bar. Levasseur didn't believe the explanation and went to explore. A hole in the ship was discovered and water rapidly filled a cargo hold. "The captain shouted, 'A snag! A snag! Quick, Lafayette! . . . my boat! . . . Bring Lafayette to my boat," Levasseur recalled. Levasseur hurried to Lafayette and reported the boat was sinking and they must abandon ship. Lafayette was dressed by his valet Bastien while Levasseur and George gathered important documents and papers. Lafayette urged them to depart while he finished dressing, but his son and Levasseur refused. "'What,' shouted George! 'Do you think that in such a circumstance we would leave you for a second?'" Levasseur recorded Lafayette was seized by the hands and dragged towards the door. Lafayette "followed us while smiling at our petulance and went up with us." Before attaining the deck, Lafayette discovered he left valuables, including his snuff-box decorated with the portrait of Washington, in his cabin. Levasseur retrieved the snuff-box.

The rocking of the ship was so strong Levasseur believed the party would not have time to abandon ship. Passengers had trouble standing on the tilting deck. The captain's longboat was brought alongside for Lafayette, but in the confusion, Lafayette could not be found. "Meanwhile, the ship leaned over more and more; each moment the danger increased; we felt that it was time to make one last effort," Levasseur wrote. Levasseur shouted "here is Lafayette" and the passengers became quiet and allowed Lafayette to go to the boat. Danger persisted as lowering Lafayette into the longboard was hazardous but accomplished. Within a few minutes Lafayette was on shore. Lafayette was frantic for a period of time because his son George appeared to be lost. Eventually George and Bastien were found safe. There was no loss of life.

Fires were built and Lafayette tried to get some rest. Before daylight a driving rainstorm added to their discomfort. During subsequent searches, a trunk containing some of Lafayette's important papers was found.

Lafayette's travels and exploits were well-documented by newspapers. An article in the *Illinois Intelligencer* on June 10, 1825, had a line that should be heeded today. The article read, "When Lafayette is forgotten our enthusiasm in the cause of liberty will have departed and the hour of our slavery will have arrived."

Despite the ordeal and the near drowning, Lafayette continued with his grand tour of military reviews, dinners, speeches and well-wishers. At Lexington, Kentucky, he visited the young women's academy, named the Lafayette Academy. Lafayette found his way to Pennsylvania, visited Pittsburgh and Erie, and headed north into New York state. Stops were made in some of the sections of the state, such as Utica, near where Lafayette spent part of the winter of 1778 during the aborted invasion of Canada.

Lafayette hurried to keep to his schedule. He arrived in Boston on June 15, in time to take part in the anniversary celebration of Bunker Hill. Lafayette didn't linger long in Massachusetts as Maine, New Hampshire and Vermont were next on his packed itinerary. Lafayette made the rounds and returned to New York City for a July 4th celebration.

At one of the ceremonies, Lafayette said: "The Fourth of July was the time of a new social order, up to then without example, founded on the sovereignty of the people, on the natural rights of man, and on the total application of the principal that a nation has the right to govern itself. Its results have surpassed the most passionate expectations."

After 10 days in New York City, Lafayette began the last leg of his trip with a visit to Philadelphia. There he took time to visit some of the battlefields of 1777, including Germantown and Brandywine. At the Cliveden estate, owned by the Chew family, in Germantown a reception was held for Lafayette on July 20. British soldiers held off the American forces during the Battle of Germantown at the Chew house.

On July 25, 1825, an intensely hot day, Lafayette was led by a large number of Pennsylvanians and Virginians to Brandywine, the battlefield where Lafayette shed his blood for American independence and where he staked his claim to being an American hero.

Levasseur wrote, "This battlefield was not renowned for a victory, as one knows, but its memory is no less dear to Americans who recall with gratitude the blood that their fathers and the young Lafayette spilled on it in the defense of their rights and their independence. Happy is the country in which events are appreciated more for their influence on the destiny of the Fatherland than for the glamour of the moment! The men who prepared the way for the independence of the United States in doing battle at Bunker Hill and on the banks of the Brandywine are no less noble today in the eyes of the Nation than those who consolidated it by the victory of Yorktown."

The next day the soldiers and the soldiers' children conducted Lafayette to Washington's encampment at Brandywine where the two oldest surviving Revolutionary War officers of the area were waiting, Colonel McClellan and Captain Anderson. At noon Lafayette arrived and crossed the Brandywine River at Chadds Ford. Lafayette recognized the exact location where Washington crossed for the first time and directed the assemblage to the spot. "The correctness of his observation and freshness of his memory excited the admiration of the numerous witnesses to the highest degree."

At Chadds Ford, according to Levasseur, Lafayette "learned that one of his companions-in-arms, Gideon Gilpin, at whose house he had passed the night the evening of the battle, was now bedridden by age and infirmities and despaired not being able to join his homage to those of his fellow citizens; the General hastened to go to the old man, whom he found surrounded by his family. In spite of extreme weakness, Gideon Gilpin recognized him as soon as he entered and showed him by tears of gratitude and affection how greatly this visit spread charm on his last moments and alleviated them."[167]

Lafayette gave his own tour of Brandywine that day. "His memories did not lead him astray for an instant," Levasseur wrote. "Having arrived at the spot where the initial combat was joined and where he had been wounded, he stopped for a moment; his former companions-in-arms crowded around his carriage; and the militia filed in front of him to shouts of *Long Live Lafayette!* During this entire scene which caused in him a

---

[167] Levasseur's account has sparked a minor historical disagreement within the local Chadds Ford community about where Lafayette spent the evening before the battle. Clearly from Levasseur's account, Lafayette and Gilpin had a connection from the battle. Gilpin's home was designated Lafayette's headquarters on the Pennsylvania state park site. Proved by Lafayette's recollection of the exact crossing of the Brandywine, Lafayette's memory was sharp and clear in 1825. The dispute comes about from a hearsay comment made by the Marquis de Chastellux, who visited Brandywine with Lafayette in 1780. Chastellux, Gimat and others stayed at an inn, three miles from Brandywine, while Lafayette went to stay with Benjamin Ring. Chastellux states Ring hosted Washington and Lafayette the night before the battle. Chastellux doesn't indicate who told him about Lafayette staying with Washington at Ring's home. The small Ring home would have been overly cramped if all of Washington's staff stayed at the Ring home. Ring's house has been known as Washington's headquarters at the park. Of course, the most important point is that Lafayette was at Brandywine, was wounded and went on to be an American hero.

profound emotion and which his modesty sought several time to abbreviate, he spoke to those who surrounded him only of the presence of mind that Washington had shown on that fateful day of September 11 and of the courage with which the soldiers and officers had supported him; but it was in vain that he recounted the names of the more illustrious leaders, and he attributed to them all the glory of having saved the army; they responded by pointing out to him the soil that he had doused with his blood, and the sight of that indestructible monument exalted to the highest degree the gratitude of the numerous spectators who accompanied him."

The tour guide, Lafayette, continued the walk on the battlefield, and he took the route by which the English had conducted their first assault. A stop was made at a house used by General Howe during the assault. The house still bore some traces of the well-directed fire of the American artillery. The owner of the home showed Lafayette a collection from the battle and some pieces were given to Lafayette. "We returned with these precious relics to West Chester, where we concluded the day in the midst of new festivities prepared by the citizens," Levasseur wrote.

At the West Chester, Pennsylvania, dinner, Rev. William Latta, pastor of the Great Valley and Charlestown Presbyterian Church, gave "a prayer very remarkable for its touching sentiments, fervid eloquence and patriotic spirit."[168] Latta's father, Rev. James Latta, was a chaplain in Washington's army. One of Washington's last visitors at Mount Vernon was Rev. James Latta, according to a log of visitors at Mount Vernon.[169]

Levasseur wrote of Latta's prayer: "Thus, how can one listen to this invocation, so simple, so touching of Reverend William

---

[168] *History of Chester County* by Futhey and Cope, pages 626, 627.

[169] James Latta supplied the family information on the Revs. William and James Latta. James Latta and his brothers Peter and Duie operate a successful trucking company A. Duie Pyle in West Chester.

Latta without being deeply moved and without joining one's pious gratitude to his?" Latta's presentation:

> All-powerful God, our celestial Father! We give you thanks for the benefits that you have heaped on the American Nation, the memory of which we recall today. We give you thanks of having poured into the bosom of our fathers the pure love of liberty, for having inspired in them, during our infancy, the desire and the strength to conquer it. We give you thanks that the very same spirit was carried to a distant land and that you put into the heart of a foreigner, whose presence we celebrate today, the desire to take up our fortunes and our dangers; that in the midst of the trials to which he has been exposed, you have spared his precious life to allow him, after half a century, to revisit our land to receive in it the tributes of admiration of the people; and to recognize there the fruits of that independence to the establishment of which he contributed so potently.

Departing the environs of the Brandywine battlefield, Lafayette headed to Lancaster, briefly the seat of government after the fall of Philadelphia, and then to Port Deposit on the Susquehanna River and then on to Baltimore. Lafayette was able to get two days of rest despite a fire in the city that greeted his arrival. Traveling on to Washington, Lafayette visited old friends in Virginia and prepared for his return to France.

A special sendoff was planned by President John Quincy Adams. Adams convinced Lafayette to travel home on a newly constructed frigate. Adams informed Lafayette that Captain

Charles Morris, one of the most distinguished officers of the United States Navy, was ordered to safely deliver Lafayette to Europe. Since frigates were named after rivers, Adams selected a river "in which you sealed your devotion to our principles with your blood. We have given the name *Brandywine*."

On Lafayette's birthday, September 6, Adams hosted a celebration for Lafayette. Lafayette spoke and his departing words were: "God bless you, Sir, and all who surround us. God bless the American people, each of their States, and the federal government. Accept this patriotic farewell of an overflowing heart; such will be its last throb when it ceases to beat."

Lafayette and his traveling party reached the ship anchored at the mouth of the Potomac during the evening of September 7. Too late to set sail, the ship began its voyage the next morning.

The Brandywine carried Lafayette home to France.

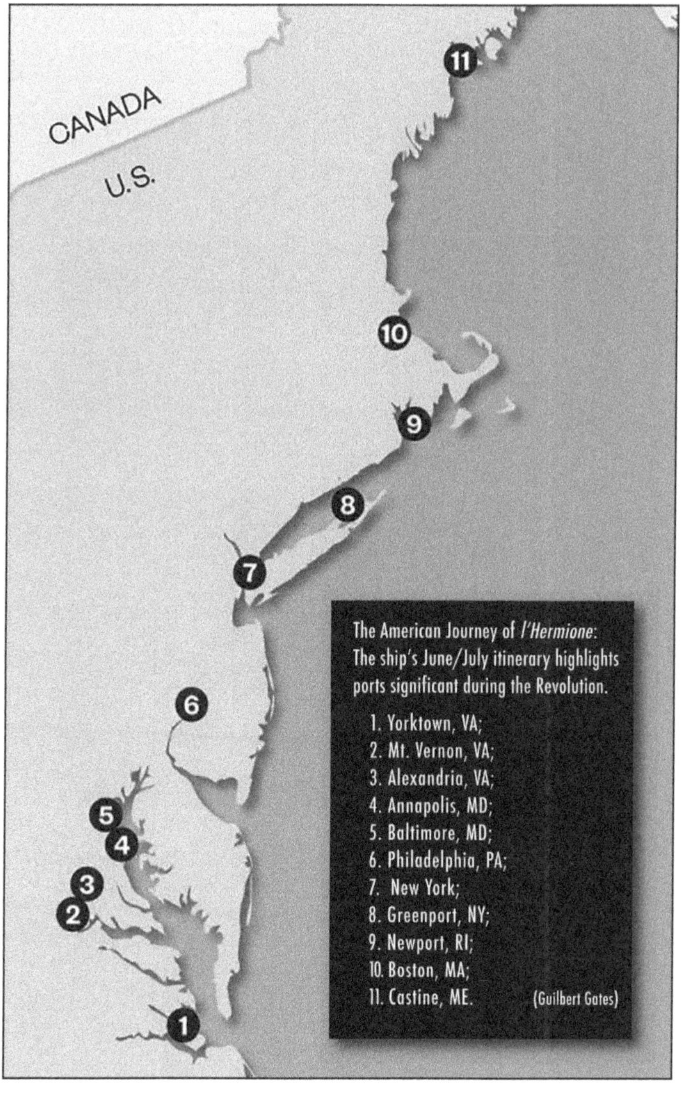
CANADA
U.S.
The American Journey of *l'Hermione*:
The ship's June/July itinerary highlights ports significant during the Revolution.
1. Yorktown, VA;
2. Mt. Vernon, VA;
3. Alexandria, VA;
4. Annapolis, MD;
5. Baltimore, MD;
6. Philadelphia, PA;
7. New York;
8. Greenport, NY;
9. Newport, RI;
10. Boston, MA;
11. Castine, ME.
(Guilbert Gates)

The Brandywine

·21·

A Hero's Death

The Brandywine sped across the Atlantic Ocean and delivered Lafayette at the port of Le Havre after 24 days at sea. Most of Lafayette's crossings of the Atlantic contained some drama, and this voyage was not without incident. A howling storm caused the ship to take on water as the rolling sea caused many on board to suffer from seasickness.

On October 3, Lafayette sighted his homeland.

The next day the captain and crew had a few surprises for Lafayette. The crew promised to have a silver vase crafted for Lafayette with decorations of the Capitol of Washington, the visit of Lafayette to Washington's tomb and *The Brandywine* at Le Harve.

The crew had a parting gift for the American hero. The American flag that flew over *The Brandywine* during the crossing was given to Lafayette by First Lieutenant Gregory, who said, "We cannot entrust it to more glorious hands. Take it, dear General; may it remind you forever of your alliance with the American Nation; may it remind you sometimes also of those who will never forget the pleasure that they had to spend 24 days with you aboard *The Brandywine*; . . . may it remind your neighbors of the anniversary of two great dates whose influence on the entire world is incalculable, the birth of Washington and the Declaration of Independence of our country!"[170]

Lafayette promised to display the flag at La Grange. Lafayette then invited the crew to visit him. If they should visit him, Lafayette promised the crew would not be on foreign soil but an American home.

France had greatly changed during Lafayette's 13 months in the United States. King Louis XVIII died and his brother Charles X became King. The rule of Charles X became increasingly harsh for the citizens of France. As the tyrannical rule gripped the nation, Lafayette was once again called upon to stand up for the rights of the individual.

In 1827, Lafayette was elected to the Chamber of Deputies. And, once again Lafayette clashed with a King. In an effort to silence Lafayette and his liberal associates, Charles X disbanded the Chamber. Of course, Lafayette wouldn't be muffled as he was re-elected to the Chamber. Lafayette's home became the center of liberal ideals. During dinners, Lafayette's daughters were hostesses, and his son an unofficial Sergeant of Arms to bar unwanted visitors.

King Charles X fumed over opposition to his rule and threatened the leaders of the Chamber with arrest if subversive steps were taken against him. The Chamber rebuffed and challenged the King. Once again, Charles X dissolved the Chamber. In the new election, the liberal members, including Lafayette, were re-elected. The infuriated Charles X dissolved the new Chamber before the legislative body even met.

The second French Revolution was on. Rioting in the streets of Paris took place, and Lafayette, then 73 years old, joined the royal protesters. Streets were again bloody as Charles X fled the palace. Another arrest warrant was issued for Lafayette. Lafayette became the recognized public leader of the insurrection and was named supreme ruler, an honor Lafayette declined the next day, as Lafayette deemed the appointment unconstitutional.

---

[170] Levasseur, p. 566.

Lafayette did negotiate the abdication of Charles X and the installation of Louis-Philippe. Peace returned to the streets of Paris.

King Louis-Philippe and Lafayette worked together for a brief period of time, but Lafayette continued to push for the rights of individuals in France and elsewhere in Europe. Eventually, Lafayette was ousted from his final position of power. Lafayette retired to his estate at La Grange as the country again veered towards royalist rule and away from the recognition of individual rights. True to his ideals, Lafayette continued his opposition to the suppression of individual rights.

In February 1834, on a chilly and rainy day, Lafayette attended a funeral of an old friend, who was killed in a political duel. Lafayette walked in the funeral procession and spoke at the gravesite. Lafayette became ill and his son rushed him home. After several weeks, Lafayette rallied enough to resume his letter writing promoting the rights of individuals.

On May 9, 1834, Lafayette was riding in an open carriage when a thunderstorm struck and left Lafayette trembling with cold. At his Paris apartment, Lafayette's doctor and family, including his children and their spouses, kept a close watch on Lafayette.

In the early morning hours of May 20, 1834, Lafayette was said to have awakened and held the locket containing the portrait of a young Adrienne. The 76-year-old Lafayette reportedly held the locket to his lips and died. Another report only had Lafayette clutching the locket. Lafayette was buried alongside Adrienne in the Picpus cemetery in Paris where victims of the French Revolution are also interned.

Multitudes of French citizens lined the streets along Lafayette's funeral procession as a hearse carried the General's body across Paris. An estimated 3,000 members, including members of the National Guard, took part in the ceremony. As Lafayette requested, only family members entered the cemetery. George Washington Lafayette covered his father's grave with dirt from Bunker's Hill, as Lafayette wished to be buried in his homeland, France, with American soil.

"The funeral procession had been an enormous tribute, but the greatest homage of all was the king's preparations against the crowds, in their grief, rising up against royal rule. The route was lined with a triple row of armed soldiers. Loaded cannon, with gunners standing by, were placed at the corners of the cemetery. It was a tribute to the power of the man and his all-consuming principle—liberty."[171]

During World War I, United States forces helped to liberate France. American General John Pershing sent his aide Colonel Charles E. Stanton to Lafayette's grave to plant an American flag. During a 4th of July celebration, Stanton said, "Lafayette, we are here."

In 1992, a French project was launched to construct a replica of the *Hermione*, the ship famous for carrying Lafayette to the United States in 1780. In April 2015, the newly constructed *Hermione* started her return voyage to the United States. The project was designed to reaffirm the relationship between the United States and France.

When word of Lafayette's death reached America, citizens went into mourning. The United States had lost "our Marquis." President Andrew Jackson ordered the same military honors for Lafayette that George Washington received. Memorial services were conducted throughout the land. Congress draped black bunting on the House of Representatives and the Senate and asked all citizens to dress in mourning for 30 days.

While Lafayette received deserved tributes in America, his death in France was not honored. King Louis-Philippe declared Lafayette was as much a menace to France in death as he was in life. No formal statement on Lafayette's death was issued by the King. The royalists considered him a traitor to the privileged class, and for others Lafayette had made too many compromises in the quest for individual rights. Lafayette departed life without obtaining American style freedom for France.

---

[171] Lane, p. 329.

John Quincy Adams offered a long eulogy to Lafayette on December 31, 1834. Adams recounted many details of Lafayette's life. He paid homage to the accomplishments of Lafayette and for holding onto the ideals of individual liberty for all in the world.

Lafayette's death was not the only time Adams spoke of Lafayette's contributions to the United States. As Lafayette was about to depart America after his grand tour in 1825, Adams said, "We shall look upon you always as belonging to us, during the whole of our life, and as belonging to our children after us. You are ours by that more than patriotic self-devotion with which you flew to the aid of our fathers at the crisis of our fate; ours by that unshaken gratitude for your services which is a precious portion of our inheritance; ours by that tie of love, stronger than death, which has linked your name for the endless ages of time with the name Washington."

Yes, Lafayette belongs to the United States as he was a genuine America hero and supreme champion of freedom. His legacy, and American independence became inevitable when Lafayette shed his blood at Brandywine.

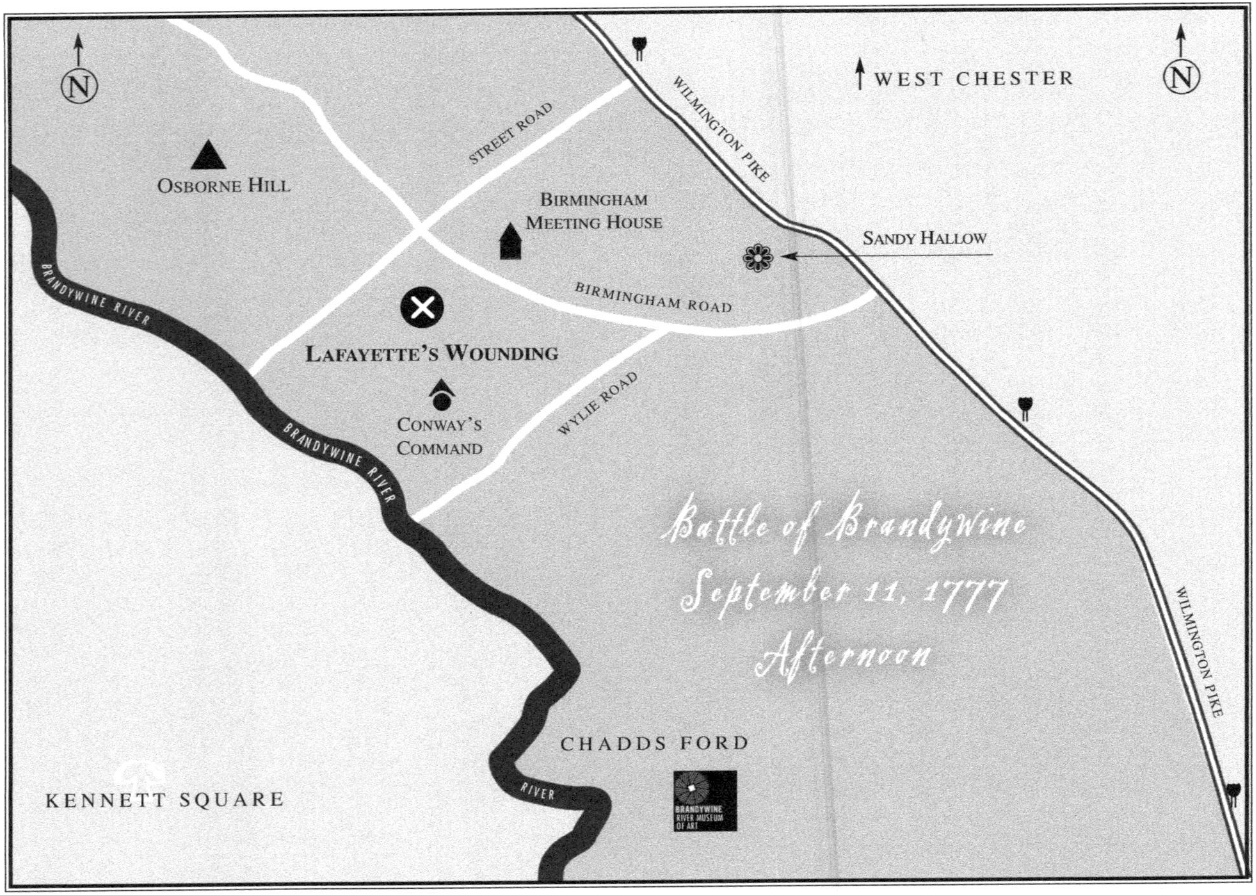
Battle of Brandywine
September 11, 1777
Afternoon
WEST CHESTER
N
N
WILMINGTON PIKE
WILMINGTON PIKE
SANDY HALLOW
BIRMINGHAM MEETING HOUSE
BIRMINGHAM ROAD
STREET ROAD
WYLIE ROAD
OSBORNE HILL
LAFAYETTE'S WOUNDING
CONWAY'S COMMAND
BRANDYWINE RIVER
BRANDYWINE RIVER
RIVER
CHADDS FORD
BRANDYWINE RIVER MUSEUM OF ART
KENNETT SQUARE

Bibliography

Auricchio, Laura, *The Marquis: Lafayette Reconsidered*, Alfred A. Knopf, New York, NY, 2014.

Billias, George Athan, editor, *George Washington's Generals and Opponents: Their Exploits and Leadership*, Da Capo Press, New York, NY, 1994.

Bodle, Wayne, *Valley Forge Winter: Civilians and Soldiers in War*, Penn State University Press, University Park, PA, 2002.

Chadwick, Bruce, *George Washington's War: The Forging of a Revolutionary Leader and the American Presidency*, Sourcebooks, Inc., Naperville, IL, 2004.

Chase, Philander D., editor, *The Papers of George Washington*, Revolutionary War Series II, August-October 1777, University Press of Virginia, Charlottesville, VA, and London, 2001.

Chernow, Ron, *Washington: A Life*, Penguin Books, New York, NY, 2010.

Davis, Burke, *The Campaign that Won America: The Story of Yorktown*, Eastern National and The Dial Press, New York, NY, 1970.

Ellis, Joseph J., *His Excellency George Washington*, Vintage Books, New York, NY, 2004.

Fleming, Thomas, *Washington's Secret War: The Hidden History of Valley Forge*, Smithsonian Books, New York, NY, 2005.

Fiske, John, *The American Revolution*, Houghton, Mifflin & Company, Boston, MA, and New York, NY, 1891.

Freeman, Douglas S. *George Washington—Leader of the Revolution,* Vol. IV, Charles Scribner's Sons, New York, NY, 1951

Greene, Jerome A., *The Guns of Independence: The Siege of Yorktown, 1781*, Savas Beatie, El Dornado Hills, CA, 2013.

Harford County, *Lafayette in Harford County Memorial Monograph 1781-1931*, Harford County, MD, 1931.

Idzerda, Stanley J., *Our Marquis: A biographical essay on Lafayette,* Lafayette College and The American Friends of Lafayette, Easton, PA, 2017.

Idzerda, Stanley J., *France and the American War for Independence,* Lafayette College and The American Friends of Lafayette, Easton, PA, 1975.

Lafayette, *Correspondence and Manuscripts of General Lafayette,* published by Lafayette's family, Saunders and Otley, New York and London, 1837.

Lane, Jason, *General and Madame de Lafayette: Partners in Liberty's Cause in the American and French Revolutions,* Taylor Trade Publishing New York, NY, 2003.

Langguth, A. J., *Patriots: The Men Who Started the American Revolution*, Touchstone Books, New York, NY, 1988.

Leckie, Robert, *George Washington's War: The Sage of the American Revolution*, Harper Perennial, New York, NY, 1992.

Levasseur, Auguste, *Lafayette in America in 1824 and 1825: Journal of a Voyage to the United States, Private Secretary to General Lafayette,* translated by Alan R. Hoffman, Lafayette Press, Inc., Manchester, NH, 2006.

Mass, John R, *The Road to Yorktown: Jefferson, Lafayette and the British Invasion of Virginia,* The History Press, Charleston, SC, 2015.

McGrath, Tim, *James Monroe: A Life,* Dutton, New York, NY, 2020.

Morgan, George, *The True La Fayette,* J. B. Lippincott Co., Philadelphia, PA, 1919.

Mowday, Bruce E., September 11, 1777: *Washington's Defeat at Brandywine Dooms Philadelphia*, White Mane Books, Shippensburg, PA, 2002.

Pisasale, Gene, *A Tale of Two Houses—Benjamin Ring, Gideon Gilpin and Lafayette At the Battle of Brandywine,* Kennett Square

Reed, John F., *Campaign to Valley Forge,* Pioneer Press, Philadelphia, PA, 1980.

Schiff, Stacy, *A Great Improvisation: Franklin, France, and the Birth of America,* Henry Hold and Company, New York, 2005.

The Gazette of The American Friends of Lafayette, Nos. 88, 89, 91.

Tower, Charlemagne, *The Marquis de La Fayette in the American Revolution,* J. B. Lippincott, Philadelphia, PA, 1926.

Unger, Harlow Giles, *Lafayette,* John Wiley & Sons, Inc., Hoboken, NJ, 2002.

Wildes, Harry Emerson, *Anthony Wayne: Trouble Shooter of the American Revolution,* Harcourt, Brace and Company, New York, NY, 1941.

Index

A NOTE ON THE TYPE

This book was set in Venetian 301 a serif typeface based off of Centaur, a 1929 interpretation of Nicolas Jenson's Eusebius face from 1469. During the 1470s his technical skill and business acumen helped establish Venice as Italy's publishing capital and in centuries since he has been celebrated for perfecting roman type, the rebirth of Latin inscription.

Centaur was designed by American book designer Bruce Rogers on the basis of Venetian typefaces of 1470 of Nicolas Jenson.

This elegant humanist face is useful for the finest typography both for book text and display matter. The Cyrillic version includes small caps and was developed for ParaType in 2003 by Dmitry Kirsanov.

Printed and bound by McNaughton & Gunn,
Saline, Michigan

Book design by Caragraphics and Carmela Cohen